CRUISING
UNDER
SAIL & POWER

CRUISING UNDER SAIL & POWER

Tony Meisel

Macmillan Publishing Company
New York
Collier Macmillan Publishers
London

For Judi, who lived through it.

Macmillan Publishing Company
866 Third Avenue, New York, NY 10022
Collier Macmillan Canada, Inc.

Library of Congress Cataloging-in-Publication Data
Meisel, Tony.
Cruising under sail and power/Tony Meisel.
p. cm.
Includes Index.
ISBN 0-02-583935-7
1. Boats and boating. 2. Yachts and yachting. 3. Sailing.
I. Title.
GV775.M45 1990
797. 1–dc20 90-30447
CIP

Macmillan books are available at special discounts for bulk purchases,
for sales promotions, premiums, fund-raising or educational use.
For details, contact:
Special Sales Director
Macmillan Publishing Company
866 Third Avenue
New York, NY 10022

This book has been designed and typeset by the author
on a Macintosh IIx and a hi-resolution laser printer
using MicroSoft Word and Quark Express.
Illustration: Clive Spong and Tony Gibbons, Linden Artists, Ltd., London.
Art Direction: Carmela Pereira
Research: Teresa Stiles

10 9 8 7 6 5 4 3 2 1

Printed in the United States of America

Contents

Introduction

Sooner or later, you wish to use your boat for more than a day. You wonder about actually going somewhere. Imagine the possibilities of the boat as the second home, new people, different sights, unusual situations. You decide to go cruising!

Cruising is all this, but it's also much more or less, depending upon your approach and your personality. Too often it becomes an unreachable ideal, a fantasy passage which quickly falls into chaos and disaster. As far as this book is concerned, cruising is the act of making a passage to a destination and staying overnight on the boat. It can last a weekend or a year. It can be on your own vessel or a chartered yacht. No matter what, it is concerned with the act of discovery: about the sea, other lands and peoples and your own inner resources.

To cruise successfully is more a matter of attitude than flashy boats or endless equipment. To cruise successfully is a matter of defining goals and achieving them. I realize this is not the usual way of looking at the process, but it will bear attention. I know people who have planned for years to cruise to the tropics. They scrimp and save, learn navigation, buy the boat of their dreams, equip her with largesse, provision her with abundance, set off... only to discover that they cannot get along in the confines of a small vessel or one gets seasick or the other cannot adjust to the lack of pacing room, etc.

One grows into cruising. If you want to see Tahiti, take a plane. If you wish to understand what exploration and adventure are about, sail a small yacht there, hopping from island to island, living with sea and stars, storms and isolation. It's not the thing for everyone. Likewise, cruising for two weeks every summer along the coast of Maine can be just as rewarding and less confining than a long ocean passage; or more confining and less rewarding. It's all depends in how you play the game.

Over the years I have made passages totalling many thousands of miles. No records set, but that wasn't the point. My goals were always to enjoy myself and my companions and to try something different

7

and challenging. Sometimes I didn't succeed; storms, breakdowns or illness forced changes or abandonment of plans. The same can happen on land. But on land you are at the mercy of other people all the time. On the water you get to experience self-sufficiency to one degree or another. It's one of the few places left.

If you enjoy being pampered you probably won't enjoy cruising... unless you are very rich. Most of us are not. We have to make do with the time and resources at our disposal. In reality this means we must modify, adapt and revise what we have, both in equipment and in physical and emotional capabilities. If you absolutely *must* have a hot shower every morning, you should seriously consider revising your priorities. It's not difficult to keep clean and fresh aboard a boat, but hot showers are a luxury available only to those with watermakers and water heaters. If you plan to cruise aboard a 30-foot sailboat, the weight, power demands and complexity of these appliances will probably be too great.

What I'm trying to get across is that successful cruising is not an extension of everyday life. If you want that, go to a resort complex. Cruising demands that you meet challenges, both those you set up and those provided by circumstance and nature. Part of the joy of living aboard and passagemaking is the element of surprise, the chance happening that forces you into seeing something in a new light or in finding the inner strength you never knew existed. It's easy to cope with the fact that Tuesday is bowling night. It's infinitely more interesting to know that Tuesday may find you in a foreign port eating foods you've never tasted before.

No one can come close to discussing every aspect of cruising under sail and power in one volume. Hundreds of authors over the past century have set their pens to the subject, and most have contributed something of value. The outstanding writers in the genre have been Claude Worth in the period between the wars in England, Eric Hiscock and Maurice Griffiths after the war, Lynn and Larry Pardey in the USA. Others have written up yarns of individual cruising, but few have accumulated the vast experience or offered the sound advice of these blue water sailors.

Note, I say sailors. Few powerboat writers are much interested in cruising in the traditional sense, yet certain types of powerboats are far superior to sailing yachts for this mission. Robert Beebe's pioneering design work in long-range powered "passagemakers" has proven beyond doubt that this is a viable way to tackle voyaging.

My purpose in writing this book is two-fold. First, I wish to convey, in a easily-understood form, the procedures and techniques that make for pleasurable cruising. Second, if possible, I hope to make clear what it is about cruising that is increasingly valuable in an information-clogged, overcrowded world. If any strain runs through this book it is "keep it simple!"

The point of going cruising is to escape from the everyday, the clutter and electronics, the powerful push toward constant activity foisted on us by advertisers and the media. One goes to sea in a yacht for pleasure, not to prove anything (although some do try). Pleasure can be exciting or sonambulent, dangerous or cosseted. It is not a repeat of one's everyday existence. If you thrive on work alone, don't get a boat. If you see options to the 9 to 5 grind, are willing to learn to be self-sufficient and are capable of drawing on inner resources, this book just may aid and abet you.

I have made no attempt to be comprehensive. In certain areas such as navigation techniques, a number of thoroughgoing books exist to guide you along the true and righteous path; equally, there is not room enough nor time to discourse herein on these topics. In other areas such as maneuvering, so much depends on the individual boat, conditions, experience and place that any attempt to offer more than guidelines would be foolhardy in the extreme.

My advice is simple: go cruising, make mistakes, learn from them and learn to enjoy the wonder and awe that can still be found on our waters. Start easy, work your way up to your dream voyage, learning along the way. Above all, plan as carefully and thoroughly as possible. You will have improved on the odds for a pleasant journey.

Tony Meisel
New Suffolk, NY

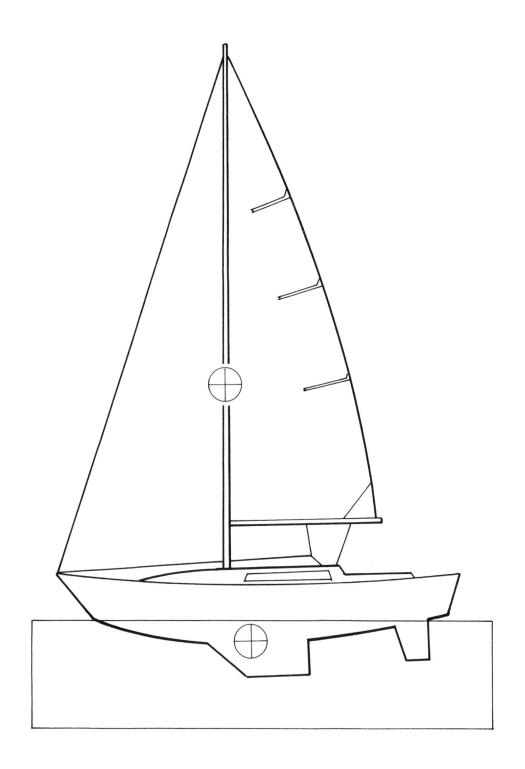

Balance is vital for a good cruising boat. This is a combination of many factors, but weight distribution, hull form, matching power to displacement and stability play a part.

The Boat

Cruising boats come in all shapes, sizes and colors. Too often, yachtsmen choose a vessel totally unsuited for its intended purpose, opting usually for the *ultimate* cruising boat. This is all well and good if you are going on the ultimate cruise–around the world, or transoceanic–but most of us have neither the time nor resources to effect such a voyage, even if we are panting with desire.

A boat is not like an internal organ. It can be replaced, modified, traded up or down. To assume that only one boat is right for every purpose and you alone is probably a major error. Owning a boat is a matter of faith, a love affair; and like most of those, it is a highly irrational pursuit. Therefore, anything I may say in the ensuing pages will probably offend someone. However, if you are going to spend more money than for anything else in your life short of your dwelling space, you might as well have the truth (as I perceive it, of course) shoved in your face at least once.

The standard given "truth" for years has been that sailing craft are the only suitable vessels for long-distance cruising, that heavy displacement yachts are best, that you need infinite storage space and other debatable formulas. Power craft, so the sages contend, are for harbor use, for weekend hops and for protected waterways. You really needed be much of seaman to run them and they cannot be trusted in heavy weather. Of course, by now you will have gathered by opinion of these statements.

Any vessel, so long as it can be battened down, will self-right and is soundly constructed can be considered seaworthy *providing the operator knows the ways of the sea and how his or her boat reacts in differing conditions.* This is a tall order. Very few of us experience the ultimate storm or endlessly long passages. But we must know both the capabilities of our boat and the extent of our own resources. The success of any voyage depends on these.

I realize you really want to hear about the romantic aspects of choosing a boat: how many berths, how much horsepower, what rigging specifications, etc. No one answer exists, and no criteria is worth noting except that the boat you choose is the best possible of its type.

SUITABILITY: Sail

The first item on the agenda, assuming you are in the market for a boat, is to decide where the boat will be used and for what purposes. If you sail in Great South Bay, off the southern parts of Long Island, where the average depth would allow most of us to walk across, a deep keel yacht will not make for much pleasure. If you sail out of San Pedro in Southern California, your keel can pierce the depths. Average wind strengths and sea conditions play a part in these decisions. If you sail where I do, in Peconic Bay at the North Fork of Long Island, you will encounter very brisk southerlies every afternoon. Having a cloud of sail will be exciting, but not necessarily fulfilling. Likewise, if you have to run an inlet or get over a bar to moor, deep draft will not help, but a powerful engine will, as will a smooth run aft.

In choosing your boat, the suitability of a vessel, in all its parameters, for a base location is paramount. Everything else must be compromised, within limits. Without the suitable hull and power, you'll end up miserable and possibly in danger.

With the advent of the Scheel keel and winged keels, draft has become something of a worry of the past, though not entirely. Centerboards are still around, though except in the smallest size hulls, their suitability for a substantial cruising vessel is questionable for several reasons. First, the sheer force needed to raise a board in a vessel over 35 feet is something to behold. If a board is properly weighted to overcome buoyancy and drop on its own accord, a certain amount of effort will be needed to raise it. Even with winches, hydraulics and all the applications of modern engineering, this is ponderous at best, tiresome without a largish crew. Second, a board *will* gather weed, lobsterpots and nets. Third, they can be broken or bent, making it impossible to get them retracted into their cases. Fourth, centerboard cases can leak or fracture, endangering the boat. And fifth, they are a royal pain to maintain; they cannot be painted without a hoist, nor can a new pendant be easily rove.

Lately, there have been a few yachts heralded equipped with drop keels. The entire ballasted keel is raised and lowered by means of electric or hydraulic winches. Unless you cruise in areas heavily populated with mechanics and hydraulic engineers, these are a dubious proposition for anything other than coastal cruising.

The Scheel keel and, to a lesser extent, the winged keel are the saviors of modern cruising sailors. They allow reduced draft while preventing leeway and keep the boat pointing to windward. The winged variety sticks out! That is, the wings themselves can seriously get in the way. Anything added invariably ends up being a problem on a cruising vessel. Personally, I would opt for a Scheel or long keel. After all,

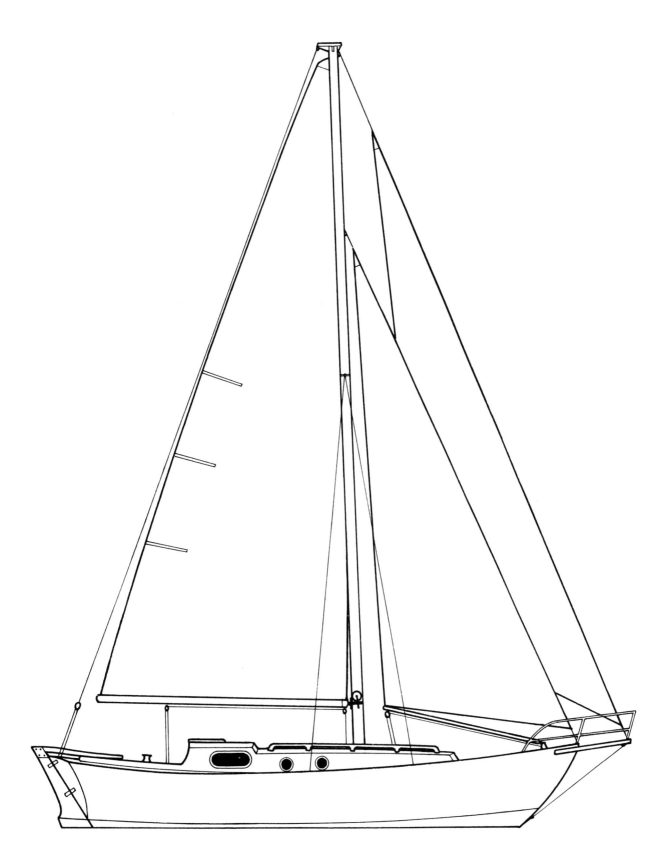

The preferred modern sailing cruiser is of moderate-displacement and cutter-rigged. It should track well and be easy for two to handle yet able to be single-handed. Equipped with a moderately-powerful auxiliary engine, and a two-bladed propeller, there should be sufficient tankage to allow a passage to be completed if dismasted.

The Boat   **13**

you're not out to win the America's Cup, and with proper design a shoal draft keel will still perform admirably.

Displacement should be given thought. Most modern production yachts tend toward lightness, with minimal wetted surface. This is fine if you're racing around the buoys or weekending. For longer hauls, and with added stores and equipment aboard, you should look at a more moderate vessel. Now, it should be pointed out that moderate today is not what it once was. As vessels get lighter and lighter, moderate displacement becomes equally lighter. At one time, a 40-footer weighing between 20,000 and 25,000 pounds and 28 feet LWL would be considered a fair cruising vessel. Today, the same boat is called heavy. What is more important is that the displacement of the vessel in relation to its length waterline and sail area is reasonable. This is not something easy to define, as displacement is not really reflected in the design figures, most of which are calculated at half-load.

When you start to cruise seriously, unless you're an aescetic, chances are you'll load a vast amount of gear, supplies, equipment and stores aboard, far more than would normally figure in the displacement figures of the designer. Fact is, a light boat will be far more hindered in performance than a moderate one. It hasn't been designed to go fast unless stripped of unnecessary weight. A moderate hull will accept weight abuse with some equanimity. The easiest way to approach the dilemma is to compare the design parameters of several different boats in the same general category.

More sail, less displacement equals better light air performance; likewise, a longer waterline will make for greater *potential* speed. Of course, these are only guidelines. Variables always creep into the picture. A heavy ship will glide along in light airs from sheer inertia. A longer waterline will aid in increasing speed downwind and on a reach. However, to windward, all other parameters being equal, two boats of equal waterline length, one with short ends, the other with generous overhangs, will not achieve the same speed. The overhangs will, as the boat heels, increase the LWL of the one boat, thus increasing its ultimate speed.

For the average cruising sailor, these fine points are probably not often considered. They will all effect the progress of a voyage, however, and should be carefully considered in the purchase of a any new boat, either sail or power.

SUITABILITY: Power

A power boat for cruising follows the same parameters, to a degree, as a sailing yacht, but distances covered effect design even more so. Not only do regular stores and water have to be carried, but large amounts of fuel, also. Thus, it would be fair to say that the faster you go, the more fuel you'll burn and the shorter your range. Most modern deep-V planing hulls are designed to go very fast for comparatively

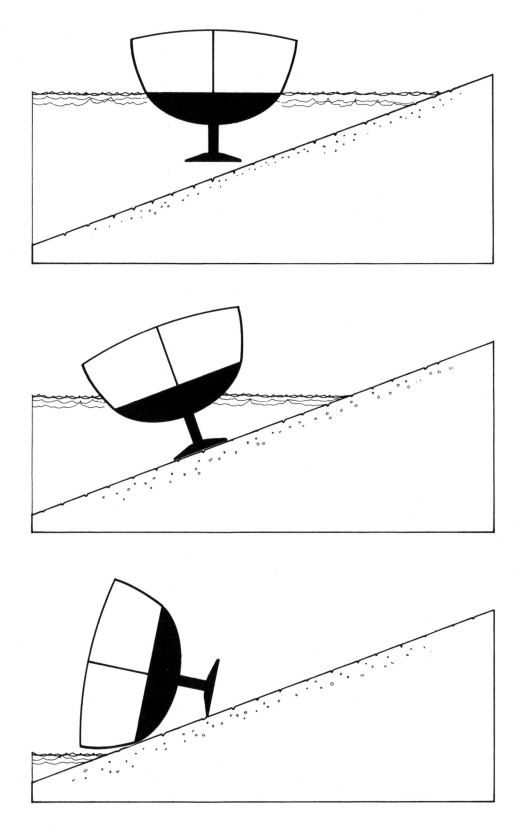

Winged-keels have a number of advantages: decreased draft, greater windward efficiency and a tendency to reduce roll when running. However, if you cruise in shoal waters or tidal flats that dry out, the disadvantages may outweigh everything. In a shelving harbor, on a falling tide, the wing will not sit upright and may cause the boat to fall on its side.

short hops. True, you have to throttle back in a head sea, and you *can* move at partial throttle, but few boaters do. Planing hulls are not suited to anything but weekend hops, unless you are willing to shell out for hundreds of gallons of fuel and many refueling stops.

At the other end of the spectrum is the pure displacement hull. Here, the speed is governed by the waterline length, the factor being the square root of that length multiplied by 1.34. True trawler types are rare, despite the advertisements. A real trawler is a most burdomsome vessel, capable of carrying vast quantities of cargo and stores for great distances. Descended from fishing boats, these boats are for the die-hard deep sea cruiser and world traveller. They won't get you there fast, but they will get you most anywhere.

A more appropriate type for most of us is the modified trawler, descended from the coastal fishing boats of both the East and West Coasts. The pioneers were Walter McGinnis in the East and Ed Monk in the Pacific Northwest. These designers took the traditional fishing vessels of their respective areas and modified them for lighter displacement, greater form stability and comfort and increased economy of operation. Most vessels advertised as trawlers are of this ilk, and will make excellent seagoing homes. However, the tendency to add accommodation at the expense of height and ultimate stability is strong. It should be resisted, if possible. The shorter and shallower the boat, the fewer decks and levels is should carry.

The semi-displacement hull will get up on plane, but will not roar off into the sunset. Generally round-bilge types, they flatten-out aft of amidships and will usually be able to achieve anywhere from 12 to 20 knots, depending on power and conditions. For the weekend or summer vacation cruiser, they are ideal. They allow you to cover distance, have good seakeeping qualities and are certainly more economical to run than deep-Vs. Additionally, they will not rut and wallow like deep-V hulls in heavy weather.

Since most buyers want all the comforts of home, designers and builders have been almost too happy to supply them, at the expense of centuries of hard-learned seagoing experience. I am sure that in the future power vessels will grow increasingly grotesque, sacrificing seaworthiness for flash and "living space" and the foolishly brave will discover the limits of any technology against the sea.

INTEGRITY

No matter what the conditions, the basic structure of the boat must be up to stuff, capable of taking the worst wind and waves can throw at it. In this day, with soaring prices for materials and labor, this is not always the case,especially in production boats.

Since most boats are sold on dry land, and sell in direct proportion to the "amenities" above and below, you will have to tear yourself away from the acres of teak, the drink holders and the large 'fridge and

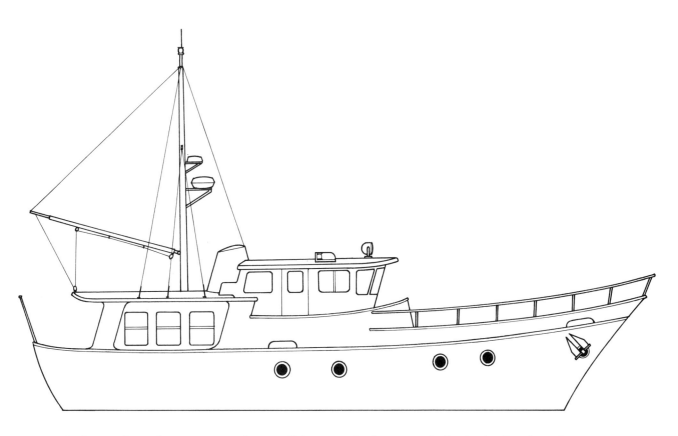

A classic, long-distance powerboat will have a displacement hull, single diesel engine (with a belting arrangement to the generator or a wing engine), a large three- or four-bladed propeller and some means of reducing roll. This can be by means of stabilizers, steadying sails or flopper-stoppers. Note the protected wheelhouse and the high bow. The first will allow you to voyage in your bedroom slippers. The second will aid in keeping up progress to weather.

try to concentrate on the basics.

Is the hull fair?

What is the lay-up schedule (if GRP)?

What hull reinforcements exist and how are they installed? How is the hull-to-deck joint made?

How well is the engine installed? Is the rigging substantial enough and is it properly anchored?

What are the arrangements for attaching deck hardware?

Are ports and hatches strong enough to resist penetration by a breaking sea?

Are metals corrosion resistant and properly protected with anodes?

Are bulkheads strong and properly attached to the hull and deck? Hundreds of questions exist. Thus, a good marine surveyor should be hired to thoroughly examine any prospective vessel. He's worth his weight in gold, especially when it comes time to insure your baby.

ABILITY

What makes a good cruising boat? Besides all the creature comforts, which depending on your needs and preferences, can make or break a

cruise, there a few points having to do with ability that must be raised.
1. Stability. This means not only static, at rest, rock solidness, but stability in any kind of seas underway. In a sailboat it is a function of hull form, ballast and rig size. In a power boat, stability is more than anything else, the ability of the boat to recover when rolled over on its side by a beam sea. Many modern powerboats are very stable under ideal conditions. All planing hulls, due to their shape and flatness aft will seem rock solid at the dock. However, though their initial stability is high, they can easily be flipped on their beam ends by a sufficiently-sized sea.

For anything other than prudent coastal cruising, one should look to a displacement or, possibly, semi-displacement hull. Most of these have been derived from fishing trawlers and, though slower, will much more assuredly get you there through thick and thin. Please note that most so-called "trawlers" are really semi-displacement configurations with hard chines and a flat run aft (Grand Banks, Albin and others).

Additionally, you must consider other aspects of the boat for stability. The least noticed is top hamper. Anything above the gunnel will have a pronounced effect on the boat's stability. Each layer of decking will add one more degree of top-heaviness. Robert Beebe, in his book *Voyaging Under Power*, has worked up a series of ratios demonstrating just what is safe for what type of passagemaking. For any powerboat owner contemplating long-distance cruising, this is one illuminating and indispensable volume.

The tendency today is to go for flybridges, large areas of glass and every possible simulation of the suburban living room. It just won't do at sea. The added weight and vulnerability of these will eventually prove fatal, given the improper combination of circumstances. The same is true of sailing vessels, of course, and every one advertised as bringing all the comforts of home with large windows and dozens of vents and hatches is subject to the same pitfalls.

Surviving a nasty roll or a knockdown is very simple, in theory. If you have minimum, truly armored glass, ports (closed, of course) and moderate hull dimensions, all should be well. The Fastnet disaster of 1979 showed the design flaws of modern sailboats to a T. Companionways open to flooding, flimsy rigs, minimal ballast and hulls designed to rating rules, not to the demands of the sea. Fact is that a very beamy hull–sail or power–has a tendency to stay upside down when turned turtle, especially when coupled with less than a third of displacement in ballast. Body weight at the rail is all well and good when racing around the buoys, but it has no business being figured into stability calculations in a cruising boat. Moderate beam–no more than one-third the waterline length–is a good rule-of-thumb when shopping for your dream cruiser.

Yes, it will mean somewhat less interior room, but, after all, most of that room is never used. It's psychological. A too-wide aisle through the cabin only encourages banging about! What's good on the showroom floor is not necessarily good at sea. As in most things in this life, moderation—in beam, displacement, power, sail area, whatever—is the best bet.

2. Stowage capacity. Although the type of cruising you do will demand more or less room for stores, water and fuel, you will be at the mercy of a marinas and yards if your boat cannot carry enough of these for at least a week with a full complement of crew aboard. If you plan to cross oceans, you will need stores and water for your crew for between 30 and 60 days. Allowing a gallon of water per man per day and ca. five pounds of food per person per day—assuming a crew of four—you must have room for 120 gallons of water plus 50 percent over for emergencies, that's 170 gallons and 600 pounds of foodstuffs plus 20 percent over for special items and snacks or 120 pounds, that's 720 pounds. The combined weight of water and food is now at ca. 2000 pounds, and you haven't even loaded up charts, clothing, medical supplies, spare lubricants, fuel and a hundred other items you or your crew simply cannot do without.

Additionally, you need room and displacement for personal possessions, spares, safety equipment, amusements and other oddments. You will end up with a heap of stuff on the dock. You've got to figure out where to stow it all. All this weight decreases the hulls stability unless stowed low, preferably in the bilges. Take this into account always. Also make sure there are several *dry* stowage bins aboard.

3. Ease of repair and maintenance. This is harder to achieve than basic design and structural parameters. Cable runs should be clean and out of the bilges. Through-hulls are easy to reach and grouped in isolated wells in the bilge. Engine access is adequate for routine maintenance. Under deck fastenings can be reached for reinforcement or replacement of deck gear. Heads are smooth-surfaced and easy to clean. Ditto for galleys. Electronics and navigation gear can be removed for storage. Electrical panels are clearly labelled for connections. Steering quadrants and other mechanisms can be reached for repair. Stuffing boxes are accessible. Go over every area of the boat with ease of entry and repair in mind. Many simple modifications can make life easier.

4. Comfort and safety. Oddly enough, a comfortable boat is more able than a cramped or ill-conceived one. Comfort makes for rest, alertness and a sense of well-being. Of course, one can get too comfortable. Passageways can be too wide, saloons too spacious. You don't want to get tossed around or thrown from one side of the boat to the other in heavy weather. Hand-holds should be located everywhere, firmly attached. Floor surfaces should be as non-skid as possible. Unvarnished teak is the ideal. Lacking that, a good non-skid paint or deck covering material will do.

Berths should be long and reasonably wide (ca. 24-30 inches); anything less will make for pains, anything wider will toss you on the floor. All cruising boat berths, even in power boats, should be fitted with strong leeboards or cloths to keep you in place in rocky seas.

Decks must be arranged for both the ease of working the boat and safety: strong rails, unobtrusive hardware, the best non-skid money can buy, handholds every step of the way fore and aft both to leeward and windward.

Whatever boat you have or purchase can be made safer, more able, more seaworthy, more reliable. Generally speaking, simplicity in design, construction and fitting out will reward you with lower initial cost, less maintenance, easier repairs and more time on the water. The tendency to bring all the comforts of home on board is unavoidable, but it won't make your cruising more interesting or exciting. The choice is up to you.

Equipment

What you outfit your boat with in terms of gear—electronics, cordage, spares, ground tackle and all the little bits and pieces needed to give you a worry-free cruise—will depend of your lifestyle, preferences, your mechanical aptitudes and your budget. Too often one is captivated by all the available goodies in catalogs and chandleries, especially in the realm of electronics, and spends lavishly to cover every contingency. Well, you cannot cover every possible contingency. But you can decide what you really need and restrain yourself from the expense and clutter of those things that are guaranteed to be used once per decade, if ever.

I am well aware that some readers will find a potential use for every known piece of gear, but some forethought is necessary to make cruising a successful pastime. If you plan to spend two weeks yearly puttering along the coast, you do not need satellite navigation systems, desalination plants or weather facsimile printers. You do need good ground tackle, a tender and a few basic instruments. On the other hand, if you are setting off for a leisurely circumnavigation, you must plan for virtually everything.

Unfortunately, many cruisers equate the dream with their present circumstances. If you know that for the next five years you will be limited to a short summer's cruise, don't get carried away with the plans for your retirement; you may change them. Spending time, effort and money—not necessarily in that order—can be fun, but getting out on the water can be even more pleasure. Think before you act.

What you will need can be broken down into several broad categories: deck gear, propulsion and/or rig, safety and emergency, navigation, living and systems. Each will be discussed in greater detail in the appropriate chapter, but we shall run down the basics here.

DECK GEAR

Deck gear includes all the fittings, lines and mechanical/electrical/hydraulic devices used to keep one aboard, tie-up, anchor or attach auxiliary gear to the deck. Cleats, chocks, anchors, winches, davits, lifelines, rails, windshields, awnings, hoses, drink holders, etc. all comes under this heading. The best advice one can give is to buy first-quality goods and attach them securely. The tendency is for boat builders to use shiny fittings, often of die-cast zinc. If your boat is so equipped, remove these and dispatch them to the nearest landfill. Since the entire point of deck fittings is to hold the boat to the land or to hold things to the boat, anything that might break or distort is not good enough. Better to have a few heavy bronze or stainless cleats, through-bolted fore-and-aft rather than dozens of useless, undersized clumps of metal screwed here and there. And all through-bolting should be accompanied by oversized backing pads of marine ply or non-corrosive metal with oversized washers installed before either lock nuts or double nuts.

Especially if you are cruising with a family crew, get oversize equipment installed, winches above all. Ideally a winch should be powerful enough so that the smallest, weakest member of the crew can haul in any sail in the wind strengths it's designed for. Remember that all deck gear is their to *ease* work; therefore, the more powerful any mechanical device is, the better. A large cleat makes it easier to fasten a line, a multiple tackle makes it easier to haul in a boom or get a dinghy back on board.

PROPULSION AND RIG

The purpose of both of these is to get you to where you want to go. Therefore, every aspect should be in as close to perfect functioning order as possible. For cruising, the least complex propulsion system you can get away with is the most desirable. In practice, this means that all sorts of go-fast sail-tweaking controls will probably complicate life. Likewise, in powerboats, every accessory which draws motive power directly from the engine, adds to the work the engine has to accomplish, decreases its efficiency and sets the power plant up for faster breakdowns.

For sailing, a reasonable sail inventory of main (with at least two reefs), working jib, 130 to 150 percent genoa, storm jib, asymmetrical cruising 'chute and storm trysail should cover all situations. What you need in sail control equipment depends on whether you are cruising or racing between ports. Cruising or racing will demand winches large enough for the weakest crewmember to haul in the largest sail in the maximum breeze for which that sail is designed. You'll need good cleats, horned and preferably of Herreshoff pattern, lots of rope, appropriate blocks with a strong mainsheet tackle and vang. Everything else is for go-fast fanatics and will not drive the boat *appreciably* faster.

Spares should include sail patches, thread and needle, a good palm, extra rope and a length of stainless wire equal in both length and diameter to the longest stay in the rig, along with bulldog clamps and ex-

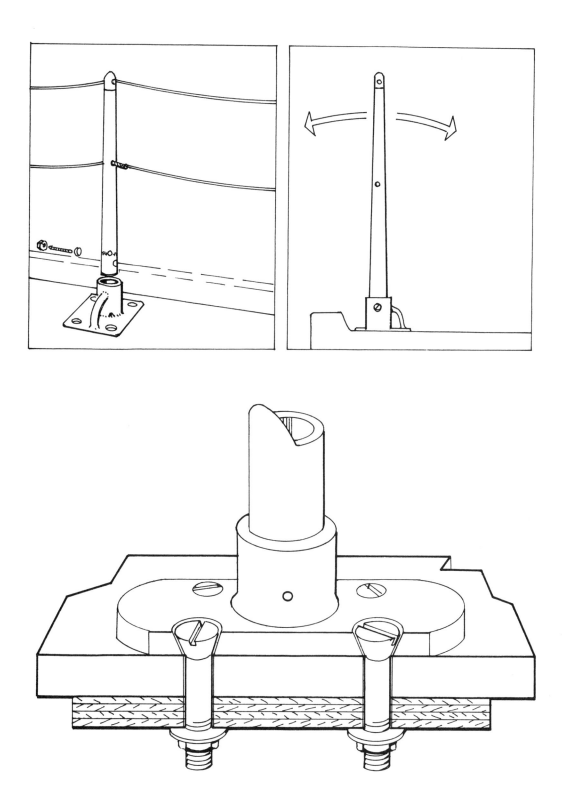

Stanchions should surround the perimeter of the deck of any seagoing boat. To be effective, however, they must be bolted through the deck with backing plates and firmly attached to their bases by means of stainless cotter pins of bolts with lock-nuts. A normal-sized person (ca. 150-200lbs.) should be able to kick or sudden-press against the stanchion without it bending or giving way. All holes for lifelines should have bushed sleeves in them to prevent broken wires and chafe.

tra rigging screws, clevis pins and a first-class cable or bolt cutter.

For powering, you need a working engine, proper shaft alignment, an effective stuffing box and a propeller suited to the hull, engine and purpose. This is harder to get right than anything else in the boat, and trial and error may be necessary to get optimum performance both in terms of speed and fuel economy. Props must be examined for wear and dings as well as alignment at least once a season. If persistent vibration or rough running is evident, you may be in need of a prop repair. On long voyages, spares must be carried for everything, needless to say. Controls should be positive and smooth-operating and all linkages secure. Be sure the rudder is fair and not bent.

SAFETY

Safe boating demands experience, attention and care on the part of the boat operator more than anything else. Nevertheless, certain items of equipment are needed to preserve body and ship. Decks need to be made as secure as possible: non-skid, rails, handholds. Everyone on board should be issued a safety harness for rough weather, and know how to wear and use it. A personal flotation device, Coast Guard approved, must be at hand for each and every crew member. A boarding ladder needs be at hand, better yet permanently attached. On the stern rail is stowed a buoy with all the accoutrements: light, danbuoy, whistle. A liferaft—for offshore—should be stowed on deck, easy to launch. Anchor and rode should be firmly secured to the foredeck ready for instant dropping.

Belowdecks, the same precautions as to handrails, non-skid and security need to be followed. Get rid of all hard or sharp edges as well. Make sure seacocks are installed on all underwater through-hulls. Fuel supply to the galley stove needs a shut-off valve located so it can be reached without reaching over the stove. Have fire extinguishers, updated and mounted in the open, at least one for each compartment of the vessel.

Engine compartments need ventilation and easy access. Wires must be routed away from any hot engine parts. Hoses must be clamped in place and double-clamped at through-hulls.

All rigging ought to be examined at least once a year. Replace all cotter pins, tape all pin ends. Look for kinks and breaks in wire rigging. Replace anything suspect. Install toggles—if they are not there already—between chainplates and rigging screws.

All emergency equipment should be located near the companionway: flares, signalling mirrors, EPIRBs, flags, etc. If you have to abandon ship, have ready a duffle containing survival supplies: extra water, fishing tackle, lights and extra batteries, food rations, charts, basic navigation tools, knife, pliers, light lines, polypropylene clothing, etc. Whatever is packed with a liferaft is usually not adequate.

Whether or not to carry a VHF or other radio depends on your need

The compass is your most important navigational tool. It must be mounted where it can be seen clearly from every possible helm position, preferably along the centerline. If on one side of the companionway, it's a good idea to mount a second compass symmetrically on the other side.

for security. I've cruised for 40 years without one, but then I cruise in areas where one wouldn't be of much use. Majority opinion supports the need to have one on board, properly installed and with at least two knowledgeable operators.

NAVIGATION

What you actually need for navigation is a compass, swung and with a deviation card made up, charts, tide tables, a nautical almanac, rules, pencils, maybe a course protractor, a lead line and a log. Add a sextant for offshore use.

What people add is a depth sounder, radar, radio, radio direction finder, loran, satellite navigation positioning system, speedometer, wind instruments, computer charting systems, fax systems and course computers with interfaces for everything possible. Anything with shiny readouts is fair game. The problem arises that 1) the initial outlay is in the tens of thousands of dollars, 2) you have to use everything and 3) you have to maintain it all. In a pinch, though electronics are getting more and more reliable, some piece of vital and necessary

Compass deviation card. The outer rose represents the magnetic course from the chart, the inner rose represents the course to steer by the compass. Read only the magnetic course on the outer rose, only the compass course on the inner rose. For each compass heading apply the known deviation and draw a line from that degree to the corresponding magnetic heading. To find the compass course, locate the magnetic course on the outer rose and follow the lines to the inner rose to read the compass course. To convert the compass course to the magnetic course, locate the compass course on the inner rose and follow the lines to the outer rose to read the magnetic course.

equipment will stop. Period. What do you do then?

Following the simplicity doctrine, the following electronics are useful and proper for the cruising boatman: RDF, depth sounder, speedometer/log. In particularly foggy areas, radar can be very useful, providing you really learn how to use it. For offshore, depending where you cruise: loran or a satellite system. By all means, add whatever you want, but most of it assumes the status of a toy, an expensive toy of limited value.

LIVING/SYSTEMS

Whatever is necessary for convenience and the performance of everyday chores comes under these rubrics. A functioning head, good and reliable stove, decent plumbing and a comfortable place to sleep are necessities. What you choose is not as chancy as it used to be, but here are some guidelines.

Heads are best chosen with an eye to reliability, sturdiness, easy of disassembly and durability. Electric heads have no place on a cruising boat. Keep in mind that all heads will eventually clog and have to be taken apart, a messy, smelly business at best. Choose one with a large diaphragm pump; this will pass large objects more easily. Nevertheless, the old dictum "only what one eats should go into a head" still holds. Cigarets, sanitary napkins and old food should not enter that sacred portal.

A decent stove will make everyone happy. Two are even better. I mean you might add a one-burner gimballed butane unit for quick boiling water for the off watch. It will save time and fuel. Otherwise, a properly installed, gimballed propane or gas stove is certainly the easiest to use. The Coast Guard doesn't like them and won't permit them on commercial vessels under US registration. Nevertheless, with proper safeguards—solenoid shut-offs—they are so much easier to use than alcohol or kerosene that choosing either of those is a matter of retro taste. Diesel is fine if you cruise in Northern climes but requires a blower. Solid fuel stoves are likewise fine for New England or the Pacific Northwest, but stowing fuel and the attendant mess of ash and hot coals is no pleasure to contemplate.

Heating units, especially diesel ones, can heat an entire boat. Small kerosene or coal stoves will keep a cabin warm. Since most cruising boats will eventually venture into cooler areas, one or the other is a good idea, though the bulkhead mounted heaters are far cheaper and don't require the complex installation of the blower-type diesel units. They don't need electrical current to operate either.

Unless you have a generator aboard, I would not recommend an air conditioning system. The drain on everything else is way beyond the means of most electrical and engine systems. If its really that hot, go for a swim!

No attempt has been made to cover every possible system. You

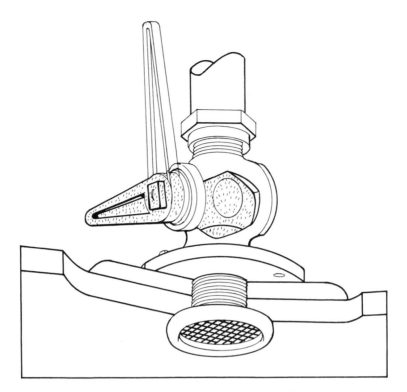

Every through-hull below the waterline must be fitted with a positive-acting seacock., properly blocked and bedded. These should be opened when needed as appropriate. A screened through-hull is recommended on engine cooling-water intake ports.

probably don't need very many of them anyway. You should search out the best your budget can stand in any category of equipment. The less of it on board, the less to maintain and repair. The less of that to do, the more cruising miles, more ports and more sights can be tucked away in the time you have available.

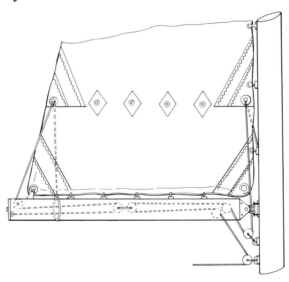

An efficient reefing system is a necessity aboard any sailing yacht. In this example one line is used to reef the sail from the cockpit, with the line led aft by means of blocks. Note the internal block and tackle arrangement housed within the boom.

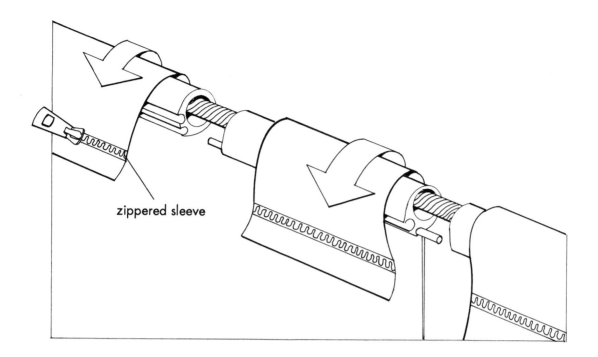

Roller reefing headsails can save much foredeck work when cruising. In this system, the mid-luff area furls prior to the head and clew of the sail, thus making for a flat set to the reef.

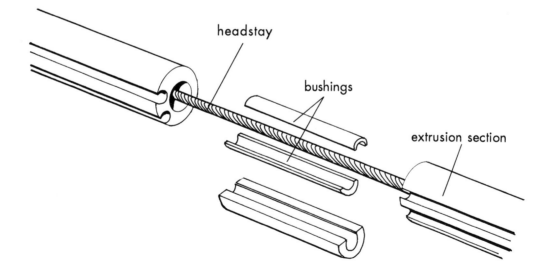

An aluminum ally extrusion fits over the existing headstay and swivels around it. This system will keep the original tension of the stay, yet present a clean entry to the wind.

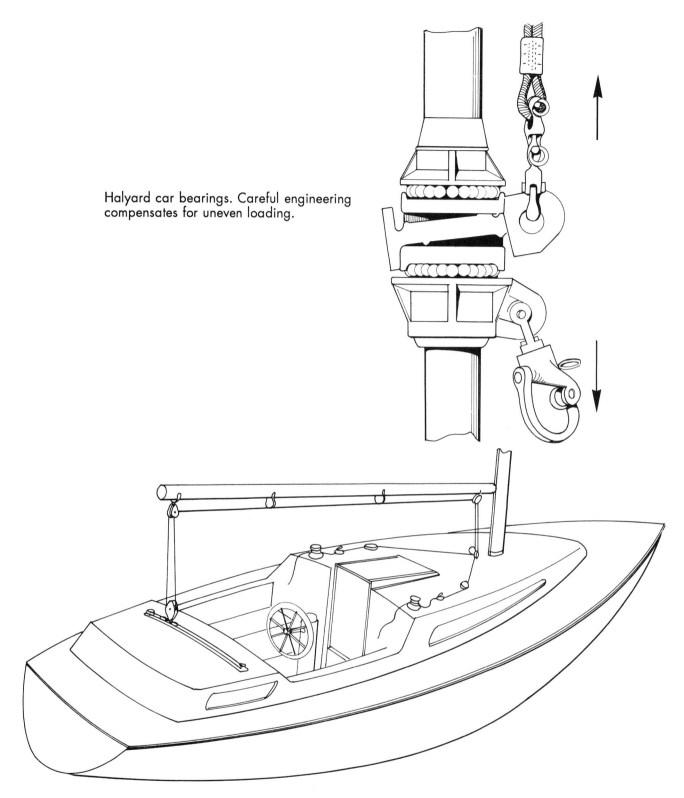

Halyard car bearings. Careful engineering compensates for uneven loading.

Optimal control is achieved through a sensitive, easy-to-use and efficient mainsheet system. Different styles are shown here. Note that all are multi-part, making for greater reduction of effort. However, the more purchase, the lesser the speed. In any cruising boat, the helmsman should be able to reach and trim the mainsheet without undue contortions. Using an athwartship traveller track with adjustable cars will allow for fine-tuning the main for differing wind strength and better balance.

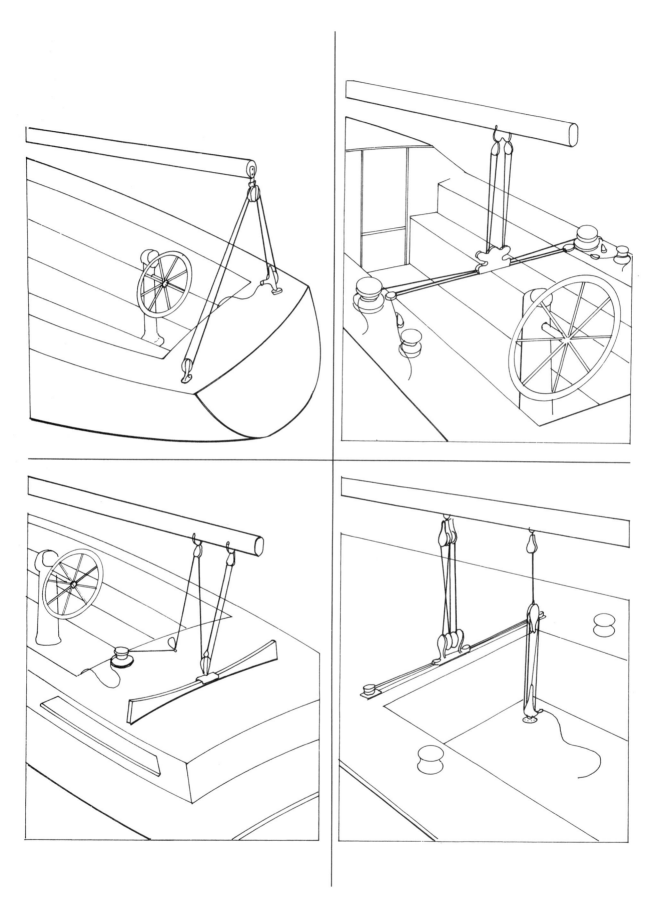

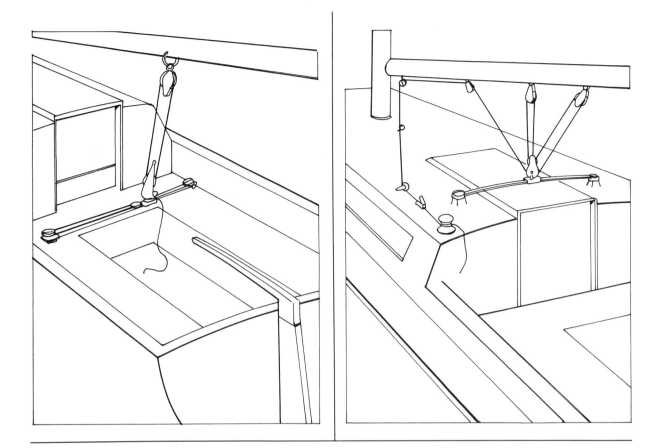

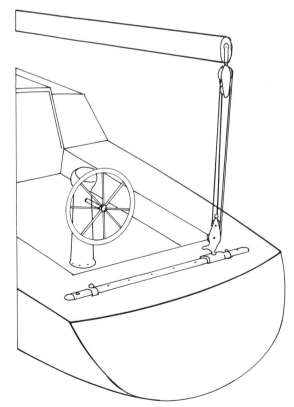

Tenders

The dinghy is your lifeline, panel truck, sedan chair, ferry and taxi in one. Without a suitable dinghy, you will sentenced to spend your cruising life either isolated at anchor or tied-up in a marina. With the every-increasing crowding of marinas and the concurrent charges, there is more and more need to have suitable transport when anchored out. Many different types of tenders are available, and what you get will be influenced by budget, size of boat, stowage area and what you want it for.

Ideally, a good tender is a weight carrier, but how it carries that weight is a function of displacement, length and shape. Since it is used most often to ferry people and supplies from land to the mother ship, a dinghy must function in a wide variety of conditions carrying an often strange collection of gear and goods. Finding the right balance of weight, handling ease, capacity and seaworthiness is not easy. If the tender is long and narrow, it will not have, generally speaking, the stability to be effective in its everyday role; however, it will be easier to propel efficiently (the greatest motion for the least effort, either manual or mechanical). If it is short and beamy, you may find it extraordinarily stable, but it will row or power like a wet slug. As in almost everything, moderation—in design, displacement, beam, depth, everything in fact—is the best course.

The perfect tender is one which will power, sail and row with equal ease. That just isn't in the cards. A dinghy may row and sail well or power and row well, but the combination of all three virtues calls upon widely differing design criteria. Some dinks have come close, but the majority will usually sail and row well. Powering wants a radically different hull shape. If you can live with sometimes severe compromise, well and good. If you want both, and have the room to spare, a sailing dinghy and a rigid-bottom inflatable together will solve your problems of getting ashore and having fun.

Assuming you must choose only one boat, decide what your requirements are before you buy it. Where will you cruise? Will you have to cross surf? Are distances too great and adverse for rowing? Will the dinghy have to be towed?

In the past couple of decades, inflatables have become the tender of choice. Very stable, easily stowed, reasonably tough, they are fine for the average boater who has only to move about for two weeks every summer. But they also leave much to be desired. Unless you are in a flat calm, they are unbearable to row, and the oarsmanship necessary to propel them is quite unlike moving a hard boat. They won't carry way between strokes and are useless into any headwind. Different types require different power. Flat-bottomed inflatables are strictly for small. low-powered motors. They have little directional stability and any attempt to plane will probably result in flipping and injury. V- or semi-v hard-bottom versions are more appropriate to high speeds as are those with inflatable keels. However, none of these will tow well, are a pain to stow without davits and are virtually useless under oar. For many of us, an inflatable will suffice. It's easy to stow, quick to set up, *can* be rowed and will carry heavy loads. It will be wet and bumpy with any kind of sea running and can flip more readily than a rigid boat. By and large, inflatables will be best powered by a small outboard motor of from two to five horsepower. They are not cheap—at least the good ones that will last—and demand a certain amount of care, especially winter storage, but one may be right for you.

If you opt for rigid tender, look for the largest you can accommodate without undue strain. A larger boat will carry more, faster than a mini. Eight feet should be considered the minimum, 10 or 12 feet in length is better. In choosing one, take into account your ability to bring it aboard. This is no laughing matter. A hard dink can weigh upwards of 150 pounds, and wrestling it on deck can be a real back-breaker. Davits are one solution, though not particularly safe or appropriate to a sailing vessel, though ideal for a power cruiser. Using the boom to hoist it will work, but you will still have to find space, clear of necessary impediments, in which to stow it. Since the smallest practical dinghy will be eight feet in length and almost four feet in beam, not to mention a couple of feet deep, this can create insurmountable problems if your boat is not long enough or flush decked. I am not suggesting you buy a larger mother ship, but the only alternative is to tow.

Hoisting a dinghy aboard can be done using the boom and main halyard, but be sure to have eyebolts mounted in both stern and bow in the dinghy to attach a bridle for the halyard to attach to. Ideally this should have an eye spliced into the center of balance to take the halyard shackle. If the eyes are mounted outside the hull, the dink can be swung upside down for stowage in its deck chocks.

Some sort of keel, even vestigial, is a necessity to supply directional stability, and the bottom and transom should be reinforced, one for chafe protection in grounding and beaching, the other to take the strains of the outboard. A strong and throughbolted towing eye,

You can't get ashore without a dinghy, but how you row it will either make the trip enjoyable or a wet, tiresome pull. This sequence shows the correct way to row a hard dinghy through moderate chop.

mounted just above the waterlines, is a must as are multiple rowing and oarlock positions. If you want the sailing option, be prepared to pay for it in cash and clutter.

The complications of centerboard or, more likely, daggerboard add weight, possibilities for leaking and obstructions to the basic boat. Then you will have to provide for mast stowage, tie downs, block mounting and more. However, there are times, particularly when you are anchored far out or when you simply wish to explore the harbor late in the day, when a sailing dinghy is ideal. Some powerboat owners might consider this option, thus acquiring the best of both worlds.

Then again, having made a basic choice, how will you move it most of the time? If you plan to clamp on an outboard and power everywhere, well and good. But remember that all outboards get wet, stall-out, foul and stop at the most inopportune moments. They are still great workhorses, especially against adverse winds or currents. Choose one with an integral tank, remember to secure it with both clamps and a stainless steel cable. And, when towing the dink, or when at anchor for any length of time, take it aboard the mother ship and secure it to a rail mount or in a vented locker. Always make sure the gasoline vent is closed when stowing to avoid leaks. Larger tenders can, of course, take larger motors and a separate tank, providing it can be chocked to the floorboards, makes for longer runs and much safer stowage. Again,

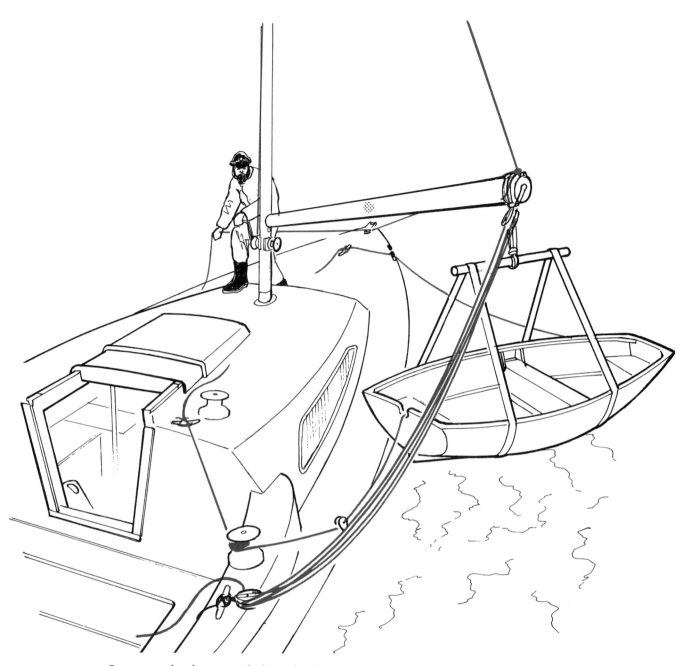

Getting a dinghy stowed aboard or launched is best accomplished using the boom as a hoist, Make sure the boom is guyed-off both fore and aft with enough slack to allow swinging over the rail. Either a sling arrangement, shown here, can be used or else a pair of hoisting eyebolts can be fitted.

never store any fuel in an enclosed, unvented space or locker.

You will need oars in any case as a back-up, and this means, among other criteria, you should look for a dinghy that can be rowed with some ease. Rowing is one of those topics that no one pays much attention to anymore, except for die-hard recreational rowers, yet it can be a pleasure, even when hauling groceries from ashore. The keys to this pleasure are a boat which is light in weight, slender (or reasonably so) for its length, with a comfortable thwart and adjustable foot brace. Additionally, you will need good oarlocks and really good oars.

Oars and oarlocks are an endless subject of debate. A good oar is, first and foremost, light in weight for its size. The best oars are made

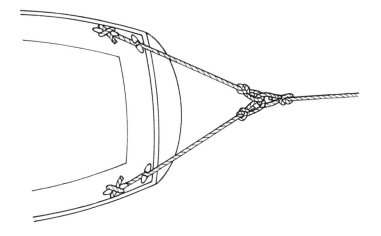

A bridle will better distribute the load of a towed dinghy. Be sure chocks are smooth and padded.

from straight-grained spruce and cost. They are long enough so that, when seated, the blades immerse without undue angle of attack and your hands do not have to cross each other when stroking, a most uncomfortable and tiring situation. Don't bother with spoon blades; they are usually too delicate for the knocks taken by a dinghy oar. Oars should have unvarnished grips and the shaft should be leathered. Do not be tempted by rubber or plastic sleeves. They don't work.

Always try to row with your back, not just your arms. It will be less fatiguing and will supply more power to the stroke. Whether you feather the blades or not will depend upon the type of boat and your skill and dexterity. Rowing against steep chop will require shorter strokes than in smooth water. Shorter oars will also demand a shorter stroke to achieve any momentum.

Probably the biggest problem a novice has is to put everything in every stroke, resulting in slipped oarlocks, very erratic progress and lost oars. Through practice, you must learn to pace yourself to the boat, sea conditions and load. A heavier dinghy will carry its way between strokes, as will one heavily loaded. At the same time, the heavier the load, the greater care the oarsman must take to avoid swamping or capsize.

A lot has been written about the hazards of towing, all of it true. But what choice have you? If you are going to use a hard dinghy or choose to tow an inflatable, if you have neither davits nor deck space, if you are making a series of short hops in settled weather then about your only choice is towing. Unfortunately, merely tying a rope between dink and mother ship will not suffice. Like everything else on the water, the vagaries of wind and weather will help determine how you set up a tow. Additionally, the size, weight, configuration and windage of the dinghy will have major consequences on the tow.

Hard and inflatable dinghies need radically different techniques

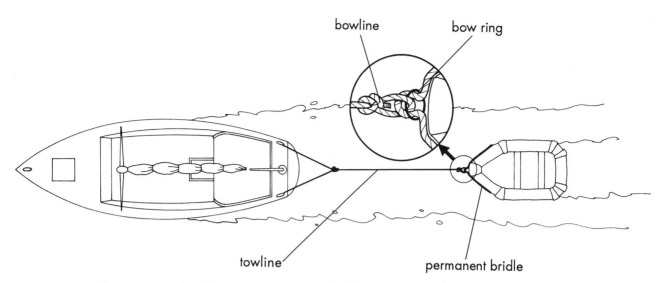

bowline   bow ring

towline   permanent bridle

Towing an inflatable, rig a permanent bridle through the tow ring of the dinghy, tying the towline through both the bridle and the tow ring. Use a bridle from the mother ship and tie the towline proper between the two bridles. This will center the tow, lessen the chances of losing the dink and help keep the dink from flipping.

applied to towing. While a hard dinghy will—depending on weather— usually follow behind, an inflatable will do its best to flip or fill with water. The surest way to protect a rubber boat is to deflate it and lash it on deck or stow it in a locker. If you're lazy or if you are making a short hop between anchorages in settled weather your best bet is to bring the bow of the inflatable over the stern of the mother ship, just level with the deck. It should be tied off with a bridle reaching from rings or the oarlocks just afore midships, in addition to the painter. This will lessen the chances of losing the tender in your wake as it slews from side to side. Nevertheless, for most passages, an inflatable should be on or below deck. Actually, in all towing operations, at least two lines should secure the tow.

Towing a hard tender demands just the opposite approach. Here the tow lines should be long enough—and adjustable—to allow the distance between the tender and the towing vessel to made longer or shorter depending on the sea state and the length of the waves. You should not have the tender burying its bows or filling from the stern. In calm weather this is not a problem, but with any kind of seaway running the possibilities for flipping and swamping are more than even. Likewise, the main towrope should be fitted with a bridle to prevent yaw and rolling. If the bridle is adjustable as well, these can be compensated for. A second tow rope is essential as a safety precaution against loss. Needless to say, no motors, oars, anchors, bailers, lifejackets, etc. should be left in the towed vessel. The only exception allowable are the oars, providing they are lashed to the thwarts or held in place by a patent oar clamp, usually in the form of a bronze double-U shaped bracket which bolts through a thwart and holds the oars by means of a wing nut and bolt.

Safety aboard must remain your primary consideration. Never overload the dinghy. If a tender is meant to carry two people, do not as-

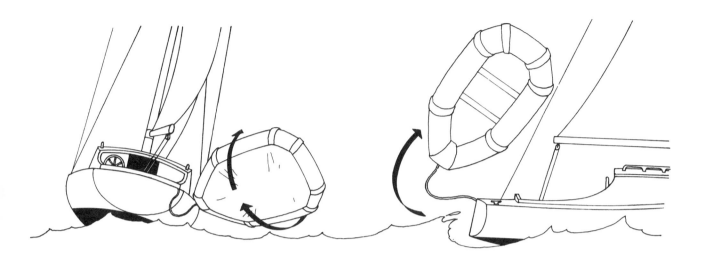

Inflatables will normally tend to flip when towed in a following sea, either over on their side or into the cockpit. Best is to deflate the boat and stow it on deck. If you must tow in a following sea, bring the bow of the inflatable over the stern of the mother ship and tie it fast.

sume you can take three and remain safely upright. Too many drownings have occurred from overloaded dinks capsizing in broad daylight in even calm weather. With the added disadvantages of chop and/or darkness, every precaution must be taken to keep to manufacturer's or Coast Guard recommendations. The same applies to groceries, and gear. If two persons and their gear leave six inches of freeboard in gusty conditions or, for that matter, any other potentially hazardous states, leave one and make a second trip. Better a touch of fatigue than a floating body.

Make sure everyone is wearing a life preserver. This should be the norm for all trips in the tender, but is often ignored. Don't! In rough water and chilly conditions or in calm water and warm conditions, you can still drown. Try to be reasonable; even the most experienced swimmer can get cramps, become disoriented or succumb to hypothermia or swift currents.

More deaths are probably caused by swamped and capsized dinghies than by anything else on the water. The average tender is perhaps 8 or 10 feet in length and cannot really hold more than three people in anything but a dead calm. In truly rough water, no more than two should attempt a journey. As well as not overloading with people, you must be careful to avoid masses of gear, especially in the ends of the boat. Try to keep the boat carefully trimmed and balanced, both athwartships and fore-and-aft.

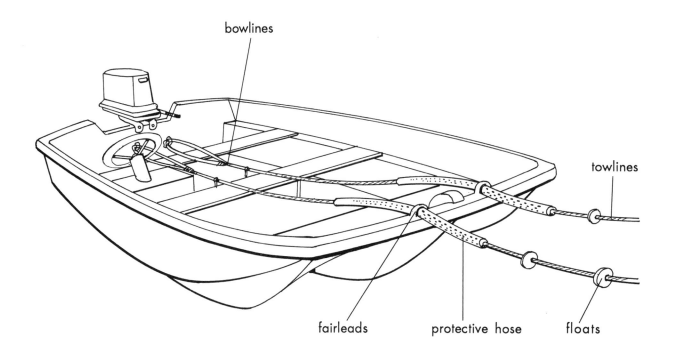

bowlines

towlines

fairleads   protective hose   floats

Towing a pram or trihedral-hull dinghy needs equalizing strain over the wide bow sections. This will also aid in directional stability in the tow. Here, fairleads—two eyebolts (or U-bolts)—have been fastened to the transom and two to the bows. Make sure all lines are chafe-protected.

Most dinghy oars are far too short, too heavy and ill-balanced. Ideally, they should fit into the tender, be made of spruce and shaped to be comfortable to use and efficient at propelling the boat. Far too few people ever bother to learn to row properly. The beamier the boat, the shorter the strokes; the heavier the seas, the shorter the strokes is a fairly sound rule of thumb. However, load, windage, sea state, wetted surface all play a part in the best (read: most effective, least tiring) way to row. Practice. And be sure that you have oarlocks, leathers and a rowing position—with foot brace—that can stand up to the job. Trial and error will find the way.

Getting the dink into the water and back on board is the first concern of the cruising sailor. It must always be tethered to the mother ship. Too often a perfect launch is followed by a perfect drift into the distance. Obviously, the method of launching is dependent upon the ship, but usually some sort of hoist and tackle arrangement will be necessary to accomplish the job with minimum fuss and danger. Always try to have an extra hand to assist. Probably the greatest danger—other than overloading—is in landing or launching through surf. This is *never* a deed to be undertaken lightly! With oar power, the difficulty will be to restrain the dinghy enough or propel it fast enough. With an outboard, the problems are stalling, cavitation and general unreliability if swamped. And that is the danger: swamping, or cap-

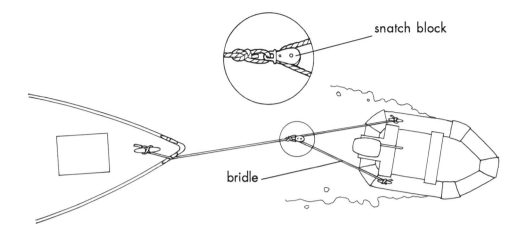

The dinghy can be used to tow the mother ship. To keep loads evened-out, use a snatch block with a bridle, as shown.

size. If the surf is running with any power, you would be well advised to stay on the ship or beach. Otherwise, you shall need a large enough boat and crew to power through. Do not underestimate the power of breaking seas. They can crack your boat into pieces and kill you and your crew.

Entering and leaving the tender demands care and technique. From either a dock or from the deck, the tender must be held steady, usually by means of both bow and stern lines keeping it beam on to the platform. The first person boarding should step quickly into the center of the dink and, in one motion, move aft, sit down and grasp the dock or gunnel to steady the boat. The second person repeats the process and moves forward, etc. Do your best to assure that everyone entering steps quickly and into the center of the dinghy. Never, never allow anyone to attempt to enter by stepping on the rail. This will surely lead to disaster: either with the person falling in the water or capsizing the dink.

Once aboard, make sure everyone is seated, balanced and secure before setting off. Release the stern line first if tied to the ship. Once the oars are in place or the motor started and warmed-up, the bow line can be released and you will be pushed by current or wind aft of the ship. Once clear, you will be able to lean into it and get going. Leaving a dock, which line is first released will depend on wind and current and maneuvering room. By and large, it's better to release the bow line first, allowing the bows to swing out and giving the oarsman room to get his oars in place and stroke. If the wind is pinning the dinghy broadsides to the dock, undo both lines, get the outboard oar in position, then push off and start to row. Remember, when under motor power, to keep all lines clear of the propeller. Also, start slowly under power; prop wash is discourteous, and speed has no place in close quarters.

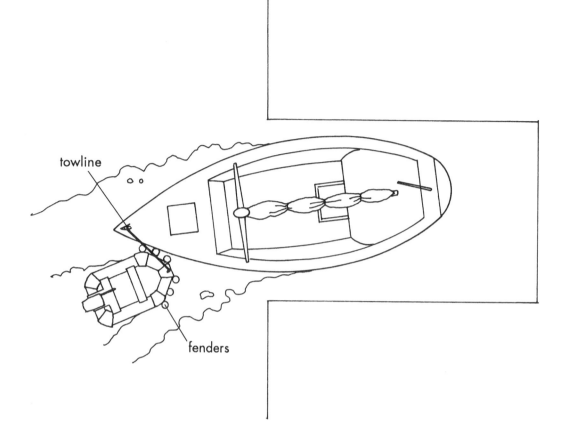

The dinghy can also be used to maneuver the mother ship in tight places, such as a narrow slip. Alternating port and starboard by means of a short towline, and well fendered, the dinghy can move surprising tonnage.

The Crew and Life Aboard

Spending even one night aboard makes you a boat dweller. Though this may seem far-fetched, the acts of sleeping, eating, washing, and cleaning turn one into a liveaboard. Whether for a weekend or a summer, living on a boat cannot be a transfer of your land-based habits to another environment, at least not for most people.

There you are, suddenly living in a very small space, with rudimentary conveniences and without the ability to run down to the corner store for a carton of milk. Generally speaking, there are two ways of looking at it. Either you go all out—assuming you have a large enough boat—and import all the comforts of home, from TV to microwave; or you leap to the other end of the spectrum and go camping with sleeping bags, portable stove and cedar bucket.

Both are perfectly alright if you can deal with the challenges imposed. Luxury demands extra systems. Extra systems demand spares and maintenance and the very good chance of breakdown. Camping, on the other hand, at least when you get to my age, doesn't hold out much pleasure, though ways do exist to make it more than minimally comfortable. Let's look at what's needed to make cruising enjoyable.

First, you need a comfortable place to sleep. Don't scoff! Most berths are too narrow, too short or situated to avoid any ingress of breathable air. For an average person, a berth of 78 inches long by 36 inches wide with a four-inch foam cushion covered in cloth is comfortable. Anything shorter will be confining. If you're exceptionally tall, you will need greater length and perhaps more width as well. Cloth cushions are the only thing for sleeping comfort. Vinyl or other waterproofs will stick and get clammy in any weather due to humidity, not heat.

Second, you need a place to cook. If you want to prepare five course, sit-down dinners on a two-burner range with a square foot of counter space, think again. Over the years, I have suggested, ever so gently, to scores of boaters, that they might be better-off modifying their diet and concept of eating, rather than attempting to duplicate their home meals. Eggs and bacon every morning will not only make a

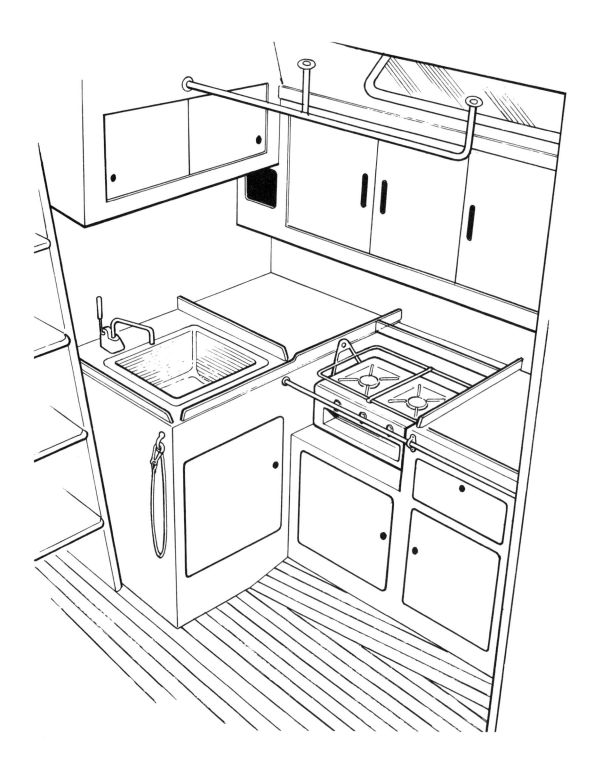

A well-designed galley is vital to the success of every cruise. Note here the crash bar in front of the stove, which is on gimbals. Also, note the galley belt to keep the cook in place in rough weather and the overhead grab rails. All counter surfaces should be surrounded by high fiddles with clean-out openings. The sink should be deep and a manual pump installed, even if you have electric water supply. Cabinet catches must be foolproof and secure. Clearance above the stove needs to be at least two feet. Floors should be the best non-skid available. If the fuel supply is away from the stove, there should be a fuel shut-off valve positioned so it can be reached without stretching over any part of the stove itself.

mess of the galley, it will also contribute to making a mess of your bloodstream, probably already clogged with fat and cholesterol. The process of cruising doesn't take much in the way of physical exertion. Plan your food accordingly. You need a stove of some sort, a sink with water supply. That's it. In the provisioning chapter, I've gone into the subject of refrigeration and cold boxes in some detail.

Third, you need a place to relieve yourself. A head is an irksome thing, to be sure, but the simpler the better. I have cruised on boats with a cedar bucket. It works, though environmental regulations will make it somewhat less useful inshore. Unless you wish to court trouble, stick with a manual head of pure and simple design. Keep spares aboard. Use biodegradable toilet paper.

The above are all you really *need*. What you want is something else, again. Besides eating and sleeping, one must have some amusements and routine to make it all bearable. The key to making a cruise, of whatever duration, really pleasurable is in creating a sense of informal order or ordered informality, whichever, you prefer on board. Just as in a more complex society, chaos leads to discontent and rigid rules lead to rebellion.

The fact is that several people are living in very close quarters, with little or no privacy. Few normal people are used to these conditions. Ex-cons are very familiar with them. The greater the number of people and the smaller the boat, the greater the chance for friction and discord. Some people, the French in particular, seem to enjoy cruising with eight people packed aboard a 35-footer. It *can* be done. One heavily perspiring crew member will make the entire boat seem like your local landfill. It's always best to plan your complement of crew around the existing boat. No production boat today is actually capable of having all its berths occupied and remain a viable cruising vessel.

Personally, I prefer to cruise with my wife or with another couple. That's it. More people aboard mean less stowage space, more stores, less privacy and more stopping in one's tracks to think about possibly offending someone. Now, it's not necessarily a crime to offend the crew, but they don't have the option of getting off at the next corner. So some sort of rules usually have a positive effect.

First, respect each other's privacy or what little exists. It's far too easy to crash in on conversation, reading, sleeping or contemplation when the other person is six feet away. Don't be tempted to interrupt just to fill empty time or space. I know this is hard discipline, but to avoid getting a sharp downward blow on the head, it helps.

Second, assign chores. Nothing will build resentment faster than one person always getting stuck with deck swabbing or cooking or rowing ashore for groceries. Work up a schedule and stick to it. If Tuesday is Jack's day for making breakfast, Jack has the responsibility to get up before everyone else and do it! And, in fact, Jack will end up basking in glory, for he has brought pleasure to the rest of the groggy,

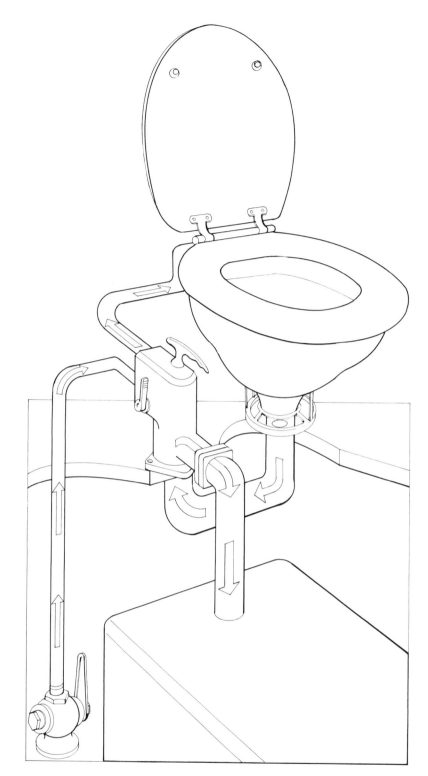

The notorious head. Keeping it functioning makes for a better cruise. Caution everyone to throw nothing in the head, other than toilet paper, that they haven't eaten. Do not throw cigaret butts, sanitary napkins, paper goods, etc. in; they will clog up the pumps and you'll be the one to have to disassemble it all. This drawing shows how it works, including the optional holding tank. The cross-section of the pump shows the location and function of the neoprene valve which prevents backflow. This can get clogged, and you should know how to clear or replace it. Once a week, pour a half-cup of bleach in the head and pump it several times vigorously. This will keep the innards clean and functioning.

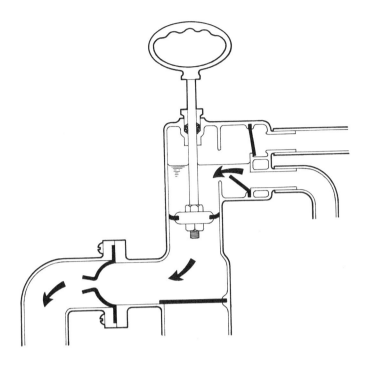

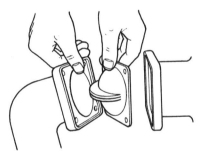

useless (at that hour) crew.

Third, let each member of the crew, especially newcomers to boating, try his hand at everything, including running the ship. Sure, they will make mistakes. Nobody expects you to let a rank amateur con the boat into a strange harbor with a fast current running, but with room and time, let them do a trick at the helm, trim sail, raise anchor or crawl into the bilge for a lost wrench. (This last one can be immeasurably satisfying to observe.)

Fourth, without coming across like a tyrant, do try to explain to the crew the nature of shipboard governance and management. Certainly the days of the absolute dictator as captain are gone. Participatory democracy does work up to a point. On board any boat, someone has to take ultimate responsibility. Take it as lightly as possible.

The Crew and Life Aboard   **47**

CREW

Unless you are a diehard singlehander, the major joy of cruising is the sharing of the experience with others. Whether family or friends or, occasionally strangers, they are all crew. Certain skippers still exist who run things like a ship of the line at Trafalgar, but, thankfully, these are an ever-decreasing minority. While few will contest that one person must have command aboard ship, the captain's relations with his crew will—more than anything else—make or break a cruise.

Dual commands do not work. Someone simply has to take final responsibility—based on knowledge, experience and competence—for any cruising vessel to run smoothly. And it is up to that person to delegate responsibility as in any corporation of individuals, taking into account the capabilities and skills of the crew. No one wants a non-cook in the galley or a mathematical idiot doing navigation.

Prior, far prior, to any voyage, the captain should poll his prospective crew members, including family, to take stock of their talents and desires. A thoughtful captain will try, from the outset, to balance his crew between experience, strength, companionability, special skills and enthusiasm. True, a bunch of hearty, beer-guzzling jocks can probably have a good time together, but most of us have to do with a wider spread of personalities. When planning a voyage, first ascertain the individual quirks of prospective crew, remembering that people who get along on land will not necessarily do so aboard the cramped quarters of an always-in-motion platform.

Best friends often fail as crew; you know each other so well that quirks and eccentricities often accepted on land come to the forefront aboard. Remember, it's harder to cater to individual tastes at sea. This goes for anyone, of course, but good friends can find the sudden changes in democratic action grating.

Family usually becomes the crew. If you have a large brood of outdoor-oriented kids and a wife or husband who relishes the boating life, all is well. Most families, however, struggle with the illusion that cruising is a great way to bring everyone together is happy harmony. It ain't so! If you function well as a nuclear family, you will probably continue to do so at sea. If the family experiences problems at home, those problems will be magnified aboard... and there's no place to run and hide. Nevertheless, every year, thousands of families go cruising with children, toys, sports gear, games, books, video tapes and God knows what else.

Hyperactive children can be a problem on board. They are never satisfied, and the basically contemplative aspect of cruising is beyond them at an early age. Frankly, it's often beyond their elders. Keeping them occupied may well lead to the ruination of your enjoyment. After all, a cruise is supposed to be relaxing, challenging, broadening and exciting. If your time is spent entertaining assorted offspring, there won't be much leftover for you.

If your children are the center of your life, a cruise can be enriching for all concerned, but it must be planned with some goal in mind. Simply taking off for ports unknown will be neither educational—in any structured sense—nor will it achieve the potential of a grand experience. Even a series of short hops down the coast can be made into a lifetime memory if planned to capture a sense of wonderment. If children are allowed to actually run the ship, a vast area of problems will be abolished. Others will, of course, take their place: errors in judgment, navigation, courses steered, docking maneuvers, etc. But no one learns except by experience and mistakes. A perfectionist father will end up with a mutiny.

Whatever crew is chosen, certain ground rules need to laid out from before the beginning of the cruise. If neophytes are coming aboard for the first time, a day's outing prior to the cruise is almost a necessity. After someone has committed to a fortnight aboard, unpleasant surprises are, well, unpleasant. If someone has never been on a boat, gets seasick, has special dietary requirements, needs regular medication, has balance problems or cannot swim, care and patience has to be exercised to avoid either hurting that person or ruining the cruise.

If one is cruising in familiar and sheltered waters, some of these objections can go by the board. A series of half-day passages hugging the coast will do little to upset most persons' routines. However, night passages, voyages of long duration and periods of heavy weather can wreck havoc with timetables and crew. Thus my insistence that crew be chosen with care and tested, especially before a long cruise.

Makeshift still.

Food and Provisioning

On any cruise of more than one night's duration, careful planning, buying and stowage is necessary if the crew is to be well-fed, cared for and happy. The food you eat on a cruise can make or break the voyage. The classic cruising diet of the immediate post-war era was meant for large, wet, tired men with rope burned fingers and heartburn in their guts. Loaded with fat and carbohydrates, it made sense for heavy work in heavy going, when everything had to be manhandled and winches, hydraulics and electrics with not even distant dreams. Dousing 600 square feet of canvas was a far different proposition than furling the equivalent Dacron sail.

Bread, bacon, eggs, meaty stews, endless coffee and untold sweets were the norm. Though there are some hearty toughs who still eat like this, the amount of sugar, starch and saturated fats contained in this sort of meal will horrify any nutritionist and will probably do more harm than good. It's no surprise that a number of long-distance voyagers have been vegetarians, with the occasional fish thrown in.

Frankly, the first reaction to the start of a cruise—at least for a few days—is constipation. This is neither comfortable or pleasant and will sap the energy of almost any man, woman or child. Thus there is a need for nutritious, tasty and *light* meals. I am not going to give directives on exactly what you should eat; after all, everyone has different ideas on what they want when. Rather, I would suggest that you do not attempt to duplicate your home eating patterns, or at least modify them enough to allow comfort and pleasure while at sea.

A few guidelines are in order:

1. Traditional breakfasts of bacon and eggs are generally not a good idea to start the day. They are unhealthy (loads of saturated fats and calories), hard to digest and likely to make one feel drowsy. Better some combination of carbohydrates and protein, say breads or grain cereals, fruit and possibly some protein in the form of cheese or lean meat or fish. Since many people want eggs in the AM, I won't scream otherwise, but I would caution you that eggs taken on a regular basis

are not particularly good for your cardiovascular system. Coffee or tea in moderation won't hurt, but don't gulp down three or four cups—it acts as a depressant.

2. Unless you are at anchor, lunches are probably best made up of sandwiches and soup or salads. On a cold day, a bowl of hearty stew will revive most anyone. However, the same cautions apply. Stay away from masses of mayonnaise, avoid bottled dressings (mostly chemicals), don't overeat (you'll get groggy) and don't drink alcohol (another depressant, and it impairs judgment—something you want to avoid when entering a harbor or navigating in dense fog).

3. Dinner is the time to go whole hog—so to speak—if you are inclined to do so. If you are moored for the night, the weather is settled and everyone has had a good day, a fine dinner with wine or beer is almost a must. But don't make it too late if you plan an early departure. Many folks, myself included, find it difficult to sleep after a 10pm repast.

4. East lots of fiber. The caution about constipation is ever so true. Changing one's habits is bad enough, but psychological considerations play a part, too. Living in cramped quarters, away from regular environments, standing watches and generally throwing caution to the winds is not conducive to regularity. Unprocessed fiber helps: raw fruits and vegetables, dried fruit, nuts, oatmeal and such will keep things moving. It will also, on a regular basis, keep your colon in excellent shape and, according to some medical authorities, aid in the prevention of colon cancer.

Since it was brought up before, I will stress the need to change your eating habits on a cruise. The notion that one needs three balanced meals a day is one perpetrated by dieticians and home economists between the wars, and one that has mindlessly stuck in the brain of generations of mothers. Nutritionists—not dieticians, there is a difference—now recognize that the balance can be achieved over the course of the day. Also, it is now understood, we simply don't need vast quantities of meat, butter, eggs, milk and cheese to locomote. If you've seen your doctor lately, he will have told you that saturated fats will promote clogged arteries, heart disease, sluggishness and probably other ailments, large and small. Protein can be extracted, by the human body, from whole grains, fish, lean poultry with an occasional hunk of lean meat thrown in. One steak a month won't hurt, but hamburgers every day, especially for someone past their mid-30s, will simply increase your chance of a heart attack. Not fun!

The same is true of fats. Butter is bad, no matter what the American Dairy Association may say. Whole milk has no place in the adult diet, unless prescribed by a physician. Use olive oil (or other polyunsaturated oils but beware of palm oil) and drink skim or low-fat milk. Likewise, avoid sugar or excessive starch. Sugar is bad for your teeth, but it also raises your triglycerides. Starch is converted by your body into sugars. Honey, jam, syrups, candy, etc. are all sugars. It don't matter! High triglycerides also lead to heart problems. Sugar ingestion also causes a momentary high, followed, especially on an empty stomach, by a crashing low. Like alcohol, it acts as a depressant eventually. Not a good idea aboard a boat.

So, what do you eat? Grains, fruit, vegetables, low-fat milk products, lean meats, fish and poultry. Snack on dried fruit, nuts, crackers, low-sugar cookies. This is not a diet for the infirm. It's a diet to promote good health, which is what boating is all about anyway. Only you, and your family, know how much to stow aboard per person per week of any given food. A good rule of thumb is to plan for each week's meals and keep emergency stores aboard for an extra week. This goes for water as well.

The usual admonishment about snack foods is concerned with sugar for the watchkeeper. Better to give him low-sugar carbohydrates and crunchy things like nuts and raw vegetables (to keep him busy chewing). Since boating is mostly about bench warming, high calorie, high bulk foods are actually a hindrance.

STORES

In addition to food, a successful cruise is made or broken by the available stores on board: fuel, water, engine oil, stove fuel, mechanical spares, amusements, cleaning supplies and the endless odds and ends which add to the everyday pleasures.

First, figure out how many days you will be away without recourse to a refueling and revictualling port. Then, knowing your boat's tankage, you can decide how much water can be allowed for showers, drinking and cooking, etc. averaging about a gallon a day per man on long voyages, proportionately more for short hops. Do take into account how much time and bother it is to refill tanks, however.

Your fuel supply can be calculated as well, knowing your tankage and consumption at varying engine revolutions. Allow extra! For an especially long passage, make sure that you can make the distance at cruising revs with at least one-quarter the distance over to allow for bad weather, getting lost and possible breakdowns. If you've planned a 100nm run, allow for 125nm. If your boat consumes 10 gallons per hour at 12 knots, that breaks down to ca. 84 gallons of fuel plus a safety margin of ca. 21 gallons or a total of 105 gallons. Don't try to stretch it. Carry approved jerry cans of extra fuel on deck, where they can vent overboard. Remember, most fuel vapors are heavier than air and will sink beneath the cockpit and into the bilges. Be very careful in handling and stowing fuel not in integral tanks.

Unless you are a purist sailor, you will use the engine, at least for berthing and fighting off lee shores. Make sure that you have spares for the essentials: filters, impellers, belts, plugs. On a long cruise consider adding a starter motor, injectors fuel lines, hoses and more, depending on the recommendations in the owner's manual. Any lubricants, especially engine oil, should be carried as well. Don't forget adjustable hose clamps and pump spares (flaps, diaphragms and hose).

Spares should be carried for most deck gear and sailing gear as well: winch springs and pawls, extra snatch blocks, coils of rope in various necessary sizes, rigging wire long enough to replace the longest stay, bulldog clips, chain, sail repair materials (see Bosunry). For a really long cruise you'll probably want to add paint, varnish and special parts not easily replaced.

Cleaning and storage supplies are a major part of any boat's stores: toilet paper, paper towels, plastic bags, dish washing detergent (which can replace soap and shampoo), cellulose sponges, scrubbers, food storage containers (plastic is best), foil, plastic wrap, etc.

Amusements must be catered to: games, cards, tape player and tapes. Things like electronic games and hockey sticks are best left ashore. Since you're all on the water, fins and snorkels, windsurfers, fishing tackle and clam rakes will be squeezed in somewhere. All these take monstrous amounts of boat space, though they will probably only fill a closet shelf or a corner of the garage at home. Plan carefully. You can actually muck-up your voyage going the overload route. There's no way anyone can possibly cover every possible contingency. Pick and choose for maximum enjoyment.

A cruise without books is inconceivable to me. Paperbacks are fine. When the weather is inclement or on a quiet evening or in the doldrums, nothing beats a good book. Whether you enjoy mysteries, horror, suspense, gothics, biography, how-to or current events doesn't really matter. But since a cruise is essentially an adventure for the imagination, why not reinforce it with the one activity that allows you to exercise yours without getting up!

FOOD STORES

What you take along, as mentioned above, depends on your diet and the amounts you and your crew normally consume, and then some. Food is a worrisome topic for all cruising sailors. For short passages and frequent harbor stops, there are few problems. But when you are off for several months in distant climes with no reliable sources of supply, problems of feeding increase exponentially. Many authors have recommended shopping lists. No one can really do this for you except yourself. Best is to decide what you need—without unnecessary frills—to feed your crew. If you cut down on meat your problems are greatly eased. Keeping fresh protein on board is possible only with large amounts of ice or with refrigeration. Both create many problems: generator or engine noise, constant supply stops, draining iceboxes and, sooner or later, breakdown or simply no supplies.

My wife and I have cruised for many years with neither refrigeration nor ice and have eaten extraordinarily well.

First, consider preserved meats and fish: smoked, pickled, canned and dried. Right off you have a choice of bacons, hams, smoked fish, canned meats and fish, canned poultry, dried beef, dried sausages, salted or pickled fish and meats... the choice is great if you're willing to try new tastes. Most hard cheeses will keep well without refrigeration, tightly wrapped and kept in the bilges. Any mould can be cut off and the cheese rewrapped in vinegar-moistened cheesecloth, then in plastic wrap or foil. Butter and margarine will keep in the bilges in airtight plastic containers. I don't eat eggs, but fresh (unchilled) eggs can be kept for a month to six weeks, provided they are turned every other day. Some sailors coat them with paraffin or Vaseline. Much easier is to plunge them in boiling water for 30 seconds (this seals the inner membrane just under the shell and prevents air from spoiling them).

Most citrus fruits and root vegetables can be kept in a cool dark place where they won't get banged around, either hung in string bags or kept in baskets in the forepeak. They need air circulation and should be checked every couple of days. Any soft or rotting ones should be used immediately or thrown away. Hard green veggies—cabbages, cauliflower, onions—will hold up as well under the same care.

Certain foods spoil very fast indeed: milk, bread, fish, poultry, fresh meat, leafy vegetables. Buy them when you can and use that day or the next. And don't forget all the dried vegetables and grains and fruits: beans, peas, rice, barley, cous cous, kasha, apricots, pears, apples, figs, dates, prunes, etc. These can all add variety to the diet and, if prepared with care, interesting tastes and textures.

Spices, herbs and condiments will make your food more palatable: vinegar, mustard, ketchup (sparingly), olive oil (which, health conscious as I am, I use instead of butter), chutneys, pickles (good source of vitamin C), olives, nuts, garlic (chopped in oil), anchovies, worcestershire sauce, Tabasco all lend a different savor to food preparation. Mayonnaise is not recommended. It will spoil without refrigeration. If you are in desperation, you can always whip some up with olive oil and an egg. Likewise salad dressings; with oil and vinegar and herbs there's no need for bottled dressings. All they do is take up space and add chemicals to your system.

Never trust your senses in a fog. Post a lookout in the bow and never proceed faster than dead slow. All signalling should be by hand, as silence is vital to safety in fog.

Navigation, Weather and Passagemaking

The essence of good navigation is knowing where you are at any given moment in time and space. Simple enough! The proliferation of electronic navigation devices has somewhat covered over the basics of the subject of late. Your concern when cruising should be to ascertain your position as simply and expediently as possible, with the least chance of losing your way or imperiling your ship and crew.

This chapter is not intended to be a textbook in piloting and celestial navigation. You should learn those prior to setting out on a cruise. What you will find here are bits and pieces to turn you into a better, more cautious navigator.

Assuming you know the basics of piloting, how to read a chart and plot a course, how to follow a course, the rudiments of tides and currents, how to judge distance-off and work speed/distance/time calculations you should be in as good a shape as most anyone, providing you practice. Like riding a bicycle, you don't forget, but you get rusty. A good navigator is, by nature, a compulsive planner. You may not like it, but sloppy piloting will always get you into trouble.

NAVIGATIONAL PLANNING

Before setting off, or even thinking of setting off, you should plan your passages. This will involve getting hold of the charts for the areas you wish to cruise in, piloting books, tide tables and cruising guides. Read everything you can on the area, its pleasures and peculiarities, especially its navigational hazards. Make sure light lists and charts are as up-to-date as possible. Do not rely on someone's hearsay or personal knowledge. Chances are it's changed since last season or, if not, it's been remembered with imprecision. Imprecision is what causes disaster in navigation.

With your charts in front of you, plot your probable courses on a buoy to buoy basis. With a reasonably fast power boat, this is no problem in the doing; you point and go. If distances are short you will have little correction to make, unless currents are strong. In a sailboat or a slow power vessel, you will have to allow for tidal streams, wind strength and direction and helming error. This last is not to be scoffed at. Any long passage will try the patience and precision of the helmsman and, without the aid of an autopilot, will eventually lead to course aberrations.

These plots will allow you to plan the time needed for each hop and the fuel and or supplies necessary for that period. In your plotting, allow extra time for clearing headlands, skirting shoals and working around obstacles. These can be gleaned from the chart and must be thought out carefully.

If you plan to sail at night, planning becomes even more critical as you will be solely dependant on lights and your own navigational aids: loran, RDF, log and speedometer and depth sounder. Offshore, the option of satellite navigation offers some repose, but you don't, of course, have to worry about hitting land!

WEATHER

Probably the most important variable in any passage is the weather. Settled weather allows you to navigate with greater precision and predict your ETA with much greater sureness. Unfortunately, the forces of nature don't often cooperate, especially during the period of a cruise. Wind and sea state can either aid or hinder your progress, though extremes of either will, if you're lucky, keep you in port.

The first thing you need to have aboard is an accurate barometer. Weather forecasts are fine, but you will have to learn, sooner or later, to predict the weather yourself. If you cruise far from radio signals, you will not have local forecasts to rely on. The best tool for this is the barometer. Generally speaking, a high pressure reading promised settled, clear weather; a low reading warns of impending storms. But many variants exist, depending where you are on the earth's surface and what geographical peculiarities abound.

Every effort should be made to get extended forecasts before you leave. On ocean passages, pilot charts can give you averages for weather systems in different parts of the ocean. Coastal passages are at vanguard of fast-moving fronts. Certainly, the ability to read clouds can help forecast weather. These fronts are much more unsettled in summer months, at least in the temperate zones. If you're lucky enough to have a weatherfax, these problems are somewhat lessened. Still, every effort should be made to log barometric pressure changes, cloud formations, wind shifts and temperature and relative humidity. These will allow you to predict, with some small certainty, a potential change. Since professional meteorologists are so often wrong in their forecasts, one can be prepared for everything and anything.

PASSAGEMAKING

All the preparation–fitting-out, new equipment, safety gear, stores,

TIME 1735
DISTANCE SAILED 3/4 M
CURRENT WESTERLY
WIND SPEED 15 knts
DIRECTION SSE
TIDE 35 M to high

Keeping a log board at the helm is advisable, not only o keep track of course and condition changes, but also to acquaint the oncoming watch with current progress. The board is best made of translucent or solid plexiglas with the categories painted on. Use a grease pencil for notations; it's waterproof, yet can be easily wiped-off.

food and supplies—is one thing; actually getting to your destination is another. Though this may seem more than obvious, very few boat owners make long passages. If you are a confirmed cruiser you will probably scoff at this contention, but statistics belie your pride. Most boats sit around, waiting for a day never to come, ever-improved, almost ready. Frankly, you reach a point in all human endeavors where you either take the plunge or you don't. If you bought this book for armchair pleasure, fine. If you are really going to get out on the water for more than an afternoon, you will have to go somewhere!

A passage of an afternoon takes as much planning—though on a somewhat different scale—as one lasting a year. You must be prepared for anything, you must know what you are doing, you must plan for the passage. Of the many areas of planning perhaps the most important is deciding where you want to go and how much time you actually have to get there and back. If you own a fast power boat, and the weather is settled, the problems are almost nonexistent. You fill the tanks, stock the galley, check systems and go, knowing the distance to run and your fuel consumption, of course. Do not belittle this point. Every summer, the water is filled with power boats out of fuel, bobbing helplessly. It's easy enough to make up a rpm/nm run consumption chart. You start by marking out a strait course of ca. five nautical miles. You then run that stretch of water at different engine speeds. An afternoon spent on three or four runs will pay off in increased confidence in yourself and your boat. If your ship can do 10 knots at 2,100rpm, consuming five gallons of fuel per hour, and you have a tank capacity of 100 gallons, you can assume that you have a range of 200 nautical miles and 20 hours running time. Of course you will cut those figures to allow for heavy weather and reserve running.

Once you know what your boat can do—and a sailor should take two-thirds of the boat's hull speed as an optimum average cruising speed—you can map out your itinerary. A good rule of thumb is to plan passages of one-half what you think you can actually make in a given time period. Weather, fatigue and the unexpected will always pop up to surprise you with their delaying effects. For a small cruising sailboat that works out to about 25 nm per day. A powerboat, on the other hand, can go as far as her speed and fuel capacity can take her.

Next, make sure the compass is correctly swung and a deviation table is made up. Spend as much as you can afford on the compass and get one as large as is practicable. Spherical compasses are most popular these days, but a good flat card traditional model is just as reliable. One etched in compass degrees with every fifth degree so noted is fine. Try to site it on the centerline and away from anything remotely liable to effect its pointing magnetic North. Cans, engines, rigging, flashlights will all effect its performance. If you plan to sail at night, it needs to be lit with a red bulb to protect your night vision.

Having stocked the boat to your likes, next brief the crew. This is more important than it sounds, though modern crews don't much like it. Nevertheless, every crewmember should be familiar with all the operating systems of the ship, emergency procedures, location of safety gear and rules and regulations as practiced on your boat. Additionally, every crewmember should be given a clear and concise briefing on his or her duties and responsibilities. If a long passage is to be made, a watchkeeping system must be set up and followed.

There are any number of possible systems, but your choice will depend on the number of crew available for watch duty and their relative experience. With only two, four hours on and four off usually works the best, as any longer will tire the watchkeeper and any shorter will not allow the off crew to get any real rest or sleep. With four crew you can go to a three hours on, five off system with a rotating clock. This way no one gets bored and watches change with some frequency. However, feeding becomes chaotic. With large crews, of course, any number of schemes can be worked out.

Most watch systems do not take into account the personal habits and needs of crew. Some people can stay up for hours, others need rest—especially from helming—every few hours. No one can tell you what's best for your boating conglomerate. You will just have to try different combinations until you find the one that best suits the available manpower.

Self-steering is not a replacement for proper watchkeeping. A couple of years ago I was a witness in an Admiralty Law case. A single-handed sailor had been run down by a tanker in good visibility. At the time, the sailor was down below. It took two years to reach a settlement, but I believe the sailor was wrong, especially as he was neither flying marks nor showing any lights at the time. Rules of the road again! Self-steering will take the load off the watchkeeper. If you don't

Sailing to windward is not usually the plan when cruising, but it will have to be done. The most efficient method of doing this is herein diagrammed.

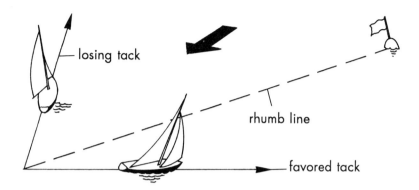

Fig. 1. The favored tack: the boat on starboard tack is making more ground towards it goal than the boat on port tack.

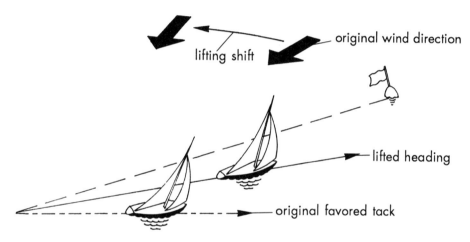

Fig. 2. Lifting shifts: when a boat already on the favored tack is lifted, she will point better and make more ground.

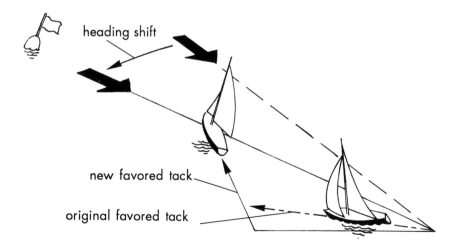

Fig. 3. Heading shifts: a boat on the favored starboard tack is is headed now on the losing tack. Coming about, the port tack is now favored.

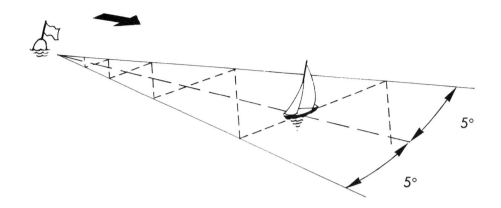

Fig. 4. Tacking cone: should the wind be dead on the nose. With the boat on the rhumb line, any wind shift is beneficial on either port or starboard tack. If the boat tacks up the cone (10°) it remains near enough to the rhumb line to take advantage of any changes in wind direction.

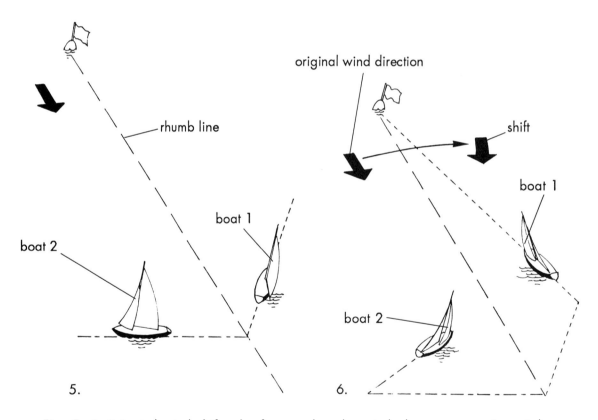

Fig. 5. Anticipated wind shifts: the forecast has the wind about to veer. Boat 1 has stood to the side of the rhumb line to which the wind is expected to shift. Boat 2 will take what comes her way.

Fig. 6. Anticipated wind shifts: after the shift. Boat 1 tacks and is able to lay her course. Boat 2 finds herself with the wind on her nose. Boat 1 will be far ahead when the two cross tacks.

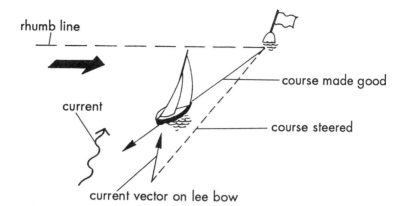

rhumb line

current

course made good

course steered

current vector on lee bow

Fig. 7. Lee bowing the current: keeping the flow of the current on the boat's lee bow, she will remain closer to the rhumb line. Here, though the wind is foul, starboard tack is favored.

have to steer, you can concentrate better, tire less and in general be more alert. Since no other ship is likely to pop-up on the horizon in under five or so minutes, you have the possibility of ducking below for a snack or to relieve yourself. And, in bad weather, you can make course corrections from within shelter, providing you have an autopilot with a remote control pad or can lead your wind vane lines to the companionway.

Once you've set up your rules and systems, you can actually cast-ff and get underway. This is no place for learning basic piloting and navigational techniques, as any number of good books or courses are available, but certain points should be stressed. First, do your chartwork. It's very easy to ignore it, especially on a relatively familiar run. But what happens when the fog rolls in? Keep a running plot at all times, and I mean at *all* times. At least at the beginning of every watch change, or every couple of hours on a short passage, determine and mark your position on the chart. Check log readings, time, speed made good. The time taken and the ease of the calculations will banish much uncertainty from your passage.

When approaching a headland or making a landfall, always take bearings and calculate distance off. The techniques are simple enough and, though they take some practice to work smoothly and accurately, are a necessity for safe arrivals. Equally important, especially when entering harbors or anchorages, is to take soundings. First, they will keep your boat off the bottom. Second, they will allow you, especially in low visibility to ascertain your position by following contour lines of established depth against the chart.

Ocean passages demand other skills. You will need to learn how to use a sextant and reduce sights. Both Mary Blewitt's classic book and the more recent one by Stafford Campbell are the clearest explanations I know. Many navigators get by with sun sights alone, but they are missing out on the fun of nighttime observations. Also, with modern

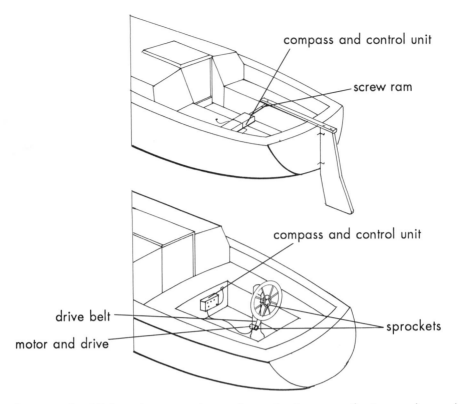

compass and control unit

screw ram

compass and control unit

drive belt

sprockets

motor and drive

On boats under 35 feet, the screw-drive, tiller-activating autopilot is popular and reliable. Since they can be installed without permanent modifications to the steering gear, maintenance and repair are much facilitated.

timepieces, calculators and instruments, much, if not all, of the mystery has been banished from celestial navigation. Equally important for the ocean navigator is dead reckoning, especially if weather is bad and visibility is down. Though this will only give you an approximation, it can be a pretty accurate one, and may be your only source of positioning for days on end.

Ocean currents are more easily calculated than coastal ones, but a set of current charts and tables is a must. The vector calculations have to be made. Don't assume that you can judge the effects of a current (which, in the middle of the ocean, with no marks, you can't) just by checking leeway. Even in a swift powerboat, current will have an effect, sometimes to the detriment of your timing and landfall.

Even with all the wonders of modern electronics, learn how to find your position the good old-fashioned way. It's actually enjoyable and, when you lose power or equipment malfunctions, you'll always have fail-safe back-up.

AUTOPILOTS AND SELF STEERING

Helmsmanship is the most exhausting of all regular chores of passagemaking. The modern boatman has the advantage of having a wide assortment of mechanical/electrical devices to take on the tedium.

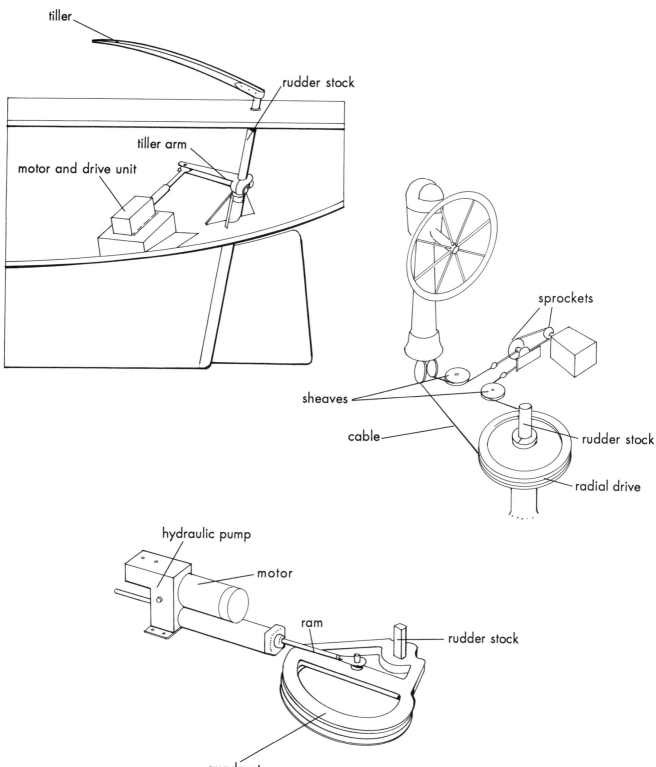

tiller

rudder stock

tiller arm

motor and drive unit

sprockets

sheaves

cable

rudder stock

radial drive

hydraulic pump

motor

ram

rudder stock

quadrant

Permanently installed autopilots make more sense for powerboats and larger craft. Here are three types of installation, for tillers, for cable and quadrant systems and for direct quadrant control. All of these systems will add a certain amount of friction to manual steering, but their reliability is greater than removeable units, protected as they are from the elements.

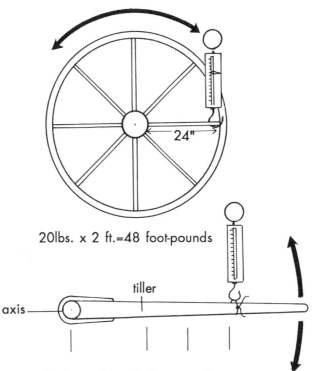

20lbs. x 2 ft.=48 foot-pounds

30lbs. x 2ft.=60 foot-pounds

To ascertain helm loads, use a fisherman's scale as shown. Multiply force in pounds times distance in feet from the attachment point of the scale to the axis. The result is foot-pounds.

Self-steering takes one of two basic forms: wind vanes or autopilots.

The first is applicable only to sailing vessels and can be had in direct drive, servo-pendulum or auxiliary rudder forms. If you are planning to go ocean voyaging one of these will be a good investment. For coastal cruising, however, its ability to steer by wind direction is somewhat hampered by constant wind shifts caused by headlands, local geography and the multiplicity of passing weather fronts caused by varying land masses. Offshore, few of these hindrances apply.

For powerboats and sailboats with suitable battery capacity an autopilot is the most logical way to go. A sensing compass acts through a series of relays and motors to activate a mechanism—push-pull arm, chain drive, hydraulic cylinder, etc.—which steers the boat on a compass course. Of course, the wind direction will not necessarily cooperate for sailors, but except dead to windward some compromise can usually be reached. These units come in sizes and configurations for any boat, ranging from simple unit-to-tiller devices up to large gear-driven hydraulic systems for large yachts.

NIGHT SAILING

Many boatmen become uneasy with nighttime passagemaking. Well, we all harbor some childhood fears of the dark, but night passages can be among the most satisfying parts of a cruise. Obviously, you have to

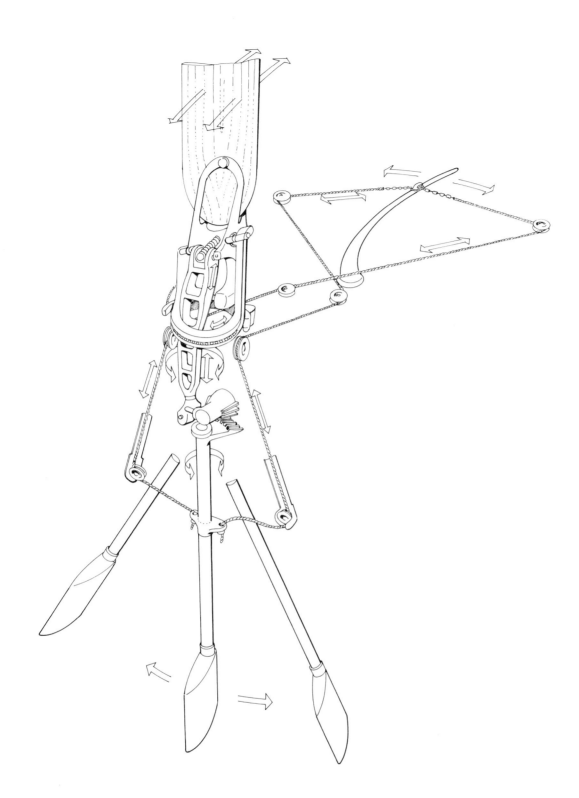

A pendulum, servo vane. The force of the wind cocks the vane, maintaining a preset course. Vanes will only sail a course in relation to the apparent wind. The servo mechanism will increase the force transmitted to the auxiliary rudder or tab in the water. For long ocean voyages, vanes will allow one to sail without dependence on batteries and charging. On coastal passages, they can be next to useless due to constant windshifts and the need for never ending correction.

Navigation, Weather and Passagemaking **67**

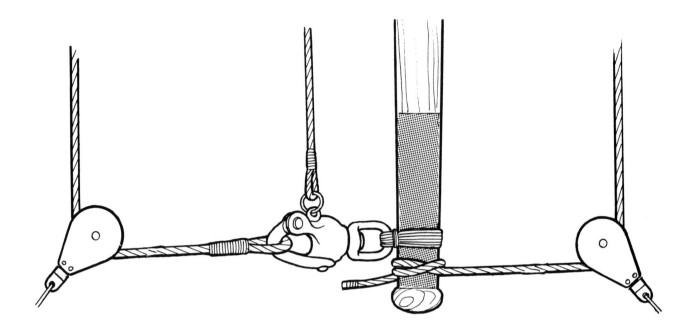

When using a vane gear alone at the helm, it's a good idea to rig a quick-release tackle, such as shown here. The line (ca. 100ft.) from the snap shackle leads overboard with a floating ring attached to the outboard end. Should the helmsman fall overboard, he can grab the ring, releasing the gear and causing the boat to round up, giving him a chance to get back aboard.

pay much closer attention to your navigation. Before starting out—and it's a good idea to start a night passage before sunset—lay out your course with precision, and chart every change an d deviation along the way. Get food and drinks ready before starting off. Don warm clothing for, except in the tropics, temperatures can drop precipitously at night.

Darkness demands your running lights are working properly and are lit to conform to the regulations for the waters you are in. Make sure your compass light is working. Concentrating at the helm can be easier at night, as there are fewer distractions, fewer ships at sea and no sun shining in your eyes to making you drowsy. Still, a proper lookout is necessary, as is taking bearings should any other ship be spotted. It can be very confusing, even for old pros, to judge distance-off and speed at night.

An autopilot is a godsend, but the same rules of watchkeeping apply. On coastal passages, shore lights can be very confusing. The necessity of plotting your passage carefully will be much more evident when you are looking for a lighted buoy and the harbor lights twinkle in the thousands. If your course has been accurate, you should, with the log working, be able to judge within a 15 minute period when you are approaching a marker. Post a lookout at the bow during that span. If the light cannot be found, stop! Recalculate your position. If you're

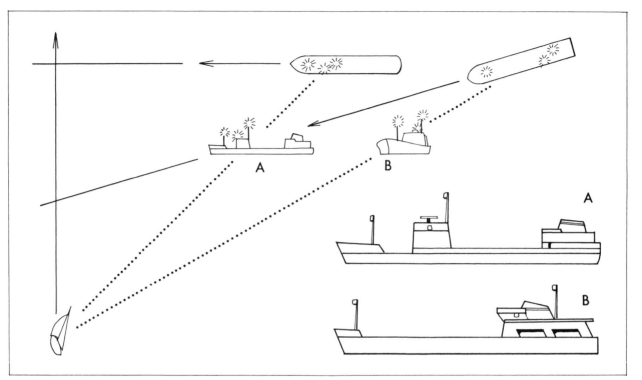

Crossing another ship's path, especially at night, is fraught with dangers. That she is showing the correct and proper lights is not to be assumed as a matter of course. The configuration of the approaching vessel's lights as well as the angle of approach is very important. Thus the need to start taking bearings immediately upon sighting. In the illustration, ship A has her lights and masts closely grouped and forward; ship B has them widely spaced. Thus A seen beam-on looks very similar to B as seen from an angle.

tired, you've probably made a mistake. Don't putter around until you've got a good idea of your actual position. Then, you can either sail on or sail a reciprocal course until you spot the mark.

Making a landfall at night, as mentioned below, should be done with extreme care, especially in heavy weather or in an unfamiliar harbor. If conditions are truly bad, stand-off at sea, either with a sea anchor or hove-to. If the weather is good, follow the marked channel with rigid concentration. Do not ever attempt shortcuts without local knowledge.

Cruising at night demands care and preparation, but it can be a romantic and extraordinarily satisfying experience.

FOG

Fog is never fun. It is threatening, causes one to mishear and misjudge distances and objects and generally unnerves the neophyte. It is one of the few situations aboard when you should *mistrust* your senses. In fact, the only things to trust in are the compass, radio bearings, depth soundings and radar. Since fog distorts sound on the water, bells and horns can seem to come from all directions. In any fog conditions a lookout should be posted at the bow. Even then, you cannot be sure that what you see is really where you think it is. Bell or horn must be sounded at intervals stipulated in the Rules of the Road.

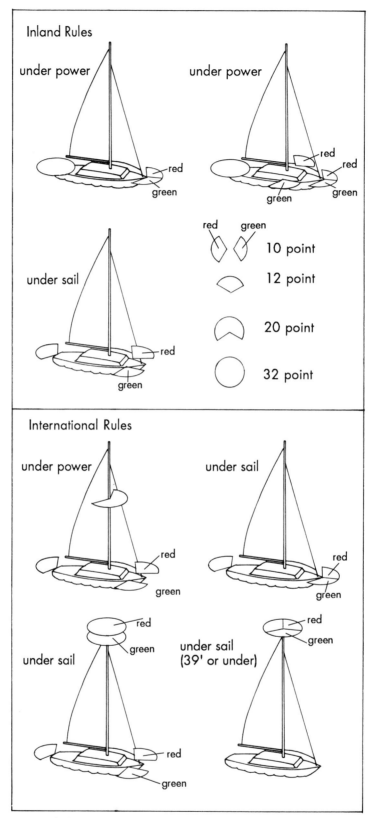

Showing the correct lights is vital to any safe navigation at night. Two sets of light rules apply in the USA: Inland and International. Inland Rules apply to waters within the inland demarcation lines on NOAA charts. International Rules apply to the high seas and coastal waters and most foreign countries. International lights may be shown in inland waters but not the other way around.

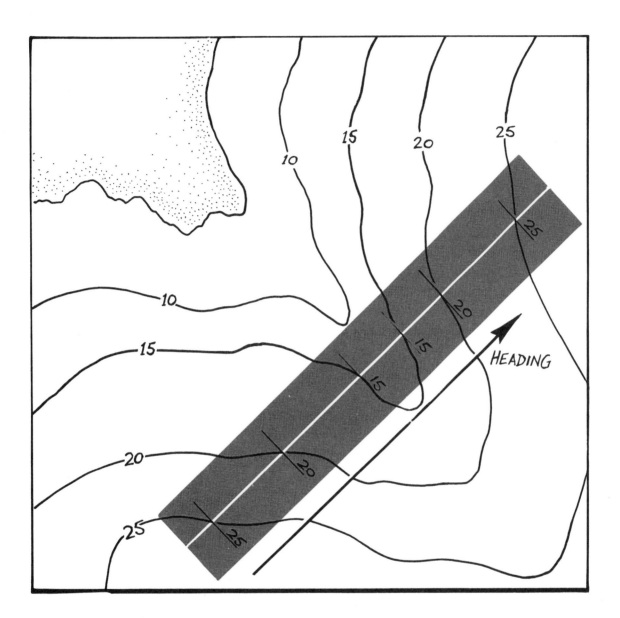

Contour navigation—following a sounding line on the chart—can be most useful in fog conditions. You must know your position, and must have an accurate, calibrated depth finder aboard, as well as an adjusted compass with deviation table. You then proceed to take soundings in a continuous run in the charted direction. Any deviation from the charted sounding line will become immediately apparent from the soundings. One person should man the chart and depth sounder and call out bearings, course and soundings to the helmsman.

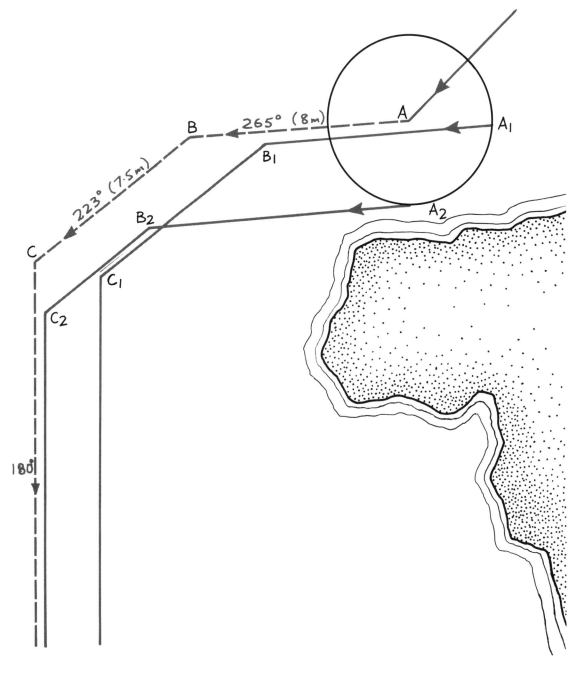

Fig. 1

Rounding a headland in fog. Accurate DR approach, you find yourself in a fog with a headland to round. Fig. 1, A is your DR plot. Give yourself a large area of uncertainty, say 8% instead of 5% of distance sailed, then take the two worst points on the circle: A_1 the most easterly and A_2 the most southerly. A, B, C would be your normal fine weather course, but if sailed from A_1 or A_2 would run you ashore. Fig. 2 shows a course 265°, 8 miles; 223°, 7.5 miles; 180° onward if sailed from A_1 or A_2 would take you clear of the headland. Points to remember:

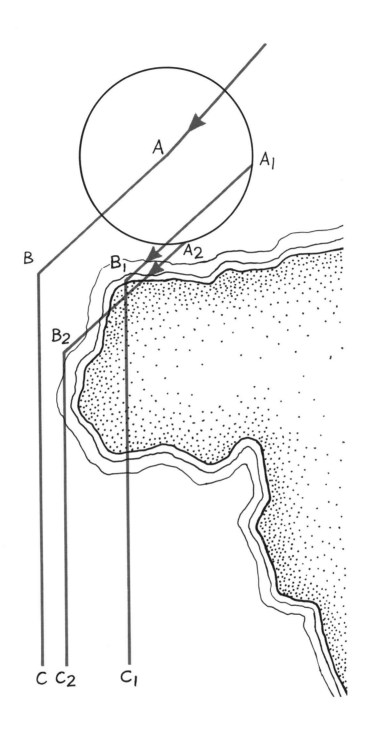

Fig. 2

1. This course must be corrected for tidal direction prevailing at the time.
2. Your area of uncertainty is growing continually, and if the fog does not lift, you should keep off after rounding the headland.
3. At all times you will be plotting radio bearings, listening for fog signals, using your depth sounder. Do not cut inside your safe course unless you are certain it is safe to do so.

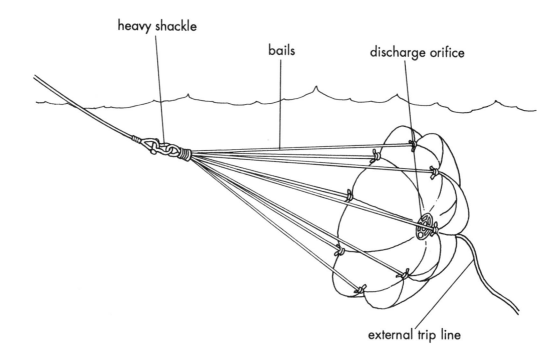

heavy shackle

bails

discharge orifice

external trip line

In certain situations, a sea anchor can be most useful to slow down a boat in heavy seas and to stabilize motion. However, the anchor must be enormous—15 to 20 feet is not outrageous, though some experts suggest twice the keel's depth—and properly streamed. The strains imposed on deck gear are exorbitant and provision should be made to take them; wrapping the line around a winch and then cleating it, with the trip line wrapped around another winch is a good idea.

A radar reflector should be hoisted at the slightest letdown in visibility. Other boats will at least know you're there, even if they cannot pinpoint your location.

In fog always proceed dead slow. Most of the time you will find fog accompanied by flat calm, but sometimes, as off the coast of Maine, fog can roll in with a brisk breeze. If under sail, shorten down to keep your speed below five knots. You don't want to surf into a trawler or a buoy. Additionally, at speed your sense of sound and its source will be even more confused. It's dangerous! Remember that *any* other boat is a danger!

HEAVY WEATHER

Sooner or later you will have to face bad weather in your cruising career. A good deal of discussion can be found in the chapter on emergencies. Few of us every get caught in the ultimate storm, but breakdowns, coupled with heavy seas and high winds can be deadly. Sailors generally are more aware of this than powerboaters. They have to rely on their wits, not their motors. When a powerboat finds itself in rough conditions, the options are fewer, since most planing hulls are not designed to move very effectively at low speed. Round-bilged hulls will take big waves better, but the average hard-chine powerboat will tend to position itself beam on to the seas. The results will proba-

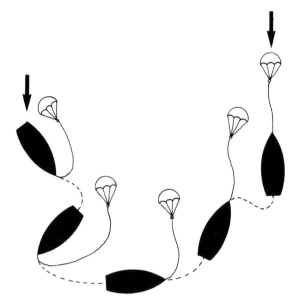

Deploying a sea anchor can take some getting used to. Basically, the boat should be headed on a broad reach, with the wind on the quarter and stream the anchor from the bow. When half the line has been payed out, jibe or power the stern through the wind and get the wind on the other quarter, then let out the remainder of the line. With the rudder amidships, let the line straighten out. As the line moves through the water, it slows the boat and brings the bow into the wind. Do not attempt to steer the bow into the wind. This would slack the line and cause the boat to fall off.

bly turn your stomach, since your won't roll so much as snap back and forth. Very soon, your stamina and courage will weaken. With that comes panic. You can prevent it.

In sailboats you can run under bare poles or storm canvas. In a powerboat you must keep her pointing somewhat head-to-wind, throttling-down to keep green water off the foredeck. If conditions get so bad that this is impossible, the next best tactic is to stream a sea anchor from the bow to keep her head-to-wind. These anchors must be very large indeed to be effective. Diameters of 20 feet are not to be scoffed at for a boat of from 20-35 feet in length. Cleats must be very strong to take this and everything that can be removed that adds windage should be got below.

Of course, if you can get to safe harbor before a blow, all the better. Secure the boat and stay there! Don't be tempted to make schedules or meet friends *unless you are experienced enough and know your boat can make the passage safely*. Novices often assume they can cope. The sea will beat them almost every time. Nothing man makes cannot be destroyed by nature. Don't chance it.

LANDFALL

Once you've gotten across a body of water you must eventually stop. Yet, too often, boatmen forget in their exhilaration on sighting land—be

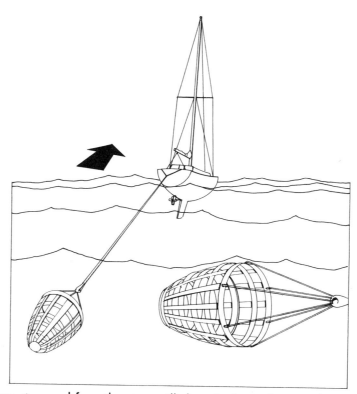

An open drogue streamed from the stern will slow the boat down and prevent rolling and possible capsize. This is a solution for running off in heavy weather and should not be used when you are simply trying to stabilize the boat by streaming a sea anchor from the bow.

it an peak visible at the end of a long ocean passage or the harbor entrance 20 miles down the bay—that the dangers of bringing the boat to anchor are greater than those of being in relatively open water. Much of this is discussed in detail in the chapter of harbors and anchoring, but it must be noted that the greatest number of problems arise from not knowing the Rules of the Road, not studying large-scale harbor charts and not reading-up in cruising guides and pilot books on the peculiarities of a harbor. you have yet to enter. All this comes before you get there. If you go plowing in, you will probably regret it.

Since you will be tired after a long passage, your first thought should be for your presence of mind. Are you alert enough to make-fast safely. If not, and the wether permits, drop anchor outside or heave-to until you feel better. Arriving at your destination at night, unless you know the harbor intimately, jill around outside until first light. There will be less traffic and you will see what you're doing. The temptations is always there to get ashore and snuggle into a warm pub. A few hours can make the difference between snuggling and salvage.

GOING FOREIGN

Even if you're chartering in the Bahamas, remember you have gone to another country. The laws and customs are different, and you are

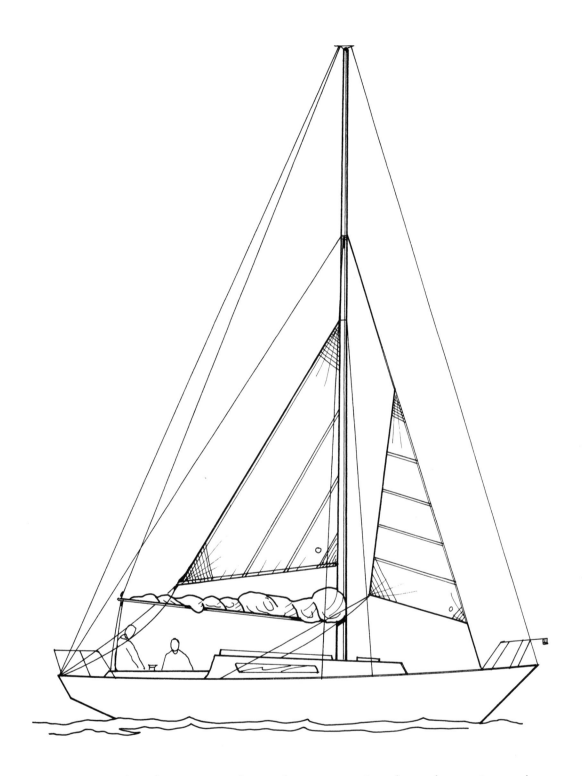

Storm canvas, though not a normal part of many cruiser's sail complement, is a real necessity for any long passages. In truly heavy wind and seas, the main, no matter how well it can be reefed, presents too many dangers from the boom and rigging. Equally, no normal jib is small enough to balance the boat against a storm trysail. The hoisting and deployment of these sails must be carefully worked out prior to any departure, especially fairleads and track arrangements for the trysail.

Navigation, Weather and Passagemaking   77

Short-handed cruising crews will most probably use an asymmetrical spinnaker for down-wind work. Actually, they are quite simple to use, if you follow a few simple steps.

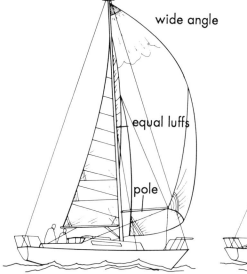

Fig. 1. Traditional symmetrical spinnaker.

Fig. 2. Asymmetrical cruising spinnaker.

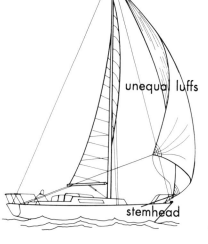

Fig. 3. Spinnaker and sock ready to be hoisted.

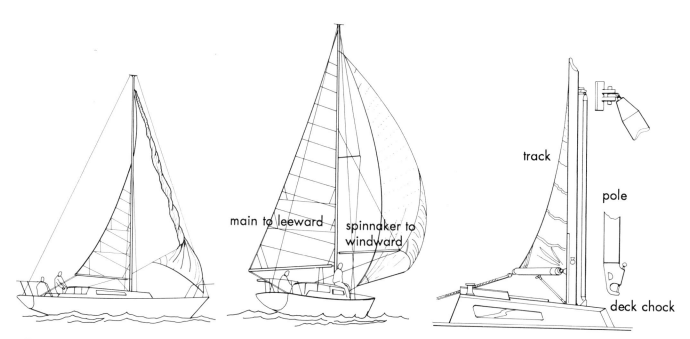

Fig. 7. Cruising spinnaker dousing with sock.

Fig. 8. Greater efficiency can be achieved dead downwind when the spinnaker is poled out wing-and-wing.

Fig. 9. Pole stowed against the mast.

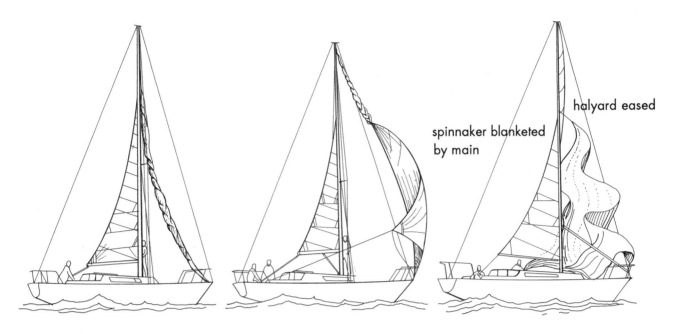

Fig. 4. Spinnaker hoisted in sock.

Fig. 5. Sock is raised while spinnaker is set with appropriate sheet.

Fig. 6. Traditional takedown without sock.

Fig. 10. Raising the pole from the mast.

Fig. 11. Spinnaker hoisted in sock and ready for release.

expected to behave yourself and follow the rules of the country you've entered. In most countries of this imperfect world, entry regulations, customs, clearance and health regulations are far stricter than in the USA. Quarantine will be enforced, with proper flags flown. Boarding will be ceremonious and you should extend every possible courtesy to the authorities. Firearms will be confiscated for the duration of your stay, liquor will be impounded, paperwork must be completed with precision, every *i* dotted, every signature in place. Passports must be surrendered. You will be expected, in most places, to pay fees as well as harbor dues, and anchor or berth where the harbormaster indicates.

He who decided to sail off into the blue and simply land somewhere is in for a surprise. There may be freedom of the seas, but there certainly is not freedom of ports. An itinerary should be made, with emergency plans, for the entire voyage. You should contact, well ahead of departure, the consulates of those countries you wish to visit and get complete information on what you will need in terms of documentation for your vessel and yourself and crew, rules, regulations, health certificates, bonded stores, costs and formalities.

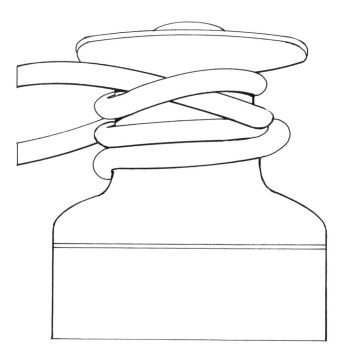

One of the most common problems with small or inexperienced crews in sailboats is the tendency for riding turns to occur due to bad fairleads for the jib sheets or incorrect tailing practice. To undo a riding turn, the tension on the sheet must first be relieved.

You should arrive with reasonable amounts of local currency. You should probably have a locker aboard which may be sealed for any bonded stores. You should not, repeat not, attempt to bribe any port official. The failure to observe any of the above will cause delays, problems and possibly confiscation of your yacht. Most countries have limits on the extent of your stay as a foreign-flag vessel. They all have strict rules on chartering. Behave yourself and have a good cruise. Infringe on their hospitality and you may be in for some very unpleasant surprises.

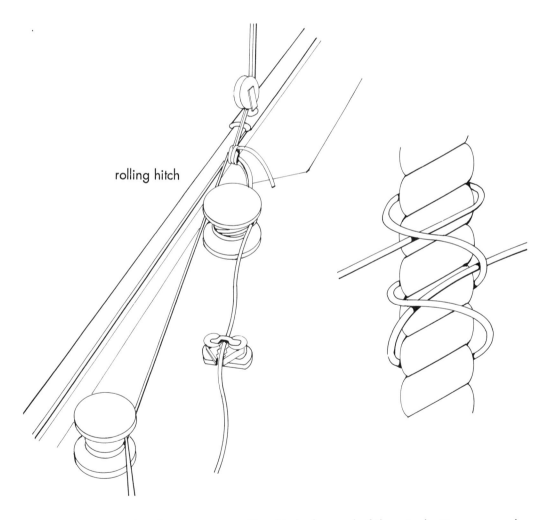

rolling hitch

First step is to attach a line, using a rolling hitch, forward of the winch. Use a secondary winch to take the tension from this line. Then you'll be able to untangle the sheet and transfer the sheet load to the original winch. The rolling hitch is used as it will hold firm yet be easy to undo. Make sure the temporary line is securely cleated to avoid whiplash from the sheet or clew.

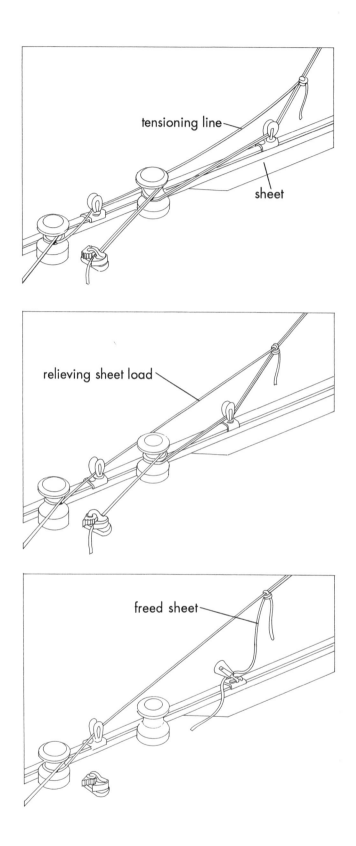

To transfer a loaded sheet or reposition a block:
1. set-up a tensioning line with a rolling hitch
2. relieve the sheet load with the tensioning line
3. the sheet will be freed for adjustments

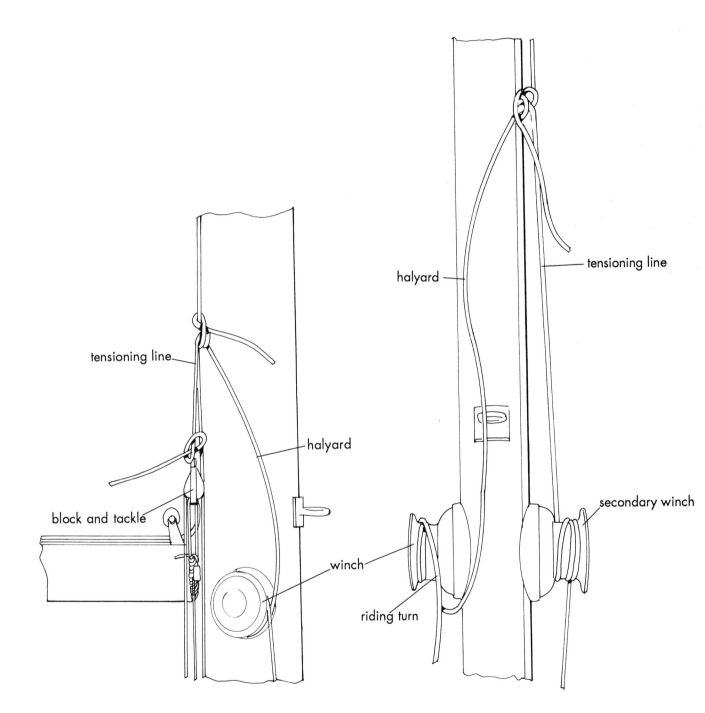

tensioning line

halyard

tensioning line

halyard

block and tackle

winch

secondary winch

riding turn

To slack halyards, use the same principle, leading the tensioning line to 1. a block and tackle arrangement or 2. a secondary winch.

Navigation, Weather and Passagemaking **83**

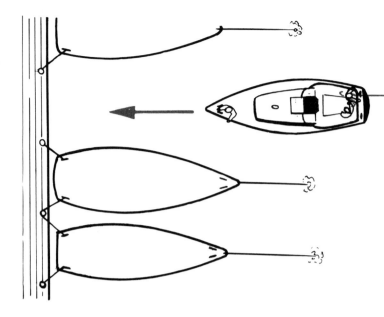

Since most boats have greater control in forward, when tying-up Mediterranean-style, it is often advantageous to drop the hook from the stern and come into the quay bow-on. You gain an added dividend of greater privacy this way, not to mention less cursing when engaged in the maneuver.

Harbors and Maneuvering

At the end of every passage, you will most probably enter a harbor. This can be an event of joy or disaster, depending upon your preparations and planning, and on the quality of your seamanship. Every harbor is different, each demands a different set of actions to be taken to moor your vessel securely and safely. Is the harbor open to prevailing winds? Are high cliffs surrounding the anchorage or to one or more sides? Is a swift current evident near docks or floats? If the bottom ground foul? Is there room to maneuver? No text can hope to prepare you for every eventuality, but following are the major points to keep in mind when approaching, maneuvering and making fast.

1. Know your landfall. Too many times, I have seen boats approaching a harbor for the first time with no chart at hand, no set of bearings on shoreline marks and at too high a speed. Every harbor has its hidden dangers, tricky currents, unmarked shoals and rocks and usually water traffic of some kind. You are a visitor. You are also not too smart if you enter blind. Study harbor charts and approaches, read the cruising guides, check out as much as possible beforehand to avoid embarrassment or worse. Do not blindly follow another boat; there's always the chance that he's as lost as you are.

2. Approach with extreme caution. Even if you've memorized every detail of a new harbor, don't count on your memory. Keep the chart at hand—and make sure it's as detailed and up-to-date as possible—take bearings *before* you enter, follow marked and buoyed channels, avoid moorings and keep to the right side of the channel. Keep a lookout posted in the bows. No matter what anyone else does, keep your speed down. If under sail, and you know it to be a crowded spot, stow sail before entering any channels and come in under power. If in a powerboat, throttle down to stated harbor speeds. If they are not posted, five knots can generally be considered a safe maximum. The local idiot in a speedboat doing 35 should be arrested (providing he doesn't kill himself or someone else first). If there's much water traffic, be prepared to maneuver quickly and without panic. If you go slow, you can see

International lights and buoyage system

Lights Periodicity: a circle=60 seconds

fixed light
range 12 nm

occulting light
light>obscured
here 1 occultation
duration of signal 4s

flashing light
light<obscured
here 2 flashes
duration of the signal 6s

Morse light
here letter A._

quick flashing light
3 quick flashing
duration of signal 12s

regular occulting light
light=obscured
duration of signal 4s

Note: radius of lights not proportional to their range

Q. fl.=quick flashing

V.Q. fl.=very quick flashing

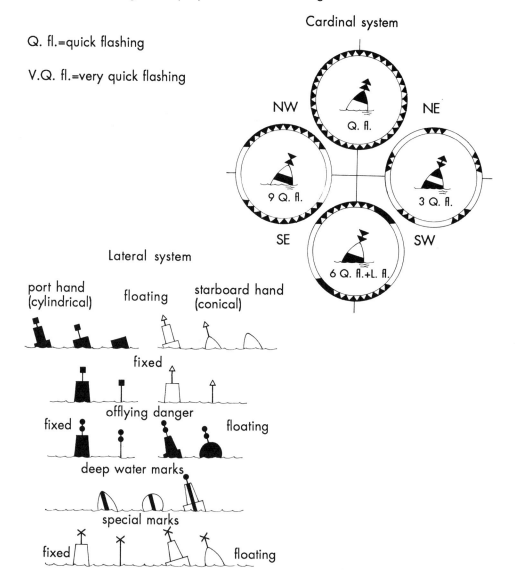

Cardinal system

Lateral system

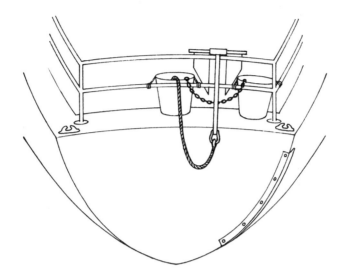

A kedge anchor kept mounted to the pushpit by means of brackets with line and chain kept in plastic buckets lashed to the rail. This can be very useful in emergency anchoring situations to stop the boat's forward motion. Equally, it can serve as a regular anchoring method for a singlehander. Be sure the rode and chain lead outside the pushpit and that the rode is secured before dropping the anchor.

more. Remember, if you've never been in a harbor before, you must be prepared for the unexpected. If the harbormaster or dockmaster waves you off, take heed. Don't pick-up an empty mooring just because it's there. Don't drop the anchor anyplace; look for a designated anchorage. Be prepared to pay for the privilege of mooring or docking.

3. Be prepared. You needn't be a Boy Scout to keep this motto firmly engraved in your brain. If you don't know whether you will have to anchor, pick-up a mooring or tie-up to a float or dock, have everything set out and at-the-ready to cope with every situation. I have seen boats go onto the rocks because an anchor could not be set in time. The anchor should be lightly secured, ready to lower. Dock lines should be at the ready, coiled for immediate tossing. Fenders should be at hand, on deck, near the rail both port and starboard. You may not know until the last minute from which side you will approach. All hands must be briefed as to all the likely possibilities. Chaos on approach will not win you any awards for seamanship.

Since the idea is to get ashore, your first dictum must be: never rush, never panic. Many boaters seem to think you can enter a harbor and settle in with the same alacrity you might park your car in a suburban lot. The fact is, many more variables are at play in maneuvering a boat through the water, taking tide and current and wind and waves

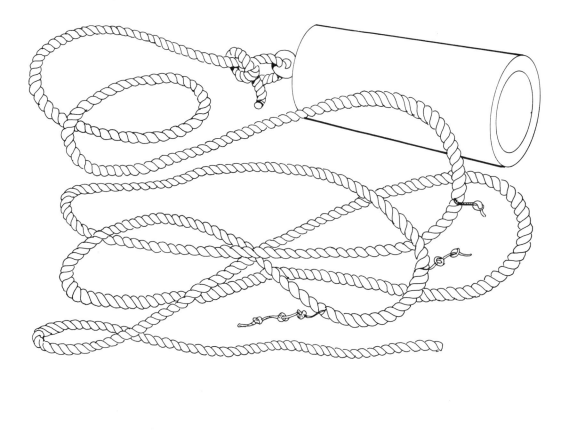

Entering an anchorage, a leadline can be more accurate and useful than a depth sounder. The line should be marked in feet, fathoms or meters (depending on your normal charts) and the weight can be armed with wax to test the bottom composition. The lead should always be swung from the bow forward, as illustrated.

into account.

Tides and currents are the bane of many a yachtsmen's existence. They vary in strength, are stronger or weaker depending on your position in the stream and generally wreck havoc with your navigation. Entering harbor, going against the tide, at least under power, is far safer than being swept in with the tide. Even a knot of added speed can screw-up your calculations, especially if you are coming alongside. If a tidal current is pushing you broadside towards a dock, beware. Unless you are equipped with a bow thruster you can end up pinned to the dock with an astounding crunch of wood and fiberglass. Small harbors are generally more dangerous in this respect than large ones; the water has less space to spread out as it enters and with a narrow entrance channel, will pick up velocity. Flushing out is easier to cope with in that the process slows the boat and, given a powerful enough engine, will allow you to maneuver with greater precision. Some harbors, especially those with enormous tidal ranges—Mont St. Michel and the Bay of Fundy are extreme examples—can only be approached or left at dead slack water, as currents can run 10 knots and tides range up to 40 feet.

MANEUVERING

Skill in maneuvering upon the water will make or break your boating pleasure. It's not something that comes naturally and it's not to be confused with driving an automobile. With ever-increasing numbers entering the boating world, and the obvious lack of education, many accidents and mishaps occur due to the lack of technical skill in guiding a boat through the water expeditiously and safely.

Unlike a land vehicle working on a fixed platform, guiding a boat through the water depends not only on the handling characteristics of the vessel, but on displacement, wetted surface, depth of keel, shape of underwater appendages, area of above water surfaces (windage), type of propulsion, seaworthiness, tides, currents, and wind strength and direction. Ignoring any of these factors can put boat and crew in peril in settled weather and create a catastrophe in bad weather.

Most maneuvers are done at slow speeds under power. Whether your boat has single or twin screws will effect what techniques you use, but the simple fact is that the slower you move, the less control you have. Since control is directly related to the force of water moved past the rudder, the less thrust, the less turning force against the rudder and the less control. In most single screw installations, this is taken care of by means of a large rudder. Twin screw boats usually have two comparatively small rudders, since they are meant to control the boat at high speeds.

However, the advantage is you can control the engines separately, putting one in forward, one in reverse and literally turning on a dime. This does take a lot of practice when maneuvering in close quarters,

Anchorage selection is always a problem. Selecting the safest place to drop the hook can be highly dependant on bottom composition, shelving and wind patterns.

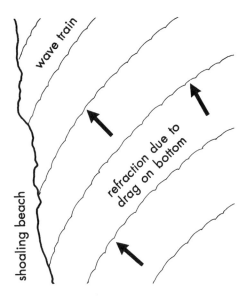

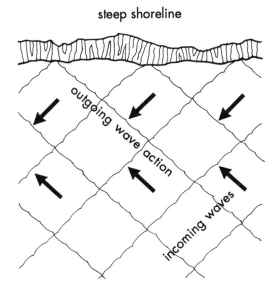

1. Refracted waves begin to drag in shallow water, altering direction as they approach the shore.

2. Incoming waves will reflect off a steep shoreline at an angle equal to that of their forward motion. Where they intersect will create nasty chop.

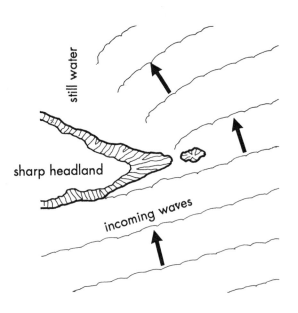

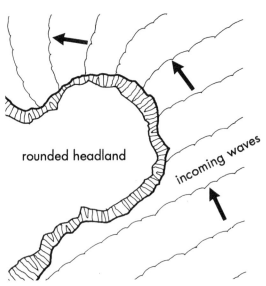

3. Sharp headlands will stall the force of incoming waves and provide protection behind.

4. Rounded headlands will promote wave action around its entire perimeter. Not a good place to anchor!

such as a finger pier berth, surrounded on three sides by tuna towers and pilings. To save nerves, all this should be practiced in open water with floating marks.

One important point to remember is that all boats have a natural inertia, based on weight, windage, hull shape and more. This inertia changes with conditions, so unless you have experienced everything, you are always in for a new set of surprises! This shows itself most when approaching a mooring under sail. Depending on the above multiplicity of factors, you will either turn into the wind and come up to the mooring or, more likely the first few dozen times, you will either overshoot it or get blown off before you can reach it.

With few exceptions, you will always have more control if you are heading more or less into the wind. Even a slight breeze, say five knots, can cause you to change tactics in any approach situation. Under all costs, you must keep enough way on to give you positive maneuverability. At the same time, be careful not to give the engine too much throttle. Combined with the inertial way-on, you may find yourself coming into a dock with an exuberant, and damaging, crunch. Coming in with the wind on your nose will help prevent that. If the only possible approach to a dock is with the wind behind or broadside, have crew stationed with lines to get ashore and around a dock cleat as soon as possible. With time, you will learn to warp your way in and out of berths. At the beginning, practice in calm conditions. A rope in trained hands can be even more useful than the engine in tight situations.

DOCKING

Approaching any dock or quay or pontoon is made more difficult by the tight quarters, proximity of other vessels and the tricks tidal streams can play amongst pilings and walls. Make due allowance for windage, drift and lost control at low speeds. Know how your ship handles! Attempt to approach to windward. With wind and tide behind you, you will have to either play with bursts of reverse on the throttle or have a crew member stationed to drop a stern anchor to slow down the ship and allow for some control. The same maneuver can be practiced with current abeam.

Cleat all lines and pass through chocks, then outboard and over any rails or lifelines. Secure all fenders overboard. If approaching a concrete or stone pier, use fenderboards. Often the pier will be quite high; a crew member should be stationed so he can scale the wall (hopefully by ladder) with both bow *and* stern lines in hand. The same is true if sailing alone or with one crew. Spring lines can be rigged after bow and stern are secured. Should the ship be tied up on the windward side of the dock, a kedge can be run out to hold it off, either from a spring cleat amidships or with two warps leading from the kedge to both bow and stern cleats.

Pile moorings are always nervous-making. Preparation is the key. Take a dummy run first, checking wind direction and strength, currents and obstructions.

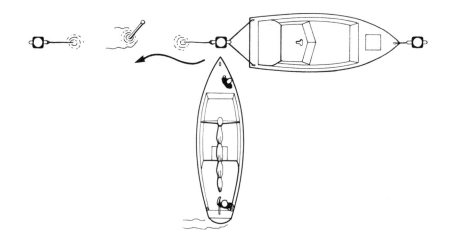

1. Look for back eddies around the piles. If you are not certain of the current, set the boat at right angles to the set of the pilings and check the drift.

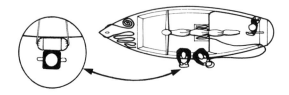

2. A fender tied-off parallel to the gunnel should be made fast to the side nearest the pilings. A fenderboard will be even better.

The stern line should be twice the length of the gap between pilings. Flake it down and take the end outside the pushpit. The crew takes that end to the windward side of the boat amidships.

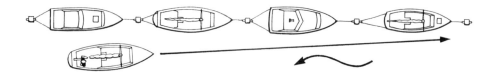

3. Go downstream and approach dead slow (maintaining steerage). Be ready to head into the wind to gauge the length necessary to bring the boat to a coasting stop.

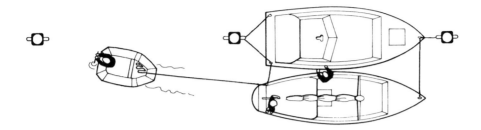

4. If space is tight, you may want to tie-up alongside another boat and carry your lines over in the dinghy. When tying-up, allow enough slack to account for the tide.

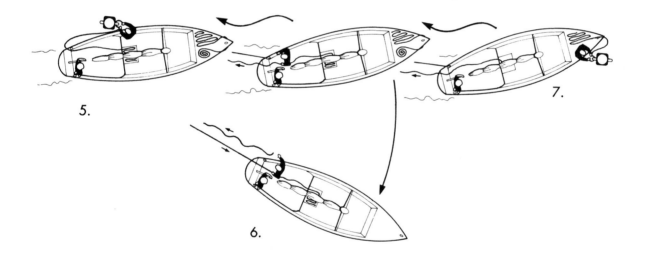

5. Turn into the wind and hold the boat against the tide. The crew passes the line around the piling and takes it back aboard.

6. Motor forward into the wind.

If there is any problem at this point, release the line, haul it in and allow her to blow clear. Then head back and make another approach.

7. Hold the bow slightly beyond the piling and let the wind hold the boat in place. Pa ss a bow line around the piling and back-down until centered.

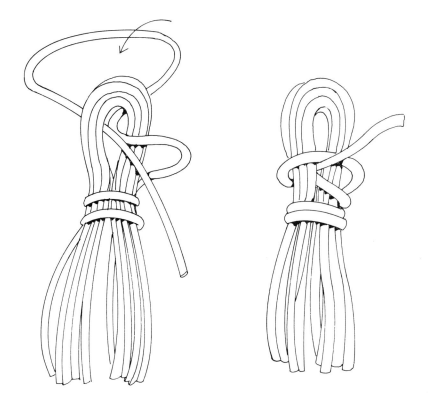

Proper coiling of lines will make stowage easier and allow them to run free when needed.

You could suddenly have to alter your intended approach or goal, either due to the unexpected appearance of a smaller, hitherto unseen boat, or to directions from the dockmaster. Lines, fenders, etc., will have to be quickly switched. If you have enough time, it pays to back off and reapproach *after* these chores have been completed. If not, and the area is crewed on first approach, it is a good idea to rig lines and fenders on both sides of the yacht. In places like St. Peter Port or Newport or Annapolis, at the height of the season, docking is always at a premium. Plan accordingly.

In most of the Mediterranean, tying up stern-to is the norm. This is accomplished by letting out the best bower about 100 feet (30m) plus the length of the ship from the quay and backing toward the dock. Unfortunately, with adverse conditions this can be at best a tricky maneuver. Better to drop the hook from the stern and go in bow first. Most boats have greater control in forward, as well as greater stopping power. In addition, should you desire such things, your privacy will be that much more. If you wish you can end-for-end the bow and anchor lines—providing there is room port and starboard—and turn the ship around. If boats are wedged in on both sides, extend the line to the quay and haul well clear of your neighbors before attempting to make the turn.

Still, before using, all lines should be loosely flaked down on deck following the natural disposition of their lay.

Should the berth be one that dries out at low tide, attempt to heel the boat slightly inward toward the quay. A line passed about the mast at spreader height and led ashore will usually do the trick. Be careful that the rigging does not come in contact with the dock, and that the spreaders will not be damaged. A block attached to a halyard and also held around the mast with a strop or loose loop of rope can be hoisted aloft to just below the spreaders *after* a line from the dock has been led through it and back to the dock or to a cleat on deck. In addition, a heavy anchor can be placed on the dockside deck of the vessel.

Be sure in any tidal area that enough slack is kept in the docking lines to allow for the rise and fall of the ship. A good idea is to lead the lines to the dock pilings or cleats in a bight and then back again to the deck cleats. In this manner, you will be able to make adjustments without leaving the deck.

Under any and all circumstances, but especially when boats are docked both before and aft of your vessel, rig spring lines both fore and aft. The forward line should be from a point about a third of the way back from the bow made fast to the dock aft, the stern line from a point about a third of way forward from the stern made fast to the dock forward. In this way, combined with bow and stern lines, there is little chance of the boat charging ahead or abaft.

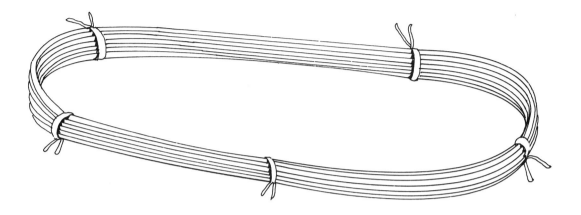

It's best to stow extra anchor rodes in large coils, tied-up in four places around the perimeter of the coil with small stuff or marline which can be broken out or cut easily.

Most all fenders are too small. The biggest you can stow should be the rule, with a minimum diameter of eight inches and a length great enough to protect nine-tenths of the topsides vertically. A fender board is almost a necessity in areas where you may have to tie-up against concrete piers.

SINGLE SCREW VS. TWIN SCREWS

The argument between the two is academic if you already have a boat. Generally, for a single screw to be effective, it needs to be large and slower turning than the usual twin screw planing boat installation. It also needs a generous rudder area to transfer propulsive force to one side or the other. True, twins will allow a smaller turning circle and can be useful in tricky maneuvering situations; but rarely, if ever, are they a great improvement over a single propeller.

You'll always applaud the system you grew up with, but a single screw configuration is generally more protected and allows for a more economical cruise. So many engine installations are possible that it's difficult to recommend one over the other, but I would opt for a twin engine set-up driving a single screw via belting or chain drive; a wing engine; or a generator installed to allow belting to the main screw.

UNDER SAIL

Picking up a mooring under sail is not a bad skill to cultivate, pro-

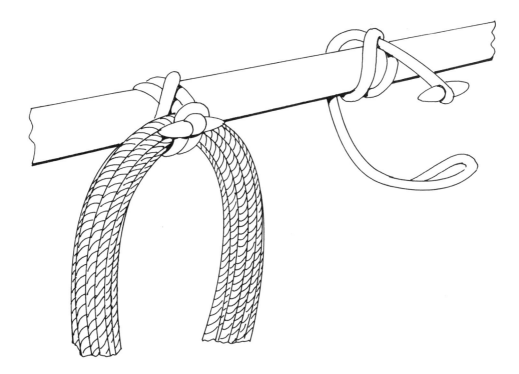

Another possibility is to stow coils of line around a rail or around a mounted dowel in a cockpit locker using bungee cords.

viding the mooring area is not too crowded. Docking under sail takes long and arduous practice. In a dinghy it's a cinch. In anything over four or five tons displacement, you court disaster unless you are able to control every aspect of sail handling, helmsmanship and deck work simultaneously. Coming into any solid pier demands that you are able to bring the boat to a stop before hitting said object. This means you must be able to judge the limit of your boat's momentum in wildly varying conditions, not something to be taken lightly when the yacht in front of you may be damaged by a flaw in your reasoning. There are times when you have no choice, such as when your engine dies. This will only work if you actually have sail up at the moment of your final approach. Roller furling and reefing headsails can literally save your life at moments like this. Pull a string, and you have a sail at the ready! Using the main to approach a dock is not to be recommended unless you have a way of dousing it instantly. A sudden wind shift, or your not letting the mainsheet out quickly enough can cause the boat to gather way again. With only the jib set (not a monster genoa unless you are in almost a dead calm), you will have greater control—providing you can reach the winches from the helm—and the ability to let the sail fly with virtually no chance of backwinding. No chance so long as the sheets don't catch on some protrusion.

Every yacht responds differently to low speed maneuvering. Wetted surface, sail area, rudder size and propeller bite all play a part in main-

A fender board is almost a necessity alongside pilings, quay walls or against any dock in an area with a wide tidal range. Note that fenders go behind the board to cushion any impact Use nothing smaller than a length of 2x6 inch stock, preferably fir or other timber that can take punishment.

taining control. The best honest advice anyone can give is to practice away from other boats and from any stationary object that might cause damage, and practice you must. I have seen highly seasoned racing sailors who fell to pieces when harbor maneuvering was called for. Likewise, boatmen who are used to docking or pulling into a marina slip are often stymied when it comes to dropping the hook securely. Never assume that a passage is finished when you get to outermost harbor buoy. It's finished when the boat is secured, period!

Spring lines are very useful maneuvering tools when coming into a dock. Additionally, they allow control when swinging out of a tight slip.

Fig. 1. Bow line used as shown will cause the boat pivot with any forward way on.

Fig. 2. If a stern line is used, the result is the same in the opposite direction. Current or wind on the bow will aggravate the problem.

Fig. 3. Using a spring line from just aft of midship will bring the boat parallel to the dock or quay. Bow and stern lines can then be secured.

A fouled anchor can be broken free in as many ways as it can be fouled. One effective way to remedy the situation is to use a docking line, carried in the opposite direction of the ship in the dinghy. Reversing the direction of the pull should break out the anchor.

Anchoring
and Mooring

Arriving anywhere after a passage is a time to celebrate—for having made it, for meeting new sights and people, for having proved your navigation skills and more. However, you've got to stop and get off the boat. You have two choices: tie-up or pick-up a mooring in a marina or anchor out.

Though many prefer marinas—after all, you get showers, a place for the kids to run around, secure berthing—there are distinct disadvantages. You will have little privacy, they can be crowded and dirty, ofttimes they are located far from shopping and, in bad weather, they can put you and your boat in danger.

Anchoring out will allow you privacy, better ventilation—you will be facing the breeze—a chance to swim off the boat, the good exercise of rowing ashore and nothing to bump into, providing your boat is securely anchored. And that's the rub. Most boaters don't devote the time necessary to mastering the skills of anchoring, they choose tackle that is too light and they usually succumb to the herding instinct in a crowded anchorage.

Ideally, any cruising boat should carry three sets of ground tackle: an everyday anchor, a lunch hook and a storm anchor. Each, in turn, should be equipped with an appropriate rode or cable. This is a point of contention, depending on which side of the Atlantic you do your boating. In the United States, a length of heavy chain roughly equal to one-half the overall length of the boat should be shackled to the anchor at one end, to a nylon rode, equipped with a spliced-in thimble, at the other. The shackles must be wired for security. The rode should be as long as is practicable, within limits of reason, and accustomed holding ground—100, 150 and 200 feet respectively for small, medium and large boats.

Using all-chain has its advantages. The catenary made by the weight of the chain acts to steady the boat, it is easier to use a powered windlass and it self-stows. However, the weight can be a critical factor in boat handling and performance, especially if the chain locker is lo-

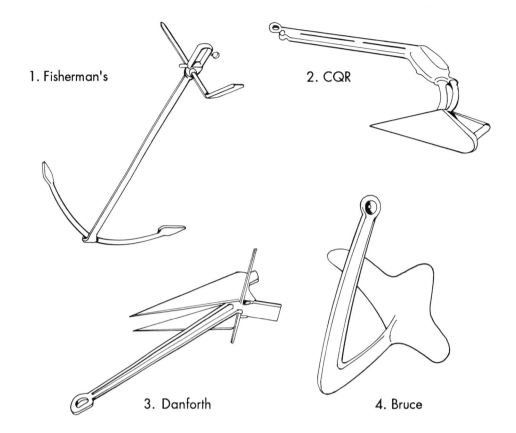

The most popular anchors.

cated in the bows. Additionally, chain gives not at all, so in heavy seas, the windlass or bits will be snapped back and forth, possibly causing damage to the ship. Some sort of snubber must be contrived to dampen the boat's pitching, usually a length of nylon line tied between the chain just forward of the stemhead roller to the chain about four or five feet lower down, making an above-water catenary of chain. When the boat surges, the rope will stretch, keeping the boat from coming up against the chain.

What is at the end of the rode is a matter of taste and experience. Four major anchor types are in common usage: plow (CQR), lightweight (Danforth), Bruce and fisherman. Each has its use, none is perfect for all conditions.

For ease stowage and a good weight-to-holding ratio, the CQR is a good choice. It will stow in a bow roller, is forged and is particularly good for weed or debris-laden bottoms. Many copies exist. Most are to viewed skeptically, specially if they are cast, rather than forged. If there's a weak link in the CQR, it has to be the pivot. Severe snubbing has been known to fracture the pivot.

The Danforth is the most used anchor in the USA. Developed originally for torpedo boats in WWII, it is light, moderately clumsy, but has the best holding properties—in sand and mud—of any anchor made. The hi-tensile versions are, in this writer's opinion, the best all-around

Stowing any anchor is always a problem, unless you have an integral anchor well. However, these do not permit instant access when you really need it. Here are some of the most popular ways to go about it.

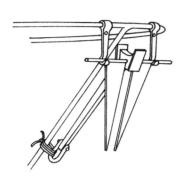

1. Patent pulpit holder for light-weight anchors.

2. Stanchion clamp for light-weight anchors.

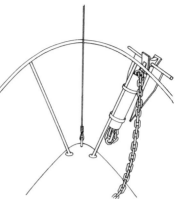

3. PVC pipe and hose clamps for lightweight anchors.

4. Aluminum lightweights can be disassembled.

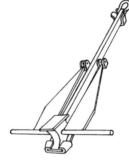

5. Chocks for deck mounting.

6. Patent Bruce roller chock.

7. Combination fitting for plow anchor.

8. Hinged double roller chock takes chain or rope and can stow different types.

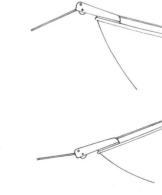

9. Roller chock extending far beyond the bow will not take heavy loading without bending or breaking.

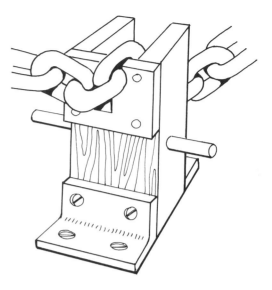

A chain-stopper will make hauling anchor easier. It can be made from thick mild steel or stainless with a notch cut to fit your size chain.

anchor for the cruising boat made today. Beware of cheap imitations.

The Bruce anchor was developed for North Sea oil rig use. They are good basic anchors, the advantage being that they are solid, one-piece tools. However, since they have blunt flukes, they are not easy to dig into hard sand; and they are clumsy.

Fisherman anchors are the old standby, rarely seen today except as storm anchors on large boats. Yet they have many advantages: nothing holds better in rock, the more sophisticated ones can be broken down for stowage and they are immensely strong. The best are made by Paul Luke in Maine, basically to the Herreshoff pattern, with sharp, broad flukes. Nicholson pattern and others usually have narrow flukes and just not enough area to hold in mud or sand.

Other patterns exist, but are not generally available or cannot be trusted in extreme conditions. If I had to choose three for my on-board inventory, I'd take a CQR, Danforth and Luke, each in the largest size I could handle and stow with reasonable ease. Too often the tables and charts published by the manufacturers and repeated—usually uncritically—in the boating magazines, tell you what the minimum size should be under headings of boat size and type, weight, holding ground and such. Go up at least one size. What the tables don't tell you is that conditions are never optimum, winds change, anchors drag, scopes are not adhered to. Better be safe than sorry.

In fact, a number of misconceptions exist as to safe anchoring. First, a large power boat will have less *affected* windage than a high-masted sailing vessel. Once the wind is freed from surface friction, its velocity increases geometrically (up to a point). It stands to reason that parts of a boat higher up will be subjected to greater wind strength than the hull or superstructure. Of course, when underway, structure heights will influence performance, but not to the degree that height does

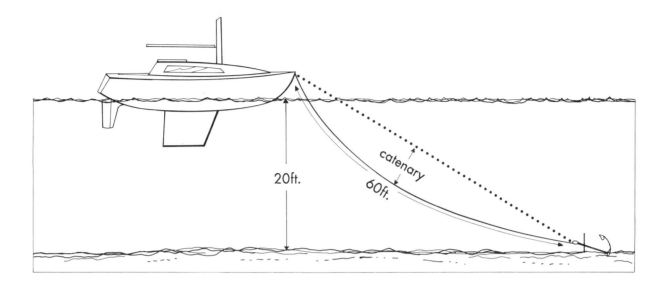

When anchoring with chain, allow a minimum of 3:1 scope. The catenary made by the weight of the chain acts as a snubber against surge and shock loads.

when anchored. Second, most boaters tend to anchor together, in small cozy groups. This is very sociable. This is not very smart, especially with threat of heavy weather. The possibility of dragging, fouling lines and collision is too great to take a chance. Spread out! Third, let out as much scope as possible—considering the conditions and occupancy rate of the anchorage. The temptation is always to be economical; be expansive, make a grand gesture and pay out as much rode or cable as is possible considering the space available and the quality of the bottom.

Deciding where to anchor is always a problem, especially judging distances off headlands, rocks and other boats. Carefully examine the harbor chart before you enter. Decide on the general area, and always have a back-up should your primary choice be full. The same goes if you are planning to pick-up a mooring or dock. Have a back-up anchorage chosen beforehand. There's no guarantee you will be able to go where you want, even if you've reserved a berth.

When first approaching an anchorage, the anchor rode should be coiled loose on the foredeck; if chain, have the windlass at the ready and no obstructions on the foredeck. It's a good idea to keep the lunch hook at the ready at the stern; it can stop you if reverse gear fails to engage. Do this no matter what, even if a berth is ready for you.

All lines should be cleated inboard and run outside the lifelines or

In heavy weather, or just for safety's sake, it's a good idea to fit chain with a nylon snubber.

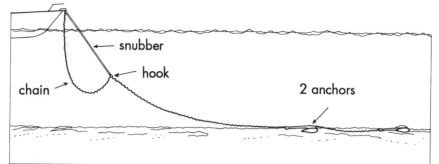

Fig. 1. Not so good. Nylon snubber is taken over the roller with the chain. Two anchors are set on same length of chain.

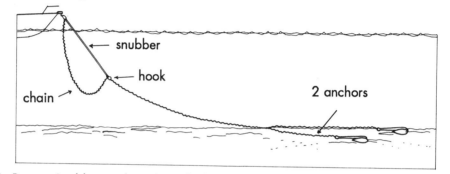

Fig. 2. Better. Snubber ends outboard of roller. Each anchor is on a separate length of chain, with the nearer one shackled to the main chain.

rails capable of being carried to whichever side of the boat is most advantageous to the side of the dock or float you are approaching. However, since the possibility exists that you will suddenly have to approach from the other side, these lines should be carried only from bow and stern. and coiled loosely on both fore- and afterdecks. Done so, you will have less last-minute panic when the time to leap ashore or pass your lines actually comes about.

Always approach anchorage, dock or mooring from downwind, orienting the boat so she will be as directly into the wind as possible at the final approach. Station crew forward and aft to fend off if necessary. Obviously, there will be times when you will not be able to head to windward. When anchoring, with the wind from the stern, run the anchor aft, allowing adequate scope. Carry the rode to the stern as well, loosely coiled, all outside the lifelines. Cleat the line twice, at the bow and then again at a stern cleat. In this way, once the hook is set, you will be able to uncleat the stern and the boat will swing around into the wind. Even under these circumstances, come in dead slow, keeping in mind the velocity of the wind and any current set. You will snub the anchor easily, but you don't want to overdo it and tear out deck fittings!

Once bow and stern are fastened, spring lines can be rigged. Personally, I believe that two springs should always be in place at a

When shorthanded, it is often best to tie-up to a dock using a continuous line, as shown. This allows one to cast-off from the boat and to adjust lines for tidal range without leaving the comfort of the cockpit.

dock to combat surges from either fore or aft. Since few boats are equipped with proper spring cleats (mounted amidships port and starboard), you should either through-bolt them yourself or be able to run lines from appropriate strong points from just aft of midships forward and just before midships aft.

The state of the tide and rate of inflow and outflow is vital to successful anchoring. In areas of small tidal range, such as the Mediterranean or the Chesapeake, this is not quite so important, but make sure you have allowed for low springs when assaying the position the boat will take when anchored. Allow for swinging room and for reversal of position when the tide changes. In areas of vast tidal range, with swift inrushing tides, such as Brittany or Newfoundland, where ranges can be upward of 30 feet, you will have to anchor far out with very long cables. In such conditions, two anchors should probably be set, especially when tides boil in at as much as 10 knots.

Bottom composition can be determined by depth sounder, chart reference or hand lead armed with tallow or grease. The bottom will determine the type and size of anchor you set. Mud, soft sand and mixed bottoms indicate a Danforth-type or plow anchor. Hard sand, as is found in the Aegean and Caribbean, will hold with either but may demand hand setting. Weed will foil a Danforth with ease, and sometimes a plow. Rocky bottoms will be best served with a good old-fash-

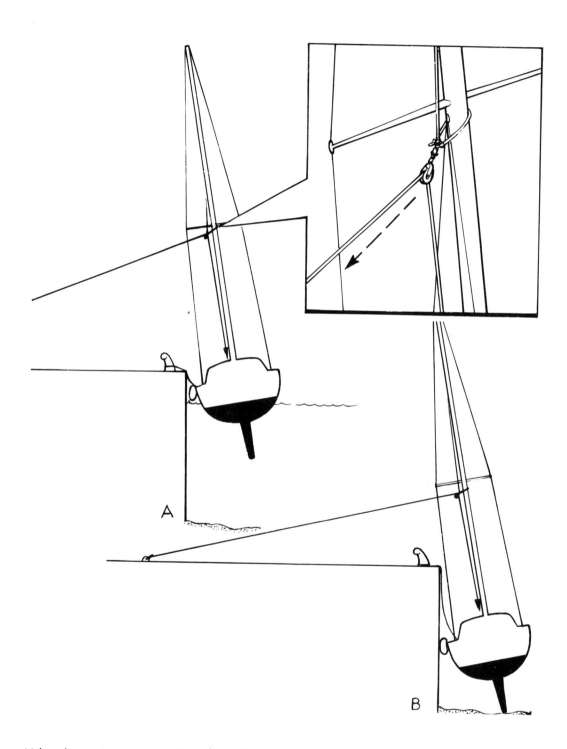

When laying against a wall which will dry-out at low tide, running a line ashore from the spreaders will assure that the boat doesn't fall on its side. Hoist the line, rove through a swivel block attached to the halyard. This will allow adjustment from either aboard or ashore.

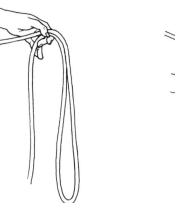 

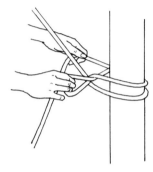 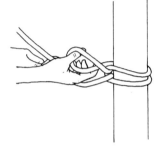

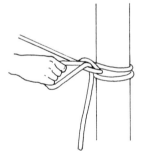 

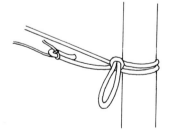

Another way to release a line from on board. The line is passed around a piling or bollard as shown. Follow the sequence, attaching a light trip line to the bitter end with a double sheet bend and passing the trip line back aboard.

Anchoring and Mooring   **109**

In confined anchorages, it's often more prudent to set two hooks. In Fig. 1, the boat is anchored with a single hook, and will swing a wide radius. Fig. 2 shows the reduction of the swing when two anchors are set. Do not set these equidistant, as that would negate any snubbing action of the two rodes.

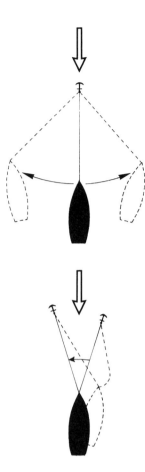

ioned fisherman (Herreshoff preferred—if you can find one) or a Bruce anchor. These two will usually dig past weed the best. If the bottom is mixed—small pebbles or shale, or weed and shale—use a fisherman; the goal will be to get underneath the top layer as quickly as possible. Coral accepts fishermen and plows best, though the shank of a plow can be badly bent by coral and chain cable is almost a necessity to avoid chafe. If it can be found, I have discovered the Northill anchor to be the most use over the widest range of conditions.

Too often anchors are tossed, dropped or slung over the bows. By carefully and slowly lowering it you will be able to ascertain the rate of drift, and will avoid permanently damaging the hull, deck or yourself.

Scope depends upon depth at high water, holding ground and whether chain or rope cable is used. All rope cables should have at least 5 meters of chain between the end of the rope and the anchor to prevent chafe and increase holding power. All chain permits shorter scope (as little as 3:1), but can snub more easily than rope. Rope, having great elasticity (nylon) will act as a better shock absorber, especially when in surging conditions. However, rope must be heavily padded—either with patent chafe gear or rags or leather—to avoid catastrophe at the stemhead, roller or chocks. The holding ground will make a difference; the better the bottom, the less the scope. Mud and soft sand will usually hold best, assuming the appropriate anchor. In any case, be

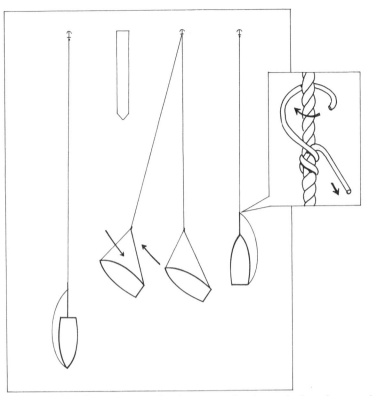

When dropping the anchor from astern, the boat can be brought head-to-wind by using a second line attached with a rolling hitch. Once the anchor is set, the boat is hauled around, using the auxiliary line, and the rode is reattached to the appropriate bow cleat or bollard.

prepared to set rope cable with a minimum of 6:1 scope and chain with a minimum of 4:1 scope. Under deteriorating weather and sea conditions, scope should be increased and the possibility of a second or even third anchor being set must be considered.

Making sure the anchor is set is the most important single step you can take in anchoring. Either back the sails, throw the engine in reverse or hand snub it when the appropriate amount of scope has been payed out. Be sure the cable is attached to a strong point below decks and is secured to the samson post, cleat or anchor winch. Even with chain cable a nylon preventer is a good idea—especially as cables have an appalling tendency to snap at the stemhead fitting or roller. Rig the preventer from a second cleat inboard to the cable a couple of feet outboard of the stem. Not only can this save you an anchor and cable, but will act as a shock absorber in heavy surge situations.

Not only should the inboard end of the cable be securely fastened to the ship, but the cable must be bowsed down in the proper stemhead fitting. In a roller, the cheeks must be high enough to prevent the cable from jumping out; a retaining pin should be fitted, and all metal should be filed down so that no sharp edges are evident at any point at which the cable *might* touch the roller or cheeks. Chain can be weakened by friction against metal! If your roller lacks a retaining pin, or if you must pass the cable through a chock, use a short length of

Anchoring and Mooring 111

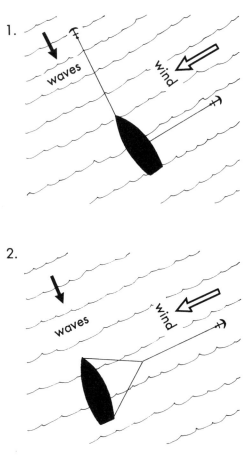

1.

2.

When wind and waves are coming from different directions you can either, Fig. 1, set two anchors, which may be uncomfortable or, Fig. 2, rig a bridle, as shown, to dampen the effects of opposing forces.

light stuff to tie down the rope or chain, either around the fitting or in some way to close off the openings and make for a rope loop.

When the wind shows signs of veering, be prepared to lay out a second anchor. The second anchor can be the kedge and can be equipped with chain and rope cable. Lower it off the bows in the direction from which the wind is veering. Pay out cable as the boat begins to swing until more or less equal strain is taken by both anchors and the boat becomes the fulcrum of an easy-swinging pendulum.

In a river where the tidal stream runs strong and will reverse or where there is little or no room to swing, anchoring fore-and-aft is called for. Anchor in the normal way, letting out double the amount of cable needed for the situation—a good reason to carry at least 75 to 100 meters of cable—and set the hook. Then drop a stern anchor and motor or winch the ship forward, paying out cable to get the ship in the required position. Be sure to station someone in the bow to take in the excess cable at the same time you are moving forward, otherwise you chance fouling the propeller or wrapping a rope cable around the keel or skeg or rudder. Allow a small amount of slack at high water, in both cables, but not so much as to make for uncomfortable movement.

Anchoring in heavy weather or off a lee shore is always a fearful and difficult experience. However, there are times when no other alternative permits itself. Two basic methods are available for effective

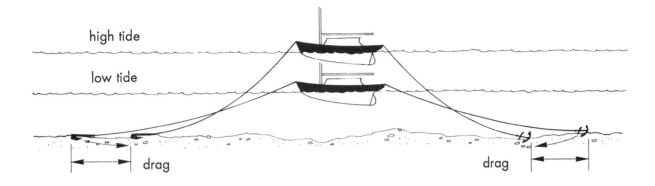

high tide

low tide

drag

drag

When anchoring from both bow and stern in a river or tight spot, be sure to allow enough scope for tidal range. Drop the astern anchor first, allowing double the scope needed. Then drop the bow anchor and back down while hauling in on the stern rode, until you are centered between. Note also that if not enough scope is allowed, the anchors may drag when the tide rises.

holding power. *First*, drop one anchor in the normal manner, paying out double the length of cable needed. Then lay a second—much as fore-and-aft technique—bringing up on the first cable. If the two anchors are laid, one to windward and one to leeward, the chances of holding in a wind shift are greatly increased, especially important when anchoring not far offshore in an open roadstead. Lay out extra cable so that both lines will not foul the underbody of the boat. *Second*, use two anchors in line. That is, attach the kedge with a length of chain to the bower ring with a shackle. Lower the kedge first, then the bower while making sternway. Or, drop the bower first with the kedge attached at least the depth of the water distance aft on the cable, certainly no less than 7 to 8 meters distance. Remember, in any storm situation the strains on deck attachment points will be excessive. Make sure that chain cable can be released instantly if you must drop the anchor and run. Buoy the chain before releasing it.

Dragging can be much more than a nuisance. On a lee shore it can be deadly. If your boat begins to drag—something you can tell from reference to landmarks—start the engine first! Then pay out more cable. If this does not work, motor up, taking in cable and reset the anchor. If the bottom is suspect, try running a riding weight down the anchor cable. This can be a patent device or a ball of chain. Just make sure that whatever weight you use is reasonably heavy, say equal to the weight

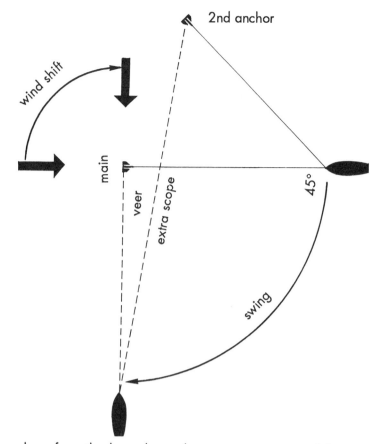

2nd anchor

wind shift

main

veer

extra scope

45°

swing

Setting two anchors from the bow demands a certain amount of forethought to allow for windshifts. This arrangement shows an effective way of doing it.

of the kedge anchor. If this does not work effectively, set a second anchor at an angle of 25 to 35 degrees.

There are times when you will foul the anchor, either on seabed refuse or underwater cables or with another anchor. First, try hauling in cable until it is vertical and taut. Then move weight aft to try breaking it out or supply appropriate leverage via a windlass. If this doesn't work, try sailing or motoring out, pulling in the opposite direction from which the anchor was originally set. So much for the easy methods. All the rest take a certain amount of real and imaginary labor. You can run a loop of line or chain down over the anchor cable, carry it out in the dinghy and then haul from the opposite direction. Or, you can use a grapnel (or a small hook) from the *anchored* dinghy to try and pick up the main anchor, or any obstructing cable. Needless to say, a member of the crew must be stationed at the bow of the mother ship and another at its wheel to cover any possibility of backward drift. If the anchor and cable are fouled by another boat's ground tackle, attempt to raise both anchor *and* cable, securing them by a line to the boat as you lift the pair higher and higher. Then try to free the anchor by hand from the dinghy (tethered to the mother ship).

When the chance exists that you will be in a crowded anchorage (what isn't these days?) or expect that you shall have to depart an anchorage with greater dispatch than you had perhaps originally

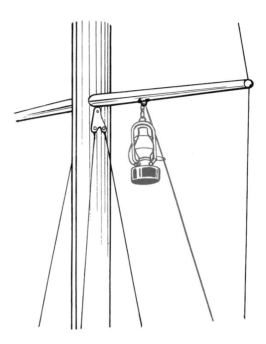

Even in a designated anchorage, it's a good idea to hoist an anchor light. Other boats may arrive late and will need some note, especially on a dark night, as to your position.

planned, it is a good idea to set up a buoyed trip line. Very simply, attach a length of reasonably light cordage (8mm) to the crown of the anchor before lowering it. To the "top" end, tie a short length of chain to steady it and a small buoy or plastic bottle. This will tend to keep other boats away; should the anchor become fouled, it will give you a ready-set method for breaking it free.

If you singlehand, setting an anchor can be a frantic experience. First, lower and secure the mainsail. You will find it much easier to handle the boat under just foresail and without the danger of swinging booms and backing sails. Pass the rode or cable outside of all stanchions and lines aft to the cockpit, making sure the cable is secured, with the necessary scope, to the foredeck. You can release both anchor and jib sheets together, calmly move forward and snub anchor and lower the jib one after the other. Release latches to drop the anchor from a roller chock are not recommended. They have a tendency to stick, or you may release the anchor and accidentally overshoot the rode, creating a large tangled mass about the underwater appendages of your boat.

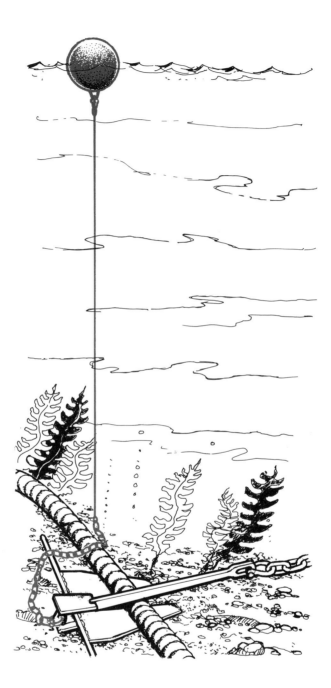

In any anchorage where you suspect a foul bottom, it's wise to rig a trip line to the crown of the anchor. Another example of reverse psychology!

Maintenance

Maintenance

Keeping a boat in Bristol condition at the dock or mooring is one thing; maintaining those same standards while cruising is quite another. At the same time, no one really wants to spend their days varnishing or head-down in the bilges trying to locate a leak. For most of us, cruising time is time for enjoyment, not repairs. Yet like all mechanical contrivances or anything that moves, boats need constant care. Just as you change the oil and filter regularly in your car (and you should), engines, rigging, ground tackle, plumbing and electronics all need periodic and regular care. If you do this at the beginning of each season, chances are certain items will need review once a month, some more often.

Modern technology has made a number of these checks and procedures less onerous than they used to be, but they still have to be done! Otherwise, you will find yourself stranded in some strange port, with no parts, no expertise and an abrupt end to your cruise. Obviously, the key to keeping maintenance less of a chore is to schedule it, and follow those schedules with clockwork regularity. Doing so will make it seem easier and quicker, even if it isn't.

The most obvious maintenance chores concern keeping the propulsion systems going, whether engines or sails. We'll cover the major points below, but these must be made as fail-safe and trouble-free as possible to assure a reasonably pleasurable cruise.

DIESEL ENGINES

Most marine engines in today's cruising boats are diesels, and the number one priority in keeping a diesel going is clean fuel. Under no circumstances assume the fuel coming from the pump is clean. Under no circumstances assume the fuel in your tanks, going through your filters or entering your engine is clean. Every precaution possible should be taken: buy from a high-turnover marina, install multiple filters, change filter elements often, install a fuel-water separator, and inspect and clean tanks seasonally.

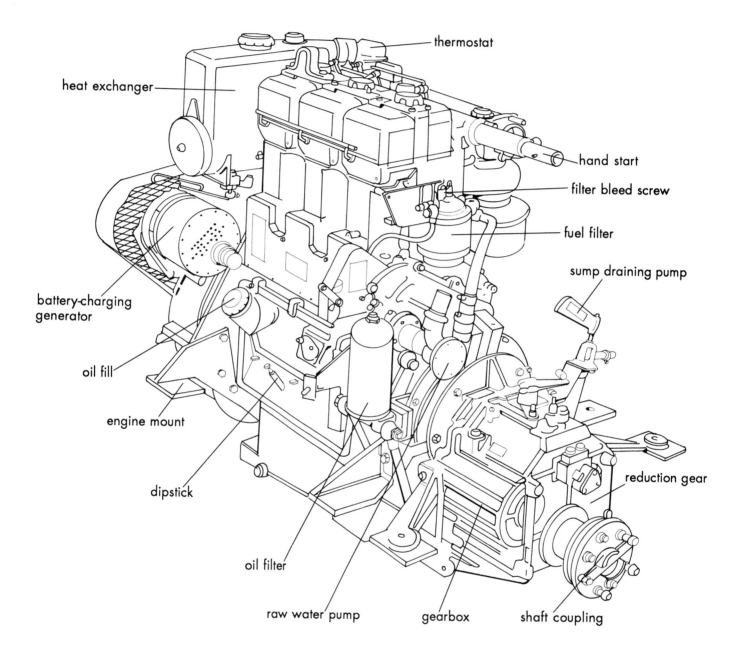

heat exchanger

thermostat

hand start

filter bleed screw

fuel filter

sump draining pump

battery-charging
generator

oil fill

engine mount

dipstick

oil filter

raw water pump

gearbox

shaft coupling

reduction gear

Typical diesel engine.

Unlike gasoline engines, they do not rely on an electrical ignition system which is subject to malfunction from the mere existence of a marine environment. However, the quality of the fuel, which is injected under high pressure into the combustion chamber, is far more critical. Since the injectors that perform this task are comparatively fine tolerance devices, any impurities in the fuel supply will likely cause clogging and possible damage to the injectors.

Since pressures build to a very high level in diesels, proper lubrication is vital to the smooth running of the engine. Engine oil levels should be checked before starting the engine for the first time on a given day. Oil should be changed and filters renewed every 200 to 250 hours of running time. A good general rule is that the faster an engine's running speed in revolutions per minute, the more frequently the oil should be changed. Consult your owner's manual.

Air is a necessity for any combustion, in especially large quantities for a diesel. Make sure vents are large enough, air filters likewise. The warmer the ambient temperature, the more air will be needed. Many high-speed engines will require more air faster, and some provision may have to be made to accommodate this requirement—either extra vents or a blower with flame arrestor.

The majority of small diesels are raw-water cooled. For this cooling to be successful, all water piping must be kept clear and free of impediments and clogging. Likewise, the pump must be working properly. Quite often the impeller—with neoprene blades—will be damaged or the blades stripped off by even a small bit of grit entering the system. A spare impeller or two should always be carried. Since the water pump is usually located at the front of the engine, this is one of the easiest repairs to make. Raw water will have corrosive effects if left standing, and all raw-water cooling systems should be flushed with fresh water at least twice yearly, more often if possible.

Water flow is controlled by a thermostat. A spare should always be kept aboard, for when this little piece of equipment goes, nothing will suffice except a replacement. Be sure you get an exact replacement, as anything else will not work or fit and you'll be left drifting.

GASOLINE ENGINES

Gasoline-powered engines also need air and clean fuel to operate properly. However, unlike diesels, they have a far more complex electrical system to contend with. As with all things electrical in a marine environment, dampness and salt air will take their toll. What with points, spark plugs, distributors, timing, cables and such, every likelihood exists for a short, current drain or power blockage. Luckily, most of the problems are much the same as with an automobile engine, accentuated by the marine environment.

In addition, gasoline engines use a fuel with a very low flashpoint and one which evaporates, forming a highly explosive, heavier-than-

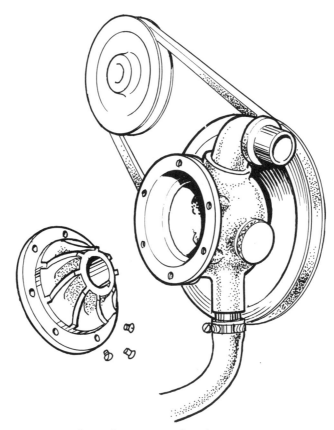

The most common cause of overheating is the disintegration or tearing of the water-pump impeller. Spares should always be carried aboard.

air gas. All engine rooms *must* be fitted with nonsparking blowers, and these must be run for at least five minutes prior to starting the engine. Do not smoke during this period or during any refuelling or maintenance procedures. Having seen both boats and owners blown to bits at fuelling docks, it is a vice to be viewed circumspectly around gasoline or any other volative fuel or material.

Always check the oil level before departing on any voyage. At the beginning of the season and, preferably, at midseason, change the oil and oil filter(s). See that linkages are lubricated regularly with good-quality waterproof grease.

Always carry spare spark plugs. One of the most common causes of engine failure is fouled plugs, due to overheating and contaminated fuel. Plugs should be chosen with an eye to the type of service expected of them: hotter plugs for trolling and slow speeds, less so for faster speeds and lighter loads. They must be gapped as per manufacturer's specifications. Newer plugs are nongapping and the initial choice is therefore more critical. Carry a plug wrench socket aboard and make sure it fits your plugs, as several sizes are available.

At the beginning of the season, check all leads and electrical cables and replace any with cracks or chafed and worn insulation. Have the carburetor cleaned and adjusted and the timing adjusted at least every two years. Points ought to be checked every 100 hours of operation and replaced if any signs of wear appear.

Since gasoline engines run at much higher speeds than diesels, lubrication is vital. Choose engine oils as per manufacturer's recommendations, but make sure that the viscosity rating is compatible to your climate and the type of operation the vessel is most likely to undergo. At higher speeds, over a prolonged period, a thicker oil will be needed to stand up to temperature increases and the faster moving pistons and shafts.

Please remember that all tanks should be located far from the actual engine and that all hoses carrying fuel should be of approved type and double clamped. Tanks must be properly vented and strapped down. Any leakages are cause for immediate stoppage of the engine. They must be isolated and repaired before restarting. You court explosion otherwise.

Like all gasoline engines, high temperatures and over-choking can cause vapor lock. If this happens, disconnect the spark plugs and turn the engine over a few times, then let it rest. Reconnect the plugs and attempt to restart.

FUEL SYSTEMS

All engines need fuel, and all tanks, hoses and pumps needed to deliver fuel to the engine encompass "fuel systems." Most modern fuel systems have both static and dynamic components: tanks, hoses and filters (though not all) are static; pumps, carburetors and injectors are dynamic. For all to work effectively, the fuel introduced into the system *must be clean.* No grit, no water, no sludge must be allowed to penetrate the system defenses.

The most effective defenses against the ingress of these impurities are the fuel filter and water separator. Most engines come equipped with a single filter; occasionally a second in-line filter will be installed. However, if one wants really clean fuel to reach the engine—and in diesels especially, this is vital to protect injectors from damage—one will install a series of multi-element filters and a fuel/water separator along the supply lines. All filters ought to be bolted to structural uprights near the front of the engine, so as to be visible, as well as keeping any weight off the fuel lines.

Fuel lines—copper piping in older boats—should be approved type, guarded neoprene fuel hose. Copper is prone to vibration and fatigue fractures. Other metals are prone to corrosion. All fuel line terminations should be double clamped with stainless steel clamps. As well, a fuel shutoff valve should be installed between the tank and first filter, accessible from the deck, to isolate the engine in case of fire.

Tanks can be made of many materials. For diesel fuel they should not be of stainless steel, as this is subject to pitting and corrosion in the presence of diesel oil. All tanks should incorporate baffles to prevent surges, and must be padded and securely fastened in place against

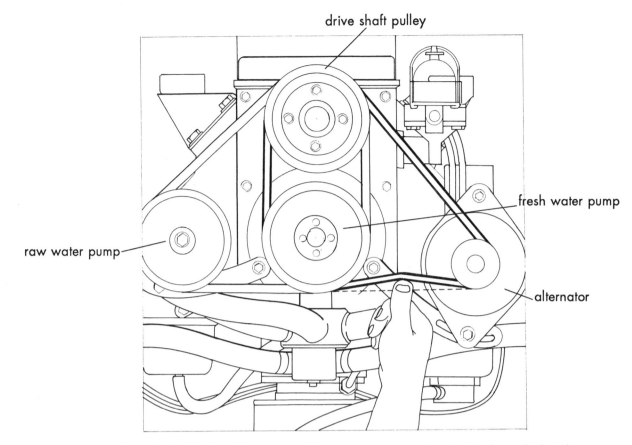

drive shaft pulley

fresh water pump

raw water pump

alternator

Engine driven belts for the alternator and water pump must be checked regularly. They should depress about a 1/4-inch with firm finger pressure.

anything the sea can throw. Without this precaution, chances are all too prevalent for breaching the hull or severely damaging structural components. All tanks must be securely chocked in place. Bearers must be broad enough and securely bolted or glassed in place and all supports and straps should be heavily padded. A ruptured tank is an unmitigated disaster!

ENGINE BEDS, MOUNTS AND COUPLINGS

Any engine, gas or diesel, must be securely mounted to the hull by means of bolting the mounting feet to engine bearers that are bolted, glassed or welded to the hull, depending on hull material. These bearers, particularly in production yachts, are often too short, the result being high-stress areas under the engine and at the ends of the bearers. If this is the case with your auxiliary, some consideration should be given to replacing or extending the bearers to help spread the loads, particularly the twisting torque, of the engine in operation.

Coupled with this is the sometimes severe vibration caused by misalignment and loose mounting bolts. The loads placed upon the bearers and the bearer cappings—metal bars bolted atop the bearers—are severe when everything is tight and functioning properly. When mounting bolts are loose, things get even worse. There have been cases where engines have torn themselves loose from their mounts. The results are

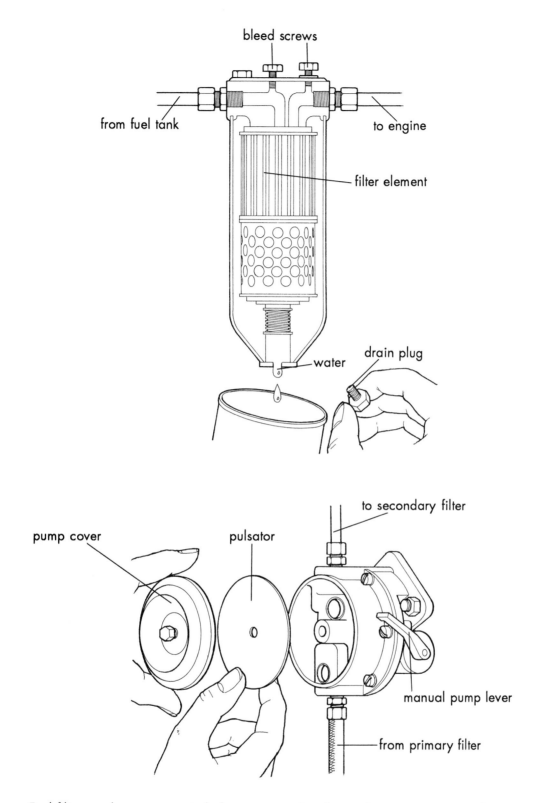

bleed screws

from fuel tank

to engine

filter element

water

drain plug

to secondary filter

pump cover

pulsator

manual pump lever

from primary filter

Fuel filters and pumps are vital elements in a diesel propulsion system. Drain the primary filter of water each time a tankful of fuel is used. Every 200 hours, replace the filter element. The fuel pump should be cleaned regularly. Small amounts of sediment should be scraped out, the pulsator replaced if it is deformed or torn, and the unit reassembled. Both filter and pump maintenance admit air to the fuel delivery system and it will have to be bled following manufacturer's instructions. A second filter, installed in-line between the primary filter and the pump, can lessen maintenance and help insure against injector damage.

worse than could be caused by a raging bull. Check the mounts at the beginning of each season and tighten all bolts.

Most modern auxiliaries are fitted with flexible mounts—synthetic rubber inserts between the engine and bearers—which help dampen vibrations, particularly in lighter hulls. Since few yachts are built to commercial standards, direct mountings are generally avoided by builders. However, flex mounts must be carefully sized to the engine and all other aspects of the installation should likewise be flexible: hoses in particular, as solid copper piping will be ruptured or yield to fatigue if fitted to a flexibly-mounted engine.

Stuffing boxes can be a source of annoying leaks. Generally, they need repacking every few years. All packing materials will compact and wear and, since one can only tighten up so much on the bolts of the box, eventually the packing must be renewed.

OUTBOARDS AND STERN DRIVES

Outboard motors have come a long way since the first rude constructions of Ole Evinrude. They can be had in 4-cycle versions, in 2-cycle (the most prevalent) with auto-oil-injection and even in diesel (workboat) workups. The basic premise is simple. Make the engine and drive train one unit and do away with installation, alignment and insulation problems in one stroke. Four-stroke engines are cared for in much the same way as any 4-stroke auxiliary.

Two-stroke outboards all work on the principle of adding oil directly to the fuel mixture. In the evil, smelly old units, this was a 25:1 mixture and produced fouled plugs, dirty exhausts and rotten fuel economy. Today's versions run on 50:1 to 100:1 mixtures and are as reliable and clean as many inboards.

The major problems are encountered when using an outboard for slow-going and heavy-hauling tasks. Since most outboards are designed for fast-planing power boats, their appropriateness for other chores is often compromised. Major problems are fouled plugs, overheating and cavitation.

Fouled plugs occur when the oil is too heavy in the mixture or when the plug is not hot enough to burn the oil/gas mixture as fully as possible. The solution in the first case is to dilute the mixture in accordance with manufacturer's instructions. In the second situation, simply replace the plugs with a recommended "hot" plug, specifically designed to use in these circumstances.

Overheating in outboards usually is caused by a blockage to the raw water intake at the base of the leg. Another possible cause of overheating is buildup of deposits in the cooling piping. This can be caused by running in very dirty water and/or by neglecting to replace sacrificial anodes, especially in salt water.

In general, maintenance of outboard engines is an easy and quick matter. Change the gear oil, replace plugs and filters every spring. Give the entire engine, under the cowl, a light spray of penetrating oil. Make sure fuel is fresh and filtered. Check that the engine wiring is sound and secure. Check the carburetor for obstructions and the valves for freedom of movement. Replace shear pins and cotters and coat the propeller shaft liberally with heavy-duty waterproof grease before replacing the prop. If the propeller is nicked or bent, have it repaired or replace it. That's it!

Of course, catastrophes can occur, the most likely being dropping the entire unit overboard. If this should happen in fresh water, dry the engine off as well as possible and get it to your OB repair man. In salt water, things deteriorate rather quickly. Wash it off immediately with fresh water and go directly to the same repair expert. Any delays will likely ruin the engine for good.

At the end of the season, the engine should be flushed out with fresh water, oiled—remembering to remove the plugs and spray some penetrating oil in each combustion chamber—drained and brought inside and kept dry.

During the season, please try to keep the engine leg and prop out of the water if possible. If not, treat the leg with antifouling paint specifically formulated for OB lower units. Most legs are aluminum and corrosion will occur if incompatible paints are used.

Stern drives are nothing more than inboard engines with outboard, pivoting propellers. Instead of going through the hull, the shafts are modifications of outboard lower units and exit the boat through the stern above the waterlines. The advantages are obvious, the disadvantages less so, especially in light of developments in all outboard propulsion units. The biggest problem with stern drives is their complex gearing and vulnerability. They are as subject to corrosion as outboards, but repair usually involves hauling the boat and their complexity makes them a poor choice for owner repair.

MASTS

On a sailing yacht, with the exception of one propelled by a kite, all sails and rigging are somehow connected to the mast—or masts—which stands vertical on or through the deck. This can be constructed of aluminum, wood—either solid or hollow—or steel or, more recently, of GRP and carbon fiber composites. No matter what the material, this column exists to allow a topmost point from which to attach sails and, in modern yachts, an after edge to support the luff of the mainsail. If the rig is not freestanding, it will be a column in compression, the forces exerted by the stays and shrouds acting to push the mast downward through the bottom of the hull if given the chance.

Most problems with masts come about from a combination of tension and fatigue. The tensions are not a constant. They vary from at rest to beating, to reaching or running; they vary with the sea state and the strength of the wind. They vary with the tune of the rig and the pressures applied by the sails and the running rigging. In other words, you cannot calculate all the variables and say with any assurance if and when something will fail.

Fatigue is a bit different. Tension can be visually demonstrated easily enough. Fatigue is due to the inherent properties of different metals, and the changes brought about to the structure of the metal by movement and oscillation, particularly by rhythmic motions. The only way to avoid a fatigue failure is constant inspection and knowing what to look for. Masts are prone to fatigue and fail at the two points of greatest stress: the partners—where the spreaders meet the mast—and at the point the mast passes through the deck.

At the spreaders, all the forces transmitted to the shrouds are transferred to the column. This is also the point at which the mast undergoes the greatest flexing. The combination of constantly varying tensions and the oscillation from flexing is astounding. In an average 24-hour passage, it can be measured in thousands of movements. Over a period of time, the mast metal can weaken and suddenly let go. You have little or no warning, and the results are not pretty. To repair this at sea is more a case of rigging a jury mast than effecting any permanent repairs.

MAST MAINTENANCE

Aluminum spars are comparatively easy to maintain. Most are either hard-anodized or else are painted with a two-part polyurethane. It goes without saying that every fall, spars should be removed from the yacht and thoroughly checked for damage, corrosion and abrasion. For winter storage, they must be supported no less than every six feet and have all shrouds and stays tied off to the spars at the same intervals. Prior to any laying down, coat the spar with a decent paste wax and do not buff. In the spring, this can be removed with cleanser, and the mast properly recoated with wax.

Both anodized and painted spars can be scratched, chipped or roughed-up. Small marks can be protected with wax. Larger scratches and scrapes may need more drastic treatment. Sooner or later, all coatings will weather and wear. A mast can be reanodized, though this is a time-consuming and expensive process. Far better is to paint it.The following also applies to repainting bare aluminum or previously painted spars.

Inspect the heel of the mast. This is an area highly susceptible to galvanic action and corrosion. The mast step should be of epoxy-coated aluminum or if not, carefully insulated from the mast with neoprene gasketing. However, even with gaskets in place, if the mast goes through the deck and the step is in the bilge, beware. Too often, steel mast steps will be installed. The combination of steel and aluminum in a salt water electrolyte will eventually spell disaster. If the steel is totally glassed in place, you are better off, but make sure there are no fractures in the GRP covering of the step.

Inspect the masthead. All fittings should be tight fitting and aligned. Spinnaker broaches and sudden gybes can sometimes knock a masthead fitting out of alignment and this will cause chafe and eventual breakage. Check all masthead sheaves for free motion and lubricate with silicon or Teflon spray. Make sure all electrical connections are tight and secure.

All mast fittings, whether riveted or bolted to mast pads, must be securely attached. Tangs should show no signs of stress or bending and the mast area around them should be free of hairline cracks. If you doubt their integrity, use a special dye to check for cracks and fatigue. Spreaders must be aligned slightly upward, ideally to bisect the angle made by the shrouds passing over them. Many spreader attachment schemes have been used over the years, but anything hinged is suspect and should be replaced with a socket arrangement or some device to hold the spreader securely at the proper angle to the mast.

All moving parts should be lubricated. The oldtime tallow and lanolin still work, though I prefer silicone or Teflon sprays. They don't gum up, they don't collect grit and dirt, and they stand up to extremes of cold and heat far better than oils or animal fats. All nonmoving metal parts should be cleaned with a mild detergent, dried and coated with a good carnuba paste wax, either a proprietary marine wax or any good automobile wax. Rubbing compounds are generally to be avoided on masts as they will wear away coatings if too much elbow grease is applied.

Occasionally, one will find stainless fittings attached directly to an aluminum mast. Remove the fitting at the soonest possible moment and install a neoprene gasket between the two, for the same reasons—though not as severe—as mentioned above about mast heels. This applies especially to mast-mounted winches made of bronze or stainless steel. Make sure the mounting pad is insulated from the mast and the winch from the pad.

STANDING RIGGING

All standing rigging is either galvanized wire, stainless steel wire or stainless rod. I suspect some will suggest rope rigging and chain, but these are only seen in either ancient or odd boats and need not concern us here. In fact, except amongst stern traditionalists, you will rarely find galvanized wire, despite the fact that it costs far less than stainless and, for a given diameter, is stronger. It needs coating with linseed oil mixed with mineral spirits (the oil to keep rust at bay, the spirits to act as a medium to allow the oil to penetrate) on a regular basis, once a month in the tropics, less often in more northerly locales. For some reason, galvanized wire is more prone to developing hooks or broken strands than stainless. This must be watched for—at least at fitting-out time—as it is a good sign that a particular length of stay or shroud will soon need replacing.

Most yachts today use stainless steel wire fitted with swaged terminals, or else with Sta-Lock or Norseman type terminals. Swaging, the process by which a tubular fitting is compressed around the strands of a wire by enormous pressure, has been around for years. It is reliable and strong when properly done. However, the same pressure that holds things together can occasionally be applied with slight unevenness. When this happens, the fitting can be weakened and can eventually fail. An bent edge to the terminal or slight cracks near the edge of the swage adjacent to the wire are signs to junk the fitting as soon as possible and refit the entire end.

Sta-Lock type terminals have two advantages: they can be applied on board by anyone with basic hand tools; they can be easily inspected for cracks and stress, and when repair time comes, the only nonreusable part is the internal cone.

Another alternative is Nicro or Talurit press-type fittings. These can be very useful on smaller boats and can be a godsend for emergency repairs. In this method, a sleeve is compressed around a wire loop or thimble, thus creating an eye for the attachment of rigging screws. These work quite well, though there is some chance of distortion if the thimble is not chosen with care or if it is galvanized and the rigging wire is stainless. Also, the wires must be kept as tight as possible around the thimble. Otherwise slippage and bending will undoubtedly occur, leading to failure.

The replacement of any standing rigging is, unless circumstances dictate otherwise, something to be done in the calm of a slip or on the hard, with the yacht hauled. If the replacement is to be undertaken with the mast in place, then halyards can double as jury rigging until the offending stay is replaced. The uppermost end of the stay must be detached, and this is a chore to be carried out from the bosun's chair. In its simplest form, this is a board attached to a bridle which can be hoisted aloft. To be both safe and comfortable, newer types are highly recommended. Those which totally support the user with safety straps in front and soft sides and back are best. In addition, some sort of pouch or tool holders should be provided for.

When using a bosun's chair, it is imperative that some sort of redundant safety factor be built into both method and system. Someone stationed at the winch below, with at least four turns on the winch, should be considered a minimum. An additional backup on deck is a good idea. A bridle should be made up beforehand to allow the person in the chair to tether himself to the mast as an added safety feature, especially if there is any movement to the vessel. Swinging into a mast from even a few feet will damage the sailor more than the mast.

FITTINGS

All the various fitments that go into rigging–turnbuckles, blocks, chainplates, tangs, exit boxes, masthead instruments, wiring, reefing arrangements, etc.—are actually the most likely sources of problems. Since each is an individual link in the rigging system, the failure of any one may well spell the demise of the entire rig. From a safety point-of-view, those parts which keep the mast up are the most vital: chainplates, turnbuckles (rigging screws), tangs and spreaders with their attendant clevis pins, split pins and shackles. Each and every part must be mated in strength to the others or havoc will result.

It should go without saying that split pins are replaced every year. Do not use brass. All should be marine stainless and sized to the job. A split pin should only project by a maximum of 3/8 inch from the clevis. The clevis, in turn, should fit snugly through its boring, and project just enough to allow the split pin to be inserted. Any greater extension will allow excess movement, chafe and metal fatigue. This goes for all fittings held together in this manner.

Turnbuckles need to be disassembled and cleaned every year and should be installed so that they are all right-turning. There will never be a question as to how to adjust them on a dark and stormy night. Threads must be greased, either with lanolin, rapeseed oil or Teflon. This last is the cleanest and most effective as a penetrating lubricant. Bent forks or screw shafts ought to be replaced as these are potential danger points. Likewise, closed-bodied turnbuckles, though they may look sleeker, have no place on a yacht. You can never tell how much screw is imbedded and I have seen masts go overboard when one popped apart. Finally, make sure that all clevis pins are secure and pinned. Split pins should not be spread open more than about 15 degrees. Too-long pins that are bent back will hamper quick removal in emergencies. Tape the pins. Turnbuckle boots are to be avoided as they trap moisture and prevent ready inspection.

WIRE

With a few exceptions, masts are held aloft by wire rope or rods in tension. Wire can be of several types, though for pleasure craft use, galvanized steel wire rope is rarely seen except for character craft. Most is stainless steel in various configurations, the pattern dictating its relative flexibility and use: 1x19 wire is usual for standing rigging; 7x19 for running rigging.

All wire is subject to great fatigue through bending and oscillation. Bending or running around sheaves will obviously cause friction wear. Repeated bending will cause stress fatigue. Oscillation fatigue is caused by the harmonic vibrations set up in all taut rigging wire by the combined action of wind and wave. Since the hourly rate can be in the thousands, there is no reliable method to gauge when the wire may be near the point of collapse. For most of us this is fairly academic. For anyone undertaking an ocean passage, however, with days at sea non-stop, oscillation fatigue can be a major concern. Wire rope should be thoroughly checked before setting out on any major voyage and any suspect lengths replaced.

Corrosion is another problem often ignored on the supposition that stainless steel cannot corrode. All ferrous metals can and will break down with time and exposure. Corrosion is most often found at terminal fittings and in the inner core of wire rope. Careful inspection and thorough biseasonal washing can keep it at bay, but once the core is corroded or a terminal fitting is highly stained, best replace the offending part of the stay.

ROPE

Whether power or sail, you cannot go to sea without endless coils of rope. This has always been so, and there is not likely to be any change in the near future. All ropes today are relatively carefree and long-lasting compared to the hemp, manila and cotton of yesteryear. However, they still need care to function at full strength.

Dacron/terylene is the standard for sheets and halyards; on larger yachts, halyards may be of stainless steel wire with Dacron tails. Dacron is highly durable and comes in any number of variants: cored, twisted, braided, reinforced with kevlar and other synthetics. All will stretch to some degree, but the reinforced types much less than everyday, twisted 3-strand line.

Nylon, used for anchor rodes and dock lines, should stretch and although great claims have been made for braided types, these will usually have less stretch than twisted lines. They are also easier on the hands, but cost close to double.

And then there's wire rope, which is rope, after all. Mcst is made of stainless steel, though you can still obtain plough steel wire rope. This must be treated with a mixture of linseed oil and mineral spirits to preserve it and keep it from rusting.

Dacron and nylon and, for that matter, stainless steel should be kept clean, as salt-free as possible and coiled when not being used. All lines have natural coil depending on how they were woven—either right- or left-handed. A rope will naturally coil one way or the other. Do not coil a line around your hand and elbow in the hope of getting a neater coil. This will invariably kink the coil. Let the coil fall naturally from one hand.

Synthetic ropes should be washed prior to winter storage in lukewarm water and a mild detergent—dishwashing liquid is perfect—then rinsed thoroughly and hung in loose coils to dry.

BATTERIES

If the time has come to replace one or more batteries, use marine batteries. Automobile and utility batteries cannot hold the charge needed to start a marine diesel or to receive repeated deep charges. Cost

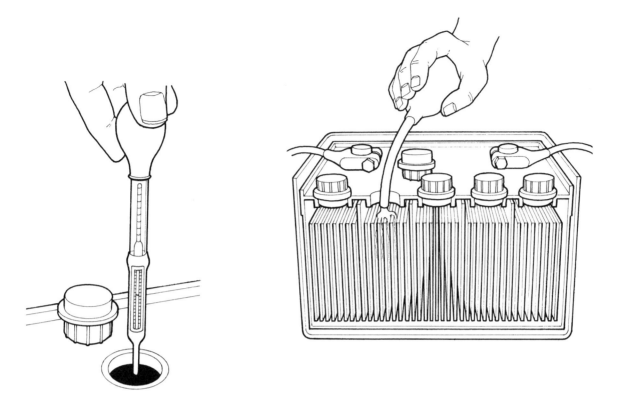

A hydrometer is used to check battery acid concentrations; a figure of 1.26 indicates a strong acid level and a full charge. When the lead electrolytes are not covered by acid, the solution must be topped-up, using distilled water. Do not overfill as corrosive acid will be spill out. Blot immediately and neutralize with baking soda in solution. In hot weather, check the battery solution level at least once a week.

should be a secondary consideration as a top-flight marine battery will last through five to seven years of heavy use. The batteries must be installed in a leakproof box, preferably above the waterline—batteries can leak hydrogen gas and, in the bilges, this is an invitation to disaster. This box must be vented overboard from both high and low positions within the box. With the newer, sealed batteries, this is not quite as insistent a requirement, but some provision to keep the battery isolated from the engine and living compartments is absolutely necessary. In addition, the batteries must be securely strapped down to through-bolted strong points.

Electrolyte levels ought to be checked weekly, more often in very hot climates. Any wet-cell battery will lose its charge faster if the plates are exposed. Likewise, batteries should be charged weekly, preferably by running the engine for a couple of hours. If you keep the boat dockside, you can use an automatic trickle charger, but be forewarned that this can short out or, even worse, the trip switch that shuts it off can malfunction. The net result will be destroyed batteries.

In fact all single-and multiple-battery installations should be equipped with a selector/shut-off switch properly rated to the *total* ampere load of the batteries. These switches should be mounted near the companionway, protected from spray and used with regularity, as a matter of course. They will save you drained batteries and make charging simpler and easier.

WIRING

Many a boat, especially purchased used, has been tinkered with. Everyone seems to think he can add whatever electrical bits and pieces he wants without any problems. What you get is a circuit board which no housing inspector would ever pass, accompanied by a jumble of mismatched, missized wires totally unidentified. My only advice is to rip out the entire mess and start over.

Boat wiring is subject to far more severe conditions than house wiring. First off, it is located in a hostile environment; humidity and water are anathema to any electrical circuit. Not only is there a constant threat of current leaks, but also the chance of corrosion of terminals and wires themselves. Now all electrical systems lose current through leaks and distant wire runs. However, boat electrical systems are more prone to current loss than most others, and guarding against this is worth as much as 20 amp-hours of battery storage in one evening's use!

One of the best and simplest ways of avoiding this is to keep wiring out of the bilges. This should be self-evident, but a surprising number of builders who should know better persist in running major circuits through the dark, dank reaches beneath the floorboards. Any wires in the bilge should be rerouted as soon as possible.

Likewise, in the best of all possible worlds, all wiring should be run through plastic conduit with junction boxes located at easily accessed points throughout the ship. These must be openable with gasketed, watertight covers and also made of plastic. Thus, if a wire needs to be run or replaced, it's an easy matter to open boxes at both ends and draw the new wire through while making any connections in the box itself. If installing conduit for the first time, insert a running line to aid in drawing the wires through, especially in long runs. Make all bends or directional changes in runs at a box, not midway along a wire.

Choosing wire is something to consider with care. The longer the run, the greater the current loss and you shall have to employ heavier-gauge wire in the installation. Use multistrand, wire with which there is much less chance of a complete loss of current and less brittleness than in single-strand wire. Insulation should be neoprene or a similar rubber compound which is waterproof and of very low conductivity.

All ends should be twisted and attached using crimped connectors.

However, each connection should be soldered as well as crimped to lessen the chance of breaking the circuit and to add to a more positive current path. Once the connectors are in place and male and female terminals are joined, cover the parts with a thin film of petroleum jelly. Do not use electrical tape to cover these connections. It will invariably trap moisture and lead to corrosion and failure.

Leads from the batteries to the circuit-breaker board or the fuse board must be sized to the maximum possible load. To calculate this, add up the total wattage ratings of all lights and appliances and divide by the voltage of the system. For example:

Lights	6 @ 25 watts=150 watts
Navigation lights	4 @ 10 watts= 40 watts
Electronics	20 watts= 20 watts
Misc. equipment	72 watts= 72 watts
Total possible load	=282 watts

12-volt system: 282 divided by 12=23.5 amperes
24-volt system: 282 divided by 24=11.75 amperes

Thus the wiring should be heavy enough to carry this load should everything be turned on simultaneously, allowing for surges in heating and motorized equipment. Generally speaking, the leads from batteries to switchboard should be on a par with heavy-duty battery booster cables (8 gauge or lower in thickness). Despite formulas for working out resistance and length, a good rule-of-thumb is to choose cable sizes up by one gauge size for each yard of running length of any electrical cable.

ELECTRONICS

Depth sounders, radars, loran, radios and other electronic devices, mostly for navigation and communication, but some—autopilots, navigation interfaces, etc.—used for active piloting, have become extremely sophisticated pieces of equipment. What used to be mechanical and highly power consumptive has become, through the use of integrated circuitry and computer chips, far more reliable and accurate and less of a power drain. However, the days when an amateur could fiddle about with a screwdriver and soldering iron are gone for good.

With a few exceptions, most electronic equipment should be installed and serviced by professionals. The sophistication is beyond most of us and the cost of repairing DIY mistakes may be as much as a replacement. Some modern equipment is designed to use plug-in circuit boards, so that when something goes wrong, replacement doesn't involve more than snap out/snap in. However, very few sailors have access to the electronic diagnostic gear necessary to decide *which* of several boards has malfunctioned.

In choosing electronics for your yacht you obviously considered whether to power the devices from the ship's system or by self-contained battery power. For certain instruments such as depth sounders and radio direction finders, self-contained batteries have much to recommend them. Should the main power supply go by the board, at least you will have the basics of navigation at hand. Logs, as well, might be battery-powered or backed up with a trailing log of mechanical pattern.

However, larger electronics or those which demand especially high power–transmitters, radar–must be connected to the main battery system of the boat. On smaller auxiliaries or power boats, the norm is now to install two batteries, one for engine starting, one for ship's systems, the two segregated by means of a battery selector switch which can isolate either battery, connect them in series or charge both or one. For any yacht equipped with a serious navigation compartment–RDF, echo sounder, log, wind instruments, loran, radar, VHF, SSB, course computers, etc.–a *third* battery specifically for electronics is highly recommended. Motor activated navigational items like autopilots and radar scanners should be isolated to the ship's systems battery, as the draw and current surges can adversely effect some electronic systems.

All electronics should be installed in a relatively dry area with protection from driven spray or rain coming from any quarter. Cables should be routed to keep them out of the bilge and all should terminate in a junction box devoted specifically to electronics, preferably near the navigation area. Certain electronic devices–satellite navigation systems, loran, radar–need grounding and this should be done by a trained electronics engineer, since interference can drastically limit the range and utility of these devices.

SAIL CARE

Sail care is actually one of the easiest bits of maintenance to undertake. First, and most important, is to keep the sails as crease-free as possible. After a headsail change, don't stuff the old sail into the bag. Push it down the forehatch and fold it below. f course, this will not be too simple with large genoas, but at least attempt to keep the sail as smooth as possible until conditions permit a proper fold. Mains should be flaked down over the boom and tied firmly but lightly. Don't try to garotte the sail with ties. You merely wish to keep it from falling into the cockpit.

Likewise, each sail should have its own sailbag, identifying the sail. Sails kept bent on–mains, club staysails–should have fitted covers to protect them from atmospheric grit and sunlight. The best material for covers is without question Acrilan, a synthetic canvas which will withstand just about any abuse. Colors are to be preferred as white will eventually get dirty beyond cleaning.

At the end of the season, all sails should be cleaned. This can be done with any mild detergent–*not* soap–and warm water. Grease and other stains that will not come out by this method can be attacked with a household cleaner or with a mild solvent. In all cases, the sail must be rinsed with copious amounts of clean water and left to dry spread out on a lawn or deck or other clean surface. Do not fold and store wet or damp sails for the winter. They will mildew (yes, even synthetics can support microorganism growth) and crease even more. After they are totally dry, fold them loosely and bag them. Store sails in a dry, room temperature space with as much air circulation as possible. Above all, don't leave them on board.

The alternative is to deliver them to your sailmaker for vetting and winter storage. You pays your money and takes your choice. Actually, this service is usually fairly cheap and repairs, if any, will be made professionally.

SAIL REPAIR

Sail damage breaks down into three major areas: tears in the cloth, broken stitching, and damage to sail fittings. Each repair can be undertaken without fear of major disaster, providing you learn some basic techniques and take your time. Sewing is one of the essentials for all sailors. Even if you can't sew a button on a shirt, you should be able to execute those stitches necessary to keep your sails in good order. Despite claims to the contrary, sail needles, except in the smallest sizes, will actually damage Dacron and nylon cloth. These are not comparable to canvas or flax and the triangular point will chafe and tear modern materials.

Instead, a round shaft needle of about 3-inch length will simply penetrate between the threads of the sail cloth. All needles will rust, no matter how heavily plated, and they are best kept in a plastic vial, wrapped in a scrap of oiled cloth and well sealed. Except in heavy cloth, a palm is not really necessary. Finding a good one is not easy! It should be adjustable, with a buckle or Velcro-fastening strap, and fit snugly. Leather is the only acceptable material and be sure to get one made for your configuration—right- or left-handed.

Thread for stitching should be of Dacron. Do not be tempted to use a spool from the home sewing basket. This is either cotton or polyester and will break instantly. Dacron thread made specifically for sails is extraordinarily strong and has been treated with an ultraviolet inhibitor. In fact, you will not be able to break the thread with your hands, so keep scissors or knife handy when you work. If you are ordering new sails, one good idea is to have the stitching in contrasting thread, as any chafe or breaks in the stitching will be easier to spot.

Since modern sail cloths are "hard," the thread that holds the panels together lies on top of the cloth, not bedded into it as was the case on old natural fiber sails. Thus, the most common area of damage is to the thread where it catches or chafes against rigging, lines or fittings. The best way to lessen this is to rig various preventive devices to eliminate or lessen possible chafe points. Baggywrinkle, the old standby, really has no place aboard a modern vessel. It is clumsy, unsightly, adds windage and will soil sails. Far better is the polyvinyl split tubing sold for snapping around shrouds and stays. It should roll freely. This will make handholds a bit less secure, but will keep the sails well-protected, cheaply and effectively.

Likewise, spreader ends must be smooth and unobstructed. Molded boots are available, but a better solution is to fit spreaders with captive ends of a hemispherical shape. The less aloft, the fewer chances for hang-ups and less windage. Also, most spreader fitments are taped on. The tape unravels during the season, trailing like a sticky serpent and allowing the boot to fly off.

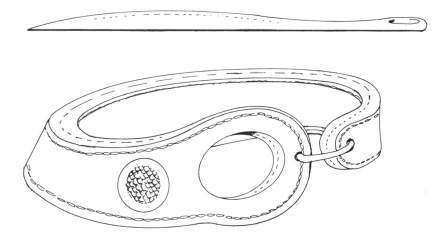

Palm and properly-sized needles are necessary for effective sail and canvias repairs. Palms are made either for right-handed or left-handed working. Needles should not be larger than needed for the work at hand.

Chartering

With the ever-increasing costs attached to boat ownership, more and more people are chartering. If you have only a couple of weeks to cruise, chartering solves a whole list of problems with minimum effort and expense. Consider, owning a boat you must pay for purchase, amortization, upkeep, slip, winter storage, equipment, upgrading, insurance and a thousand bits and pieces. Most likely, you'll use the boat a few weekends and a couple of weeks per season—unless you live in the South or West—and there's no way to justify that expense rationally. I realize that reason is not the major point of being involved with boating, but it should, unless you can throw money around, play some part in your deliberations and decisions.

Deciding if you can charter is the first consideration. Charter companies will be more than hesitant to simply accept your word as to your competence. Most will accept certificates from recognized sailing schools, yacht club membership or proof of ownership of a similar vessel. Five years of Sunfish sailing will not qualify you to charter a 40-foot cutter or trawler! Individual, private charters are a different story and must be arranged through the owner or his agent. These, due to insurance considerations, may be even more stringent in their requirements. Be honest, no matter what. Your own liability, should an accident occur, will be all the greater if the owner can prove you misstated your experience. Some charter companies will check you out prior to handing over the boat. They are within their rights to do so, and you should cooperate. If you fail muster, they may deny the charter or demand you hire a qualified captain.

Assuming your competence and experience can be proven, *before the fact*, you can then decide whether you actually wish to charter. Chartering does allow you to see places you would not get to in an average lifetime of cruising. It allows you to concentrate on boating, not on maintenance, and actually getting to a particular cruising ground. In fact, in today's world, with less and less time for leisure, chartering maximizes your time on the water.

In the past, chartering was limited to a few popular areas or to private charters in odd corners of the world. Currently, there are virtually no interesting cruising grounds in which it is not possible to charter some sort of boat. Be forewarned, however, to expect boats and equipment different from what you may be used to and, especially in foreign countries, customs, rules and regulations which may occasionally be perplexing or downright odd.

To give one example, a few years ago my wife and I decided to charter in the Tyrrhenian Sea out of Elba. Everything was arranged through a reputable broker in Italy. When the charter contracts arrived, we noticed a requirement for a "Sailing License." We queried the broker, but his reply hadn't arrived before we had to leave. Arriving in Elba, we were greeted by the delivery captain with the stark fact that in Italy, any vessel under the Italian flag has to be skippered by someone with an Italian Sailing License. We had no choice but to hire the delivery captain to accompany us. He was a remarkable host and the trip turned out to be beyond our expectations. You must be prepared for this sort of unusual event or, given time, make all arrangements, leaving nothing to chance, before you go.

When considering a charter in an area you've never been to, make enquiries from national tourist authorities, check several charter companies and read local yachting magazines. This last is especially important if you are planning to go foreign, as customs, government regulations and piloting will be different from *your* norm. Don't rely only on nautical publications. General tourist information, history, geography, natural history, in fact almost anything touching on the area and your interests can become part of your background research.

In the course of all this research you will, of course, keep in mind your own abilities and limitations. Nothing can ruin a holiday more than unwanted challenge, read disaster. Be honest with the chartering company; after all, your pride can wreck their investment. Don't plan an itinerary you cannot realistically complete. If you're a tyro and plan to spend 14 hours underway daily, think of the others in your party who may actually want to stop and swim or go ashore. Planning for more than a couple of hundred miles in a sailing vessel or a few hundred in a powerboat per week is utter madness. You will be exhausted, the crew in tatters, tempers frayed and a good holiday ruined.

Chartering will also demand that someone in the crew can take over fully should you be disabled. This means that your wife/husband, child or best friend must have the same level of skill as you do. If one of them doesn't, teach them or have them study, before shoving off. All this should be clarified with the charter company before you even send in a deposit. This cannot be overstressed; too many tales of helpless crew, left at the mercy of the elements, not even knowing how to call for aid or fire a distress signal, are on the books.

Once you've decided on an area, found a charter company or a private yacht, you will still have to decide where within that area you will go and what are the hazards to navigation, weather patterns and sea conditions at the time of your trip. For this you'll need charts, pilot books, tide tables and as much other information as you can get from the charter company. If they are hesitant to provide it, you should question the possibility that their other services may be lacking. Sailing in the British Virgins is a lot different than sailing in the Outer Hebrides, to say the least. Remember, this is a holiday. If you are totally unaware of the "niceties" of your proposed charter location, think long and hard. The sunny, trade wind reaching in the Virgins will be replaced by wet, grey hard beating to windward in the Hebrides.

All this should be ascertained before you go, with the charter company. They will also walk you through the intricacies of insurance, bond and financial obligations. After all, you may be sailing off with over $100,000 worth of yacht. No right-minded person would do so without covering his rear in the most complete manner possible. Different companies have different policies. Some demand a percentage deposit in cash or certified check. Some may ask for the same as a credit card debit. Others will offer insurance or a combination of insurance and deposit. Read the fine print and ask questions if you don't understand something. Better to go through the tedium beforehand, rather than face the music later.

The charter contract, which varies greatly around the world, must be read with the utmost care. I know this is a vacation, but you are transacting a piece of business just as complex in its ramifications as signing a lease for a car or a house. What are both parties' obligations? What are the financial demands placed on the charterer for lateness in return and/or damage? Is provisioning available? Are there proof of experience requirements? Again, question everything and, if in doubt, consult your lawyer.

Assuming all the above has been answered satisfactorily (and you've gotten over the shock of this complication for a vacation), you can go! First, decide how you are getting there. The cost of flying to many destinations will equal the cost of the charter, and this must be figured in to the calculations. What are you taking with you? This will depend on the detailed description of what is supplied in the charter. In certain areas, notably the Mediterranean, bedding and linen is not supplied as a matter of course. Carrying sheets, pillows and towels for six people can defeat even the best planning. Ideally, you will go to an area with a settled climate. In the tropics this means shorts, tops, a sweater, bathing suits and maybe one dressy outfit. In tougher climes you will have to keep warm. Evenings are always cooler than daylight hours and you must plan accordingly. In any area north (or South) of the tropics you will probably need foul weather gear. If you are taking children, bring along safety harnesses to fit. Also, try to pack in collapsible duffles; hard luggage takes up too much space on board.

If the charter is victualled, and you've approved menus, it's still a good idea to bring along favorites special items to keep the crew happy, especially foodstuffs not generally available in the charter area. A number of common fruits and vegetables are not to be had in many areas and cuts of meat will be different. Try to expand your culinary horizons and go native as much as possible. You and your crew will learn a lot and have fun in the process.

If you are provisioning yourself, find out ahead of time what to bring from the charter company, as they will know local conditions best. Alcohol will usually be expensive, except for locally produced drinks. Sweets and meats will be expensive. Paper goods can be outrageous. Plan ahead and you can save yourself time and money.

When you get to the boat, most charters will give you a complete run-down and check-out. Following is what you should familiarize yourself with:

On Deck: General
operation and location of running rigging
location of spares
operation of engine controls
rigging of awnings
working of anchor windlass and anchor stowage
location of docklines and fenders
ladders and man-overboard equipment
working of liferaft
placement of deck fills for water and fuel and location of key
length of the anchor rode
location of emergency tiller and steering system checks
operation of dinghy engine
procedures for stowing dinghy
working of roller furling systems

Belowdecks: General
locations of all through-hulls and stuffing box
working of all expandable furniture
watertank capacity
location and working of all pumps, especially bilge pumps
location of all safety gear (PFDs, flares, fire extinguishers)
stove operation and location of shut-off valves
location of fuel and gas tanks
peculiarities of refrigeration
operation of heads
operation of shower and sump pumps
function of electrical panel switches
operation of battery switches and top-up procedures

Belowdecks: Navigation
charts and cruising guides,
light lists
tide tables
Nautical Almanac
documentation, insurance documents, customs procedures
working of radio
working of navigational devices aboard

Belowdecks: Propulsion
procedure for starting and stopping engine
location of repair manual and tools
how to do basic engine checks
proper engine revs, temperature and oil pressure
fuel capacity

The charter staff will familiarize themselves with you. Be expected to show your knowledge in chart reading, basic piloting, boat handling and anchoring. Keep your cool; this is all for your eventual benefit. If, for some reason, the charter company is not satisfied with your performance, they are perfectly within their rights to insist you hire a captain then and there. Thus, the need to be absolutely truthful in your application and pre-charter conversations. Otherwise you will find yourself standing at the dock, forfeiting your deposit and perhaps your entire fee.

If you feel insecure in your skills for the area involved, consider either hiring a crewed yacht or flotilla sailing. Crewed yachts cost big bucks, but can be the ultimate in luxury. Since this book is about you going cruising, we shall mention no more; a reputable yacht broker can help you find what you need. Flotilla sailing involves a group of individual yachts and a lead boat with company rep, spares, etc. aboard. You go to preplanned stops, but how you get there is up to you. Usually, you'll be in radio contact with the company captain, who will also supply tips, local knowledge and psychological support.

The key is to have fun. Chartering can offer it without the initial investment in a boat. Equally, you can go anywhere in the world and go boating without spending a year getting there. With the lifestyles most of us live, there is not the time to take a year or two off. Chartering can give you the pleasure without the headaches.

If you're thinking of buying a cruising boat, chartering can help you make the decision. Trying out a particular boat for a week is a safe and relatively inexpensive way to decide whether or not it fills your needs.

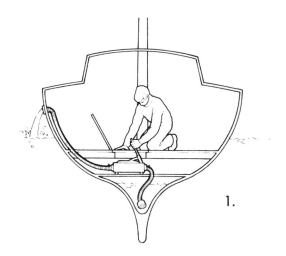

1.

2.

3.

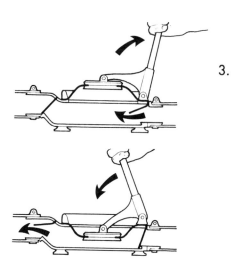

A primary safety tool is the bilge pump. It should be large capacity, minimum 25 gallons per minute. Fig. 1, how a diaphragm pump works. Fig. 2, non-returnable outlet flap valve. Fig. 3, discharge line must be looped above the waterline to prevent backflow. Pump should be located where it can be worked with minimum effort and protected from the elements. Ideally, one should be located in the cockpit, another below.

Safety

Safety at sea, and in port, should be your primary consideration at all times. This is not meant to sound stuffy. The ease with which one can be injured on board, getting aboard, or getting ashore is astounding, ranging from cuts, bruises, broken limbs, concussions and drowning.

The key to safe passagemaking is to always think out potential problems beforehand, to prepare the boat as best possible and to plan a conservative passage. Watch the weather (see Weather chapter) and if at all in doubt of conditions along your proposed route, stay put. Trying to battle the elements can start out being fun, but in short order both the conditions and the strength of yourself and your crew can deteriorate to the point of disaster.

Preparing your boat for the worst is time consuming and expensive. Preparing it for all but the worst may be futile when the worst comes along. But let's try to run down some of those things that can be done to prevent accidents.

DECK GEAR

The old saw of one hand for the ship and one hand for yourself is an absolute dictum. Even when moving about at the dock, be prepared to grab on to something. The wake of a passing launch, a sudden gust of wind can send you off balance and overboard or against some hard object. Hope that something is there to grab on.   Almost all stock boats are underequipped with railings, handholds and stays. As a general guide, you should be able to move both above and below decks–from stem to stern–with a grab rail at hand. This means rails must be through-bolted to cabin tops on both port and starboard sides of the deck, preferably at waist level. They can be either along the top of the house or freestanding. Further rails should surround the cockpit and the foredeck, as well as lifelines or solid rails around the perimeter of the side decks.

Almost all lifelines are too low, usually between 18 and 27 inches from deck to top of the stanchion. This means that the actual guard

Safety gear.

Boat Size	Under 16ft.	16-26ft.	26-40ft.	40-65ft.
Personal Flotation	I or II or III or IV	I or II or III or IV	+ one for each person + one for throwing	
Fire Extinguishers	if tank carried inboard or fuel vapor can be trapped		without fixed system or / with fixed system	without fixed system or / with fixed system or
Sound Audible for 1/2 mile	or		+ or	
Visual Distress Day	none	or / 3 orange smoke flares— hand-held or floating		
Night	SOS light or	or / 3 red flares– hand-held, meteor or parachute		

wire is usually at least an inch lower. Ideally, guard rails should be at least 30 inches off the deck and 36 inches if possible. Additionally, a second, intermediate, wire should be strung halfway between the top wire and the deck. These wires must pass through bushed holes in the stanchions, unless you have welded railings instead. Stanchions can be made of bronze, galvanizes steel or stainless steel, but make sure that they are thick-wall extrusions and that the bases are strongly reinforced. A good test is to sit on the house, rest one foot against a stanchion and suddenly push forward with your leg. You would be surprised at how easily it can be made to distort and bend. Powerboats should have fixed rails around the perimeter of the deck, preferably 40 inches high with gates port and stern. Patent gate hardware is readily available.

Non-skid must be effective. The best is teak decking, but this is very expensive, needs much care and adds weight where it's least needed. Next best is a patent deck covering such as Treadmaster, a cork/rubber composite that will keep your martini glass from rolling overboard. Painting over GRP is not often done these days, but it is still more effective, and easier to renew, than molded-in patterns. To work at all, the paint must have silica granules or silver sand mixed-in prior to application. This, if the paint is a thin enough consistency, is preferable to scattering the sand over wet paint, letting it dry and vacuuming the excess. It is also less abrasive.

On all boats, sail and power, some means of attaching harnesses should be installed to allow a crewmember to move fore and aft without unhooking his lifeline. Jackstays of some sort are the best bet, but they should not interfere with movement on decks or waterways. Best install them on the trunk cabin top in a sailboat. On a powerboat, much will be decided by the nature of the superstructure. Generally, the best location is along the house side, just below any eyebrow molding and heavily through-bolted with backing pads. This location will interfere less with window glass and should allow for attachment without having to bend over. Be sure the aft end of the jackline is as far aft as possible, so crew can clip on prior to leaving the safety of the cockpit or, better yet, the companionway.

SAFETY BELOW

Getting below on some vessels demands gyrations just short of the acrobatic. Companionways must have rails mounted both above and below decks and ladders must have non-skid treads on the steps. Gloss varnish has no place on any place your foot may rest. Treads cab be Treadmaster or simply rubber stair treads, to be bought in any hardware store, trimmed to size. Ladders must be equipped with sides and interior railings should be graspable by the smallest (read children) crewmember.

Once below, a rail should be installed on the overhead either on or

In heavy weather, any crewmember coming on deck should secure his safety harness before leaving the companionway. Rails, as shown, on either side of the companionway, will greatly aid this procedure, and allow crew time to secure themselves before clipping on to the jackstays.

just off the centerline. Handrails along the cabin sides are not very useful in heavy weather, though they can be a help in getting out of a bunk or settee. Vertical pillars running from counter tops to the overhead are equally useful. Make sure, though, that they can be gripped fully around. A six-inch diameter post will not make for a firm "hands-around" handhold.

All counter corners should be rounded and conceivably even padded. It is very easy to be thrown across a saloon and crash into something hard and painful. The saloon table is another area of concern. If any part of it folds, provision must be made to fasten the leaves or flaps, preferably with non-rattling hooks or positive catches. All table edges should be chamfered, also to avoid injury.

In the same vein, all hardware should be protected from random meetings with the human body. Handles, bolt heads, fasteners and catches must be covered or out of the way. Incidentally, if any cupboards or locker doors are held closed with friction catches, remove them and replace with positive closures. Friction and magnetic catches have no place aboard a boat. If any heavy items are stowed in a locker, one good roll of the boat can cause them to break open the door and the ensuing chaos of flying debris can be dangerous and messy, too.

The tendency of boat builders to cover the cabin sole with slickly varnished ply or teak boards is most unfortunate. Floorboards can be painted with anti-skid grit added or they may be bare wood. Anything else is asking for trouble. Carpet will slide about, get wet and holds dirt. Linoleum—often seen on older boats and workboats—is too slippery when wet.

The galley is prime territory for accidents, some of grave potential danger. Stoves must be fitted with guard rails strong enough to take the weight of a person falling against them. Galley belts ought to be fitted also. Even in a relatively stable power boat the chance of an unexpected roll or pitch cannot be ignored. Stoves should be fitted with a positive fuel shut-off *in front of the stove.* The last thing you want to do is reach through roaring flames to shut the thing off!

Should a fire occur, the following are good guidelines for coping:

Both stove and tank valves must be closed. If stove valve cannot be reached because of flames, shut off tank valve and attempt to rip out hose. Some modern installations have remote control valves, either mechanical or electrical. These can be wired to simultaneously cut the fuel supply at both of the valve locations.

Alcohol, though rarely used except in the USA, has a low flash point and can be extinguished with water. However, the splashing water can also carry flaming alcohol with it, possibly igniting curtains, upholstery or even the container of spirits used for preheating the burners. Fiberglass or other flame-retardant treated blankets can often successfully be used to smother flames. They must be close at hand.

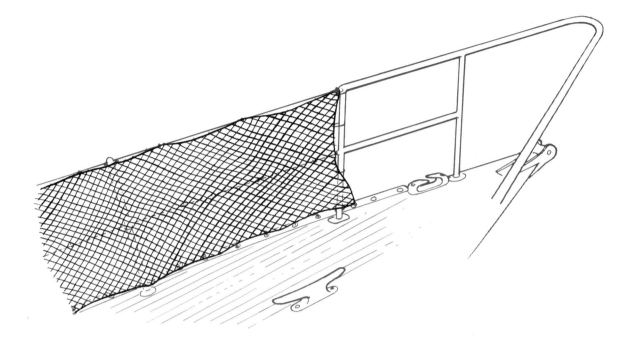

Nylon netting lashed between the lifelines and toe rail will not only prevent sails and small objects from going overboard, it will keep small children—who should always be in a safety harness and attached to a strong point—from frightful danger.

Wood and coal fires can, of course, be put out with water. However, it may be handier to keep a container of sand nearby. It will be safer—no steam—and usually easier to clean up afterward. This applies to both heating and cooking stoves.

Propane and other gas fires are the most dangerous. Flames can travel these fuel lines much faster than with other fuels. A fail-safe device must be fitted to the stove, and every precaution must be made to keep all equipment in prime operating condition. Explosion is the greatest risk. If a flare-up occurs, immediately shut off the gas and apply a fire extinguisher. Use the utmost caution when lighting a gas stove. Constantly check the system for gas leaks. With the exception of compressed natural gas (CNG) this entire class of fuels is heavier than air, and can be ignited by the simple act of striking a wrench against the engine block.

Keep the stove clean! A grease fire can cause just as much damage as any other. Either smother it with a fire blanket or use a fire extinguisher. In addition, always keep a fire extinguisher to hand near the outside perimeter of the galley, and make sure it's inspected yearly for a full charge.

All galley surfaces above, beside and behind the stove must be insulated with nonflammable materials clad in stainless steel (for ease of cleaning). This is especially the case with overheads; flaring flames can easily set curtains and deckheads alight.

While we're on the subject of galleys, we might as well tackle the water supply aboard. Since this is vital to the well-being of all on board, its purity and the avoidance of contamination is of the utmost importance. Most boats today will have either stainless steel or GRP water tanks connected to the various pumps with sanitary, flexible tubing. All tanks must be cleaned yearly. Ideally, they ought to be fitted with watertight inspection hatches that allow for manual cleaning. Lacking these, the addition of ordinary household bleach, one cup to 100 gallons of water, will sanitize tank interiors. Of course, the tanks must be thoroughly flushed afterwards and refilled.

While the bleach solution in in the tanks, operate all pumps aboard, allowing the solution to pass through hoses and pump mechanisms. Since most water hoses are transparent plastic they can easily become breeding grounds for bacteria without the sterilizing effect of sunlight. Since that's unlikely, the bleach serves the same purpose.

Heads, likewise, can be centers of bacterial growth and should be treated with bleach or chemical wash at least once a month, following the manufacturer's instructions. Also, for safety's sake, make sure the seacocks in the head are properly installed and fully operable. I know of at least two boats which sank, on their mooring, from a neglected head seacock.

CHILDREN

If you are cruising with children, a whole new dimension emerges in safety considerations. Try to remember when you were short and without great strength. It isn't easy. Likewise, it isn't easy for a child to move about a ship with the same sureness as an adult, especially if the child has no previous experience aboard. It's best to acclimatize children with the ship at rest. Spend a day or two, picnicking at the dock or mooring. Learning to move safely is an acquired art for children who are used to unbridled enthusiasm, frequent fearlessness and general lack of forethought.

Safety and emergency equipment is good if it works. Though this may seem self-evident, it's surprising, not to say frightening, how much gear kept aboard for emergencies doesn't function properly or at all when it is truly needed. And since we have become so dependent on the *idea* of its necessity, and we have gone to the expense—considerable in most cases—of actually purchasing and installing it, we really must take the trouble to make sure it is in working order.

LIFE RAFTS

In dire emergencies, when one is forced to abandon ship, the life raft is probably the single most vital piece of equipment. Unfortunately, it is also the one piece of equipment aboard that no one has ever tried out. Now, admittedly, it is an expensive process to test a life raft as the CO_2 cannister must be recharged, the raft refolded and the whole repacked. Considering the purpose of the equipment, though, it really ought to be checked out by a certified raft servicing facility once a year, at the beginning of the season. Too often, this is done in the autumn and the whole kit is left in some damp place over the winter and God knows what can happen! In fact, the most usual failure point in a raft is the inflation valve(s). Since any metal valve can corrode or oxidize enough to limit free movement, this must be carefully checked and coated with the recommended lubricant. Do not use just anything at hand! Viscosity for valve lubricants of this sort must be low enough to allow for no possible thickening in cold or wet.

Where a life raft is stowed has a major impact on its proper functioning. The ideal is a ventilated, waterproof locker. Since this is a virtual impossibility aboard most vessels, the best solution is in a cockpit locker which may be opened instantly, no matter what situation the yacht is in. Mounting the raft on the forward end of the coach roof or the foredeck is to court malfunction. And no matter what, a moulded cannister is the only reliable containment for a raft. Soft valises can allow breakage, corrosion and actual material tears and rips.

Remember also that many of the contents of a survival pack are liable to deterioration over the course of a season. Emergency food and water supplies are particularly susceptible. Anything even slightly suspect should be discarded, as to survive only to come down with food poisoning is not exactly a fair trade-off. Likewise, knives and fish hooks that have corroded, lines that have frayed or plastic evaporation stills that have cracked or ruptured will do no one good. Rarely can these items be repaired. They should, at the time of repacking the raft, all be coated with rust preventative or a light oil—providing the coating will not have a detrimental effect on the raft materials!

All fastenings that hold the raft to the deck or raft cradle need yearly inspection also. Often a raft is held in place with lashings. These must be inspected for chafe and for proper knotting. Any knot must be of a sort that is releasable instantly. Patent latches should be checked for corrosion and kept lubricated and free-moving.

HARNESSES

Personal safety harnesses should be considered a must for small children, night sailing and any passage offshore in heavy weather. Basic requirements include strength-tested specifications, positive and tested hooks and a secure means of adjustment. Yearly inspections should include checking the carbine hooks for hairline cracks, the

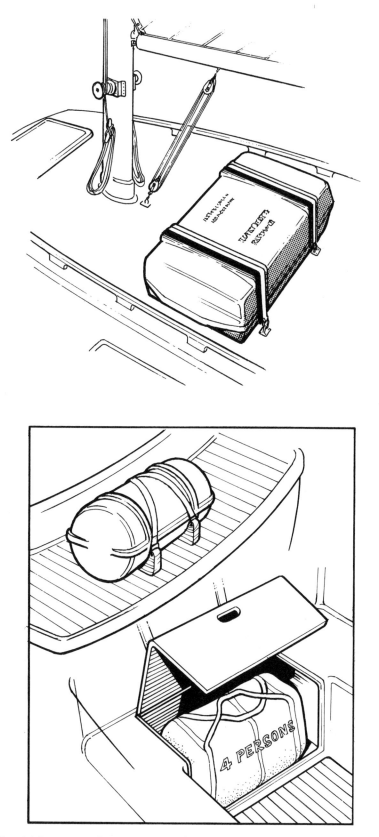

Life rafts should be stowed in waterproof containers, lashed to the cabin op or in the cockpit away from any obstructions. Lashings should be patent, quick-release types or else rope which can quickly be cut free. Do not ever stow a liferaft in a locker or where access to it may be impeded by rigging, deck gear or lines.

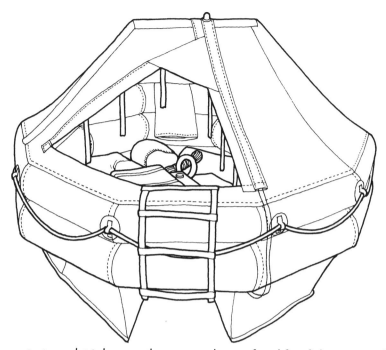

Despite many tests and trials over the years, the perfect liferaft has yet to be manufactured. The best is one produced to SOLAS specifications. These are generally commercial and very expensive. All should offer protection, multiple buoyancy chambers, an insulated floor, access from the water and a supply pack. This last must be supplemented with charts, extra water and food, compass, in fact anything you can think of to make survival easier and more prolonged.

stitching in the body webbing and that which hold the rings in place, and making sure no chafe or fraying has damaged the tether. Stitching can be easily renewed, but make sure to use Dacron/Terylene thread, doubled.

Any damage to the hardware indicates the immediate need for replacement. A distorted hook or D-ring can only lead to fracture or failure under stress. Since most of these hooks are made of stainless steel, and this alloy is subject to fatigue, every effort must be made at constant inspection. If in doubt, the fitting can be saturated with special dyes made to locate hairline cracks.

Tethers take the most abuse—whether nylon rope or webbing—and splices in rope are apt to chafe against deck gear, shrouds and lifelines. The same precautions apply to all lines.

Harnesses that are integral with foul-weather jackets are more protected, needless to say, but also hidden. If the harness cannot be removed from the garment for inspection, don't buy the jacket! Otherwise, check out all the parts as above.

MAN OVERBOARD LIGHTS

If crew goes overboard at night, no light—either personal or attached to a dan buoy—will be of any assistance to recovery if it doesn't work.

In a pinch, a very secure safety harness can be made from a 15-20ft. length of 1/2-inch diameter nylon line.

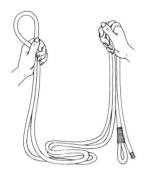

Fig. 1. Double the line, placing the ends together.

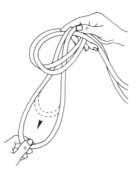

Fig. 2. Think of the loop end as the working end. Tie an over-hand knot to create a down-ward-hanging loop ca. three feet long.

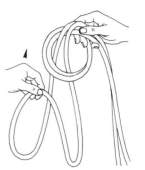

Fig. 3. Bring the three-foot loop up and over the standing part.

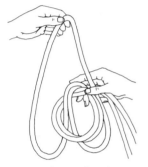

Fig. 4. Place the loop to be held securely as shown.

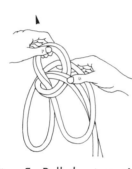

Fig. 5. Pull the two sides of the loop, where they pass through the overhand knot, upwards to form a bight.

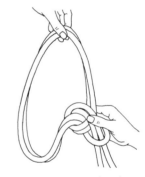

Fig. 6. Even up the loops and tighten the bight.

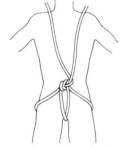

Fig. 7. Step into the loops, one for each leg.

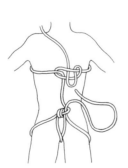

Fig. 8. Circle the chest with a half-hitch, and secure it with an overhand safety knot, forming a loop.

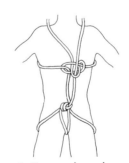

Fig. 9. Reeve the other end of the line through the loop and tighten to secure.

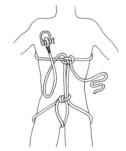

Fig. 10. Secure a shackle to the first line end.

When singlehanding or alone in the cockpit, what do you do if you fall overboard? Streaming a polypropylene line with a buoy attached to the end can at least give you a chance to grab on to something, and haul yourself back. The line should be 50-100ft. long and end in a brightly-colored float. Poly line is used as it is yellow and easily spot in the water and it floats.

Of course, all members of the crew should have flashlights/torches when on night watch. In addition, it's a good idea to equip each crew member with a personal safety light to clip on to his or her foul-weather gear. This is in addition to the self-activating light which must be permanently and securely attached to the life ring or horseshoe.

Any and all of the above must function without fail when needed. This is not as simple as it sounds, as very few so-called waterproof lights are truly shielded against the ingress of moisture. Taping battery compartments closed is not a good idea and often ineffective. Better, purchase a good light to start with, make sure the seals are tight and replaceable and that any openings can be clamped or screwed closed. Snap-apart fixtures have no place on a boat. Batteries should be replaced at the beginning of each season and discarded at the end of the season whether or not you have actually used the lights. Batteries left in place over the winter can swell, deteriorate, explode or leak. Likewise, bulbs should be changed at the start of the new season. If one should suddenly burn out when needed, a life can be lost.

DECKS

In any sort of seaway, in fact in any weather, the antiskid properties of a deck are your most immediate aid in preventing injury or going

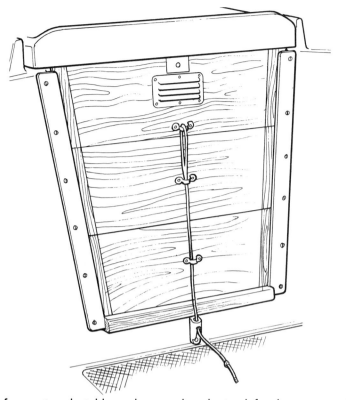

Some means of securing hatchboards must be devised for heavy weather. If a boat takes a wave below, or is knocked down, she stands a chance of foundering. Large volumes can enter through the companionway, and hatch boards can fall out. This method, made from a length of line, a few padeyes and a cleat, is cheap and effective.

overboard. Sadly, very few stock boats have proper antislip decking. Most are moulded-in patterns of varying effectiveness. All have some sort of gelcoat in places. And gelcoat is the enemy of sure footing. It looks good, and will continue to do so for a few years, but once the gelcoat has worn you will have grubby-looking decks and still not much protection from spills. Better you should attack the problem at its source, and go about making your decks truly safe.

Probably the best antiskid decking is teak. However, in today's light-displacement boats, the weight of teak is a real safety hazard, not to mention the expense and care needed. A more practicable solution is to install Treadmaster or similar material. This is sold by the sheet, weighs little and is impervious to most anything. Compounded of cork and rubber, Treadmaster is put down with a special two-part epoxy adhesive and, providing the deck is properly prepared, will last for years.

If that is not cheap enough—and for a large deck area it most certainly is not cheap—the best method of saving your neck and other parts of the anatomy is to paint the decks and sprinkle sand, microballoons or ground walnut shells over the still-tacky paint, letting it dry, then vacuuming up the excess. This will need replacement every few years, but the cost is minimal and the labor can be done in one week-

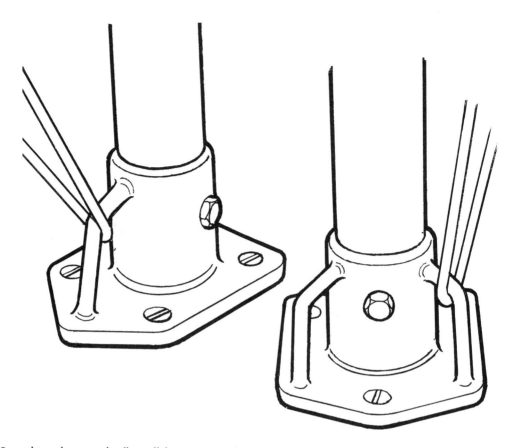

Stanchion bases ideally will be equipped with welded bails. These allow for attachment points for lines, blocks and safety harnesses.

end. Although it's fashionable to demarcate different areas of the deck with bands of gelcoated GRP, better to cover the entire deck with non-skid; then there should be no question of slipping on a hatch surround on a dark and wet night.

Besides the deck, cockpit seats should be sheathed in teak—especially if you value your posterior. Coamings, which get trod upon constantly, should likewise be sheathed or have self-adhesive nonskid strips affixed to them. Cockpit floors are much helped by teak gratings and, though expensive, they will repay the cost in resale value and comfort, especially keeping your feet out of collected water.

LIFELINES AND GUARDRAILS

Provided you have a secure deck under you, there is still a need for some means of restraining yourself from going over the edge. Lifelines and guardrails—in theory—serve that purpose. Nothing, however, will do any good if the uppermost line is too low. And in many production boats this is all too true. Twenty-four inches will catch most people just above the knees, acting as a perfect fulcrum to tip them over the deck edge. The bare minimum should be 30 inches and, on larger yachts, even higher.

To make any rail effective, it must be anchored so firmly to the deck that a large person thrown against it will not make it give way. In practical terms this means that all stanchions must be of thick wall or solid tubing and through-bolted even on a wood deck. No screw, no matter how long, will hold under the wrenching stress of 200 pounds going at high velocity. In turn, the bolts used should be sized to the mounting holes in the stanchion bases and long enough to extend through the deck and backing plates and still allow length enough for a washer, nut and locknut beneath that. Since stanchions get jerked around a lot, they will need rebedding every few years. Don't try to squeeze silicone in cracks. The entire base must be removed, cleaned with solvent (as well as the deck area it rests upon), and reattached with a generous spread of sealant under the entire base area. This is a two-person job, unless your stanchion bases are drilled for stove bolts, in which case everything can be put in place and the job can then be finished off below.

Check stanchion bases for corrosion. Quite often a stainless steel base will be used with an aluminum stanchion. Invariably, the two will fuse after a couple of seasons. This may not affect strength, but it will make it impossible to replace one or the other. Once a year, remove the stanchion from the base, clean it and coat the end of the stanchion with silicone spray or light grease. Make sure drain holes are kept clear and replace as necessary

Wire lifelines, especially those covered in plastic, are subject to chafe and corrosion. Especially inspect the end fittings, usually swaged. If there are cracks visible, replace with Sta-Lock or Norseman terminals. Make sure the stanchion holes through which the lines pass are burnished and that lower lifeline guides are fitted with bushings. While you're at it, check over all line anchoring points on stern rails and pulpits. Usually welded, these welds are subject to twisting strains and if any sign of a break or fatigue appears, have the yard reweld the eye or loop in the rail.

ROPES

Though it may seem odd to include ropes and lines in a discussion of safety, they are vital to the well-being of the ship. For docking, anchoring, sail control, kedging and warping, if a rope breaks both you and your yacht can be put into a position of grave danger.

All lines should be checked every season. Since virtually all rope used today is synthetic, mildew and rot are no longer problems, but ultraviolet deterioration is, especially in nylon. Any rope which passes over a sheave ought to be reversed end-for-end once a year. Anchor lines, especially, must be inspected carefully where they pass over rollers or through chocks and also at the thimble end shackled to chain. If any chafing appears around the thimble, cut it out and splice a new one in. Any other chafe must also be cut out. If any fraying shows up in the middle of the rode, cut it up for docklines and get a new one.

Too often docklines are tattered and in very lowly condition. They are oddments demoted from other tasks. Demote, for sure, but please use sound rope. Docklines are in constant motion and need to be especially strong and free from defects to cope with the stresses put upon them from wakes, tidal surge and sharp edges. Though it's usual to have large eye splices in docklines, an unspliced length is both stronger and more useful. A loop can always be tied in with a bowline. Best use rope of a larger diameter than usual for any lines used to hold the boat for longer than usual–wintering, for example–or in anticipation of a storm. By larger than usual I mean up one or two sizes, i.e., 3/8 inch to 1/2 inch (8mm to 10mm) increase.

FIRE EXTINGUISHERS

Not often thought of as safety equipment, the various appliances in engine compartments designed to extinguish fires or prevent them are as important as anything in keeping vessel and life together. Since most engine compartments–except in outboard-powered boats and workboats–are enclosed to a greater or lesser extent, their ability to contain a fire is directly related to the ability to cut off oxygen from the engine intakes, as well as the speed at which any extinguishing system works and the amount of fireproof materials surrounding the engine room. A steel boat is best able to contain a fire; a GRP boat least able, due to the extreme flammability of GRP as a substance.

The first thing to check out is the fire extinguishing system installed in the engine compartment. Is it functioning? Do the valves work freely? Was the powder or foam recently recharged. All charging should be clearly dated and renewed according to manufacturer's recommendations. Placement of the outlets for the system are very important. Make sure that they do not spray indiscriminately over the block, but are directed to the air inlet, so as to cut out combustion as soon as possible.

The two most common types of permanently installed fire extinguishing equipment are foam or dry pressurized cannisters and Halon gas systems. Both will work under ideal conditions, but certain precautions should be taken. Halon, especially in the earlier installations, would often be exhausted through the engine before it could work. Current systems have a solenoid-valve activating device to close the exhaust on the engine just prior to activation. Halon works by robbing the oxygen needed for combustion from the engine proper and is highly effective. Dry powder and foam systems may be better for electrical fires.

Ideally, both systems should be installed as well as a number of hand-held extinguishers of an approved type at key locations around the boat. There must be a minimum of one in every separate compartment of the vessel, including for good measure the cockpit lockers (especially handy if the companionway is blocked by flames and smoke). All hand-held units should be recharged at least every three years or according to manufacturer's specifications.

Not only a fire extinguisher but a fire blanket should be located near the galley stove. Alcohol and kerosene (paraffin) stoves do flare up now and then and the danger is that some part of the overhead will catch fire. Have no curtains in the galley, and be sure that the overhead is insulated with fireproofing material covered with a stainless or aluminum sheet, allowing at least 1/2 inch of air space between the overhead and the fireproofing. Ceramic spacers made for home wood-stove installation are particularly good for this purpose.

Make sure the forward hatch is always accessible. It's is the only safe means of escape in the event of a galley or engine fire blocking the companionway.

Helicopter pick-up is dangerous at best. Follow loud hailer directions from the 'copter exactly, and remember that wind and waves will put you at jeapardy at every moment.

Emergencies

The last thing you want to cope with when cruising is a major emergency and, if truth, very rarely does one occur. You must be prepared for the eventuality, nevertheless. The fate of your ship and crew will depend upon your knowledge and skill, and the only way to acquire it is practice. I'm not suggesting you go out searching for a gale, but you can work on various maneuvers in calm water, even at anchor. Try to at least get the basics down so that when a crisis does occur, you'll be able to have the outlines of procedures in your head. It helps.

ABANDONING SHIP

If, and only if, the mother ship is in imminent danger of sinking, inflate the life raft on deck or by tossing overboard to activate the CO_2 cylinders. Do not attempt to right the raft until necessary. Extra water, food, etc., should be packed at hand in a duffle. Tie it to the raft if possible. Ship's papers, passports, etc., should be in a waterproof pouch, the responsibility of the captain. If at all possible, get extra flares, radio emergency beacon and a compass aboard, as well as charts of the area. All this takes preplanning.

Hypothermia is one of the surest ways to quick death. Keep fully clothed, including hat and boots. Water within the oilskins will have something of a wetsuit effect, and the wet clothing, especially if wool or polypropylene, will have a high insulating effect. Move as little as possible, only as much as is necessary to stay afloat. Attempting to swim, no matter how strong a swimmer you are, will result in heat loss on a massive scale, unconsciousness and death.

Leave the raft tethered to the ship. Too many people have been lost attempting to leap from ship to raft. Only when every member of the crew is aboard should the tether be cut. Take what care you can not to cut the raft also.

A dinghy can be used if the life raft is not functioning or if there is none. It should be fitted out beforehand, especially with a strong and sufficient size sea anchor to hold it bow to wind. However, since no

Backing sails in shifting winds, be prepared to drop all sail quickly and watch out for the possibility of accidental jibes. Using the foresail alone will negate that possibility.

Setting a kedge. Row the anchor and rode out from the mother ship. Be sure the rope is coiled or flaked down loosely to allow for smooth pay-out.

Legs can be rigged from oars, balks of timber or a spinnaker pole in drying out situations. make sure they are lashed securely and guyed as well to prevent collapse. Make sure all lashings can be released from on deck.

When aground, weights suspended from a swung-out boom can help in reducing draft just enough to allow floating off. Make sure someone is stationed at the mainsheet to haul you back aboard; with a double-ended sheet, of course, you can do so yourself.

dinghy (or virtually none) is designed for life-raft use, certain precautions are necessary. First, a rigid boat will need to be heavily fendered to avoid damage from the mother ship. Second, boarding will be extremely difficult and dangerous in anything approaching heavy seas. Third, an enclosed form of protection—canopies, dodger, etc.—will be necessary to avoid boarding seas and exposure. Fourth, permanent flotation is an absolute need. To board a dinghy, be sure to coordinate your stepping aboard with the rhythm of the two boats; otherwise you may step into thin air and descend rapidly to break limbs upon your sudden entry. Do not untether from the yacht until all members of the crew have boarded.

If no life raft or dinghy exists, put on your life jacket, and enter the water from the windward side of the boat. From any other point the boat can drift down, or back down or slip to windward, endangering anyone in the water. Keep all clothes on, and assume a fetal position to conserve body heat. A light, whistle and knife should be attached to the life vest. Try to stay calm.

Pickup by ship or helicopter is a dangerous, touchy and frightening maneuver. Inevitably the ship will be larger than your vessel, and the chances of collision and dismasting are great, even in calm seas. You will be distraught and tired. Try to be hoisted aboard, rather than climb a ladder. Leave the yacht from bow or stern and time the move up to coincide with the crest of a wave. In heavy weather you will probably be safer in the lee of the larger ship, but you must move fast. Do *not* worry about your yacht! It can be replaced. Helicopter rescues demand even more thought on your part. Clear the cockpit and release any rigging located there, even if the mast goes over forward. Do *not*, repeat *do not*, fasten the helicopter line to any part of your vessel! Grab the harness lowered and, as quickly as possible, help each crew member into it. At each pass of the copter be prepared to snag that line. In heavy seas it will be difficult, in strong winds even more so. Signal green if prepared to leave, red if not. Another possibility and perhaps safer is to be picked up from the dinghy or life raft towed astern. However, this makes you a smaller target, and gives a less stable platform for the pickup.

AGROUND

Backing sails can lead to accidental jibe. Be prepared. You may be better off dropping the jib and backing main. This will keep the foredeck clear for anchor handling. Onshore winds can vary in strength, of course. In a gale the engine will probably not be sufficiently powerful to pull you off the ground. You will have to set a kedge. Do it carefully in heavy conditions. If you plan to kedge and power at the same time, be wary of fouling the propeller with the kedge warp. Either keep it taut or use floating line.

If the tide is falling rapidly, best prepare to dry out as comfortably as possible. With fast ebb and heavy seas you may have to prepare to abandon ship, especially if the boat is on rocks. If the tide is rising and you are on a lee shore, get the kedge out as fast as possible or you may be swept further ashore.

Much depends on the profile and configuration of the boat's keel. If a long, sloping keel, you will have less trouble backing off. If a fin keel, you may be able to spin the boat about and reach or run off into deeper water. Twin-keel boats should not be heeled, as you will only increase the draft. In calm conditions, prepare to sit out the tide. In heavy going, you will have to kedge or power off.

Heeling a single-keeled boat can be accomplished in several ways: move the crew to the shallow water deck; swing crew or loaded dinghy off the boom end. In a very small boat, you may be able to use the main halyard taken ashore for leverage. (Beware: masthead fittings cannot take much abuse. Do not try this maneuver in a heavy-displacement vessel.) You may be able to reduce draft by lightening ship. Remove heavy gear to the dinghy, possibly drain water tanks. In a light displacement boat, this could decrease draft by the inch or two needed to free the keel.

Hauling off can be done with a bow anchor while the crew heels the boat. May also be accomplished by an aiding vessel. If another ship can help, first make sure that questions of salvage are resolved. Then, depending on your position, pass *your* line to the assisting vessel. First make the line secure to foredeck bollard or stern cleats with a bridle, or secure it around the mast or cabin house. Instruct the other vessel to slowly pull you seaward without any surge of acceleration. This is most important. A quick application of throttle could result in torn decks or dismasting. When you are free and able to maneuver, request your line freed. For such tows, polypropylene cordage, because it floats, is best employed, lessening the chances of fouled propellers and rudders.

CHAFE

A sheetbend is the quickest way to take care of a serious chafe, though it must be remembered that knots will never be as strong as the original or as a splice. Using two bowlines will have the advantage of easy undoing of the knots no matter how heavy the strain on the lines.

The easiest thing to do is to end-for-end the line, although, depending on the application, this can cause further chafe and weakening of the line. However, with modern fiber rope this is rarely a problem, and top-quality polyester rope will last as long as twenty years with proper care. Better, get rid of the original cause of the chafing: unfair leads, rough edges (especially on metal fittings, the application of a fine-toothed file will achieve wonders), and so on.

Padding—whether plastic tubing or hose, rags, leather, a sacrificial rope whipping or baggywrinkle—is as old a practice as the sailor has.

Where sail chafe is involved, the best recourse is to have the sail recut or reinforced. Baggywrinkle is ugly, soils the sails, and creates a surprising amount of windage. It is better is to use shroud rollers or spreader tips. No matter what method is chosen, the padding must be secured, either with tape or whipping.

The most secure method of repairing a chafed line, short of replacing the line altogether, is to cut and splice it. A short splice will be stronger, but will not be able to pass through a block sheave; a long splice will be close to the original diameter of the line and will pass, providing the sheave is large enough in the first place.

COLLISION

If bearings remain constant, chances are you are on a collision course. Taking bearings at night can be especially difficult. Try to keep one set of the approaching ship's range lights in line.

Chances are that a large ship will not spot you until after you have spotted her. You will probably have to take evasive action, but you should attempt to signal first: five or more short blasts of a horn will be taken as a warning. At night, either five short flashes of a strong light, or the Morse code "U" (2 short and 1 long flashes). Also, a torch shown against the sails or a white flare will indicate your presence.

Warning signals:
  One blast: I am altering course to starboard.
  Two blasts: I am altering course to port.
  Three blasts: I am going astern.
  Five blasts: Watch out! *or* I do not comprehend your intentions or actions.

Evasive action does not mean sailing until you see the whites of their eyes! Make all maneuvers with decision and positively. Course changes should be large and the new course should be held. Do *not* constantly change course; you will only confuse the oncoming ship. Always try to pass astern of the approaching vessel.

Despite all the rules of the road, you should not hold to etiquette. Forget everything you ever learned about sail over power, etc. You should be the one to avoid the other vessel. Especially with large ships at sea, not always, but often, the watch will be short-handed or they will not be manning the radar, in particular with flag-of-convenience registry. Right of way is only of import if the other vessel responds in kind; otherwise, assume she is going to make mincemeat of you and act accordingly. If there is a chance of a head-on collision, both vessels *should* alter their courses to starboard. If the other does not, take immediate evasive action, under the fastest means possible, full throttle ahead.

If a collision is unavoidable, try to present the smallest area of your ship as is possible to the oncoming vessel. This will, hopefully, lessen the impact and the resultant damage. If you are struck, the other vessel—a large tanker, say—may not even know she has hit you. Get off distress flares as fast as possible. Sound horns, bells, sirens—anything to attract attention. Have the crew stand by to abandon ship.

DISMASTING

A mast that has gone overboard presents a serious threat to the continuing integrity of the hull, especially in heavy weather. In calm seas, you and the crew may be able to hoist the mast back on board. If the mast is sizeable and therefore heavy, a better procedure will be to lash it to the hull. Hoisting will necessitate securing the spar on at least three points along its length, and rigging tackles fore, aft and amidships, using winches in the cockpit, perhaps the vang to the maststep and the anchor windlass with appropriate jury-rigged fairleads. Station crew at each location and be sure that the hull is appropriately fendered; in this instance, every fender aboard should be secured to the rail on the hoisting side. Chances are that the lifelines and stanchions went by the board when the mast went over, so safety harnesses are *de rigueur*. Since most masts will add considerable weight to the side to which they have been lashed, it may be necessary, especially in a light-displacement boat, to rearrange the stores and weights below deck. In addition, metal masts, unless foam-filled, will sink fairly quickly. It is imperative to move with dispatch.

If you decide to lash the mast to the side of the yacht, a large part of the rigging will have to be cut away. This can be done either by undoing the rigging screws (which will most likely be bent out of shape by the shock) or by cutting the rigging wires, either with cable cutters or with a cold chisel and hammer against a steel block. Be warned: rod rigging will not be so easy to part. That rigging which can be left—lower shrouds on the side of the vessel on which the mast went over—should be kept as added security. Remember, however, that it may be necessary, in increasingly heavy weather, to cut the mast adrift. Those remaining attachment points will hamper any efforts to do so.

An additional thought: the mast can be left trailing from bow or stern to act as a sea anchor. In truly atrocious seas, this may well be the best way to retain some steerage and control. This must be accompanied by constant watch, for the errant spar could well be flung onto the ship by breaking seas. In such a case, the mast should be secured with rope cordage, rather than by rigging wire, since cutting it loose if necessary will be much simplified if an axe can take precedence over a pair of cutters.

Should the mast fall aft, chances are the crew in the cockpit will be injured, wheel or tiller will be broken, the cabin house may fracture. Get any injured crew below and commence appropriate first aid. The mast should probably be cut away as soon as possible.

Preventing chafe always makes cruising easier. Nothing is more annoying than constantly renewing lines and rigging. Fig. 1, two bowlines can quickly join two lines. Fig. 2, spreader ends should be smoothed and taped. Fig. 3, a long splice is necessary when the line must pass through a sheave. Fig.4, taping or using patent chafe protectors for turnbuckles and spreader tips. Fig. 5, sheaves must be sized to the wire or rope passing around them to prevent seizing or chafe. Fig. 6, whip all rope ends to prevent unraveling.

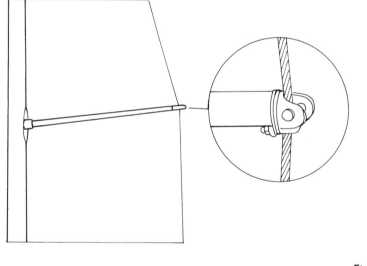

Fig. 1

Fig. 2

Fig. 3

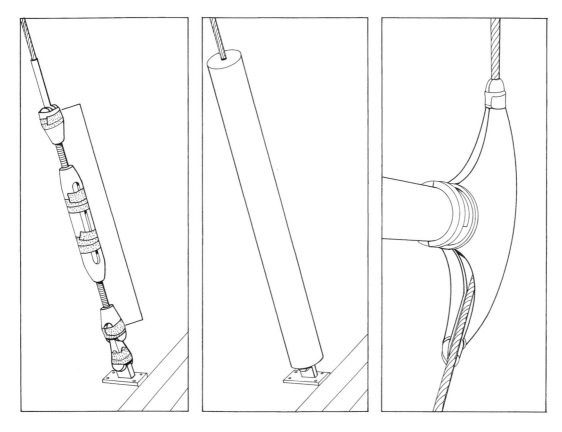

Fig. 4

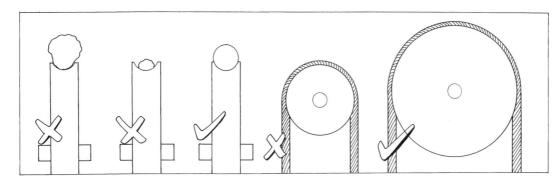

Fig. 5

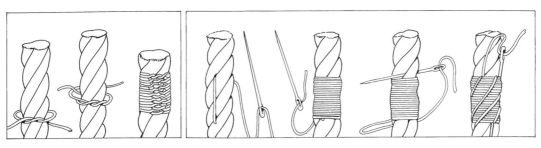

Fig. 6

Emergencies   *169*

Breaks at the spreaders are more common than one would wish to imagine. Due to the number of fittings, terminals, etc., at that point, the mast can be weakened. If the mast should fracture and the upper portion come tumbling down, lash it to deck and proceed to JURY RIGS: MASTS. If the mast is left dangling, lash the upper part to the portion left standing; trying to cut down the top and maneuver it to the deck can be a tricky and dangerous job.

Move fast to avoid damage to the ship, but not so fast as to endanger the crew. Think out your actions first and instruct the crew carefully and clearly on what must be done.

DIVING

Attempting to dive when the boat is in motion is foolhardy in the extreme. Any additional movement will make any underwater task extraordinarily difficult for the diver. The most usual reason for having to dive is either to unfoul the anchor or to clear the propeller. In either case *be sure the ignition is off.* Since few people can remain underwater without artificial breathing apparatus for more than 45 seconds to one minute, especially when exerting themselves, a safety line is a must.

The person on deck should have prearranged signals with the diver: one jerk on the line, pull up; two jerks, help; etc. A line without a tender is useless. The person on deck will often sight danger before the diver: shark approaching, squall coming, etc. Always have a boarding ladder secured before the diver goes in. He will know where it is and there will be no fumbling when it is needed. Make it as long as possible and weight the bottom rung.

ELECTRICAL FAILURE

It is a sorry fact of life afloat that sooner or later salt air and moisture will have a detrimental effect on your boat's electrical system. You can guard against run-of-the-mill failure by checking all connections, wiring, fuses, junction boxes, circuit breakers, battery installations, etc., at the commencement of every season and at least twice during the course of the season. Battery terminals must be cleaned and, after reconnecting, coated with a thin layer of waterproof grease. Check all wire clips to see that no breaks have occurred in the insulation. Any wires running low in the ship, especially in the bilges, should be rerouted away from any possible water contamination. Overhaul the alternator and generator. Replace all fuses and lamp bulbs once a year as a matter of course. See that all connections and connecting clips are free from corrosion and coated after cleaning and reassembly. Top up batteries and secure. Make sure they are properly vented. Check engine wiring harnesses and make sure all wires are securely clipped and away from any excessive heat sources.

Assuming you have done all the above and the power fails, what do you do? First check the battery. It may be dry. A connection may be vibrated or torn loose. The alternator may not be functioning. A fuse may be blown, or a cable may have shorted out. Having checked this, and found the situation beyond repair, the following are all reasonable alternatives: Use a kerosene/paraffin lantern hung in the rigging instead of navigation lights. At worst you will be thought a fisherman! Or use an electric/battery anchor light. If the engine has no handcrank starting capability, and a second battery is available, jump or reconnect the cables. Sail.

ENGINE FAILURE; Diesel

If the engine stops on its own accord, switch off the ignition. Check the fuel system. Filters must be free of dirt and water. They should be filled with oil. The possibility exists that the tanks are empty. The filters may be only partly filled if this is the case. However, partial filter filling may also be due to a fuel line blockage. If the engine won't restart, you will have to bleed both filters and possibly injectors. Consult your owner's manual.

Overheating is the most common problem with diesels and is most often the result of a torn or failed water-cooling pump impeller. First, though, check the water inlet for debris and blockage to the water pump and make sure the propeller is not fouled. This is the place to warn you: *always carry a spare impeller*. Changing it is a ten-minute job at most, but for want of a spare, you may be disabled until you can signal for a tow (in a powerboat) or the breeze picks up.

Additionally, overheating may be due to a blockage in the raw water inlet or within the cooling system itself. Check the inlet, make sure exhaust water is being discharged through the exhaust pipe. Check all water piping going to and coming from the engine for leaks. You may be able to repair minor leaks with heat welding tape or even duct tape. Major leaks or cracks will demand replacement of the piping. It's a good idea to carry lengths of heat resistant, reinforced neoprene hose in the proper diameters for just such cases. Also make adjustable stainless steel hose clips.

Oil pressure dropping can indicate a major problem. Check the oil level and top up. If water has mixed with the oil, the head gasket may have ruptured. Do not run the engine above very low rpms (no higher than 1500 rpm in most modern marine diesels). If there should be a crack in the crankcase, shut down the engine at once. Without proper lubrication the engine stands a good chance of seizing or grinding itself to bits.

If the engine will not start, yet the starter motor is turning over, the glow plug may need replacement. Uneven running may be due to a clogged or broken injector. If possible, replace; if not, run engine very slowly.

A full spare kit as well as the manufacturer's manual should be aboard for anything more than a day sail. Read the manual before setting out on a cruise. Make sure you have the necessary tools on board. As mentioned above, should anything seem wrong–high temperature, rough running, frequent stoppages, oil pressure fluctuations–*stop the engine immediately*! Failure to do so may cause major damage. Remember that anything that moves needs maintenance. As much as you might hate the "iron jib," it is part of the yacht and needs the same care as the brightwork and winches.

ENGINE FAILURE: Gas

Check the electrical system. The battery may be dead, especially if the starter motor will not turn over. A connection between the battery ignition switch and starter motor circuit may be defective. Check the spark plugs and distributor head. Often, only the plugs will have to be cleaned or replaced; always carry spares.

If the engine stops with grinding and clanking noises, serious damage is probably at hand. If no noise occurs, an electrical fault is probable and should be traced as above. If the engine hesitates and stops, the fault is most likely with the fuel system. Check as per instruction manual. The fuel tank may be empty. If not, there is probably a blockage in the line, or the fuel pump may have malfunctioned. Blow out the fuel line. If still no result, dismantle or replace the pump. Additionally, the carburetor may need adjustment. If you have the tools and expertise, go ahead.

Overheating will be caused by a blocked water inlet, a broken pump, low oil level or a fouled propeller. In any case, if the temperature rises, turn off the engine immediately.

If there's a drop in oil pressure, stop the engine and check the oil level. Refill as necessary. Do not run the engine unless absolutely necessary. Uneven running is probably due to a fouled plug or bad timing. Replace the plug. If unevenness persists, have the mechanic check it out. An obvious cause is a loose HT lead. Make sure all leads are firmly seated on the plug ends.

FIRE: Engine

In the event of fire, it is vital to stop both fuel supply and ignition as soon as possible. This is especially true of gasoline/petrol engines, as explosion can occur both within the engine and back to the fuel tanks which, since they are usually located beneath or alongside the cockpit, can cause serious injury or death.

Please, please inspect and, if necessary, replace all engine room extinguisher valves at least twice each season. Since engine spaces are usually the most ignored places aboard–at least on sailing vessels–they are subject to all the ills of bad boat husbandry: oil accumulation, severe damp, grit and old rags. Valves can not only be corroded, they can be blocked by grease and debris. Likewise, all wiring for all sys-

When fighting engine fires, always stand well clear of the opening. Your first problem will be to actually get access to the engine. Be very careful in opening hatches and access panels, as flames can shoot out with considerable force and heat. Aim with care and discharge the extinguisher while bracing it against the floor or some cabin furniture.

tems should be kept clear of the bilges, not run near or over working or hot parts of the engine, secured carefully and have all terminal fittings lightly coated with waterproof grease. If any of these precautions are ignored, very likely the system will fail when you most need it.

Using hand-operated extinguishers is not difficult, but does demand calm and intelligence. Everyone on board should be thoroughly acquainted with their operation, and you should have fired one off in practice, with crew present. The important thing is to hold them steady, pointed directly at the source of the flame. If necessary, brace yourself against a bulkhead or counter.

Engines are, of course, rarely out in the open. They are covered by hatches, companion steps or casings. If you are in the cockpit when the fire commences, get below before you open the engine compartment. You will not be able to direct your firefighting from above and unless there is a readily removable engine hatch in the cockpit sole, don't try! Actually, cockpit engine hatches probably should not be opened, as the flames shooting out will be sure to burn someone.

If the fire gets out of control while you are below, *Do not attempt to escape through the companionway!* Use the forward hatch, and prepare to abandon ship. In the event of *any* fire, have the crew prepare the life raft or dinghy to stand by. Unless you are aboard a steel or aluminum boat, the chances of a runaway blaze not causing the boat to founder are minimal. Fiberglass, unless laminated with fire-retardant resins, will soon turn into an inferno. If you cannot contain the fire, don't fight in vain. *Get off the boat!*

FOG

Fog is usually accompanied by little or no wind. However, there are times and places where dense fog will coexist with strong breezes. In such situations, decrease throttle if under power or reduce sail more than you would normally. In dense fogs, visibility may be down to less than 100 meters, and anything other than dead slow ahead poses a real threat to the vessel and crew.

Human senses become less than reliable in foggy conditions: sounds are distorted, shapes appear and disappear, ships creep in and out of banks that suddenly close in. The only reliable navigational tool in such situations is the traditional ship's compass. Of course, you have made sure it is corrected and compensated before setting out. TRUST IT! No matter what your senses indicate, the compass is a safer bet. It is not subject to psychological pressures, it doesn't drink, and it won't fall overboard.

Fog signals: international rules:

One blast: I am turning to starboard.

Two blasts: I am turning to port.

Three blasts: I am going astern.

Five blasts: Beware! I am in doubt about your intentions.

Short, long, short blasts: Warning! Danger of collision.

These are to be sounded on a horn or whistle. The ringing of a bell signifies a vessel aground or at anchor. If attempting to home in on an audible signal, remember that fog can distort apparent sound direction. Proceed with utmost caution. Always post the best-sighted person in the bows. He will be able to give some warning of impending danger. Prearrange signals with the helmsman.

Radar is not often found aboard small yachts, but recent developments are putting it in the range of affordability; and scanner size and power requirements are decreasing. Radar takes practice, but if you have a set, you will no doubt have figured out how to use it. Depending on range, it can show you exactly what is ahead of you in most, if not all conditions.

HEAVY WEATHER

When the weather deteriorates to a point where ship handling under reduced sail becomes difficult, when the size of the sea endangers the integrity of the ship, or when progress in a safe direction becomes near impossible, you are in danger. These three criteria are not the only ones, but they can serve as a good guide to the next set of maneuvers. All are dependent on weather fronts, winds and depressions. The size and displacement of your vessel will have some bearing upon the meeting of the above conditions. Obviously a ketch of 15 meters LOA will be able to cope with large seas with greater assurance and safety than a power vessel of 10 meters LOA. Any sound vessel, however, can undertake precautionary maneuvers to allow more or less equitable coping with bad conditions.

When the wind pipes up, the first thing to do is to reduce sail. However, balance is equally important, especially when reaching or beating to windward. The larger vessel will be able to hold a course longer than a small boat, due to displacement, sail-carrying ability and a larger crew. A powerboat, without the ballast or lateral plane of a sailing yacht, will have different problems to cope with. The key is to keep green water from coming aboard. Running in a powerboat demands keeping speed at one with the wave length, plowing to windward invariably demands throttling back, whilst progress in beam seas is very much a function of the dynamic stability of the hull. When the weather is truly nasty, an appropriate reduction of speed is invariably the best seamanlike judgment.

Everything on deck and below must be secured in heavy weather. Sails, anchors, lines, life raft, crew must be attached to the boat in a manner that precludes loss overboard. Crew especially should be in life harnesses. Anchors should be given double lashings with heavy line: a loose object of such shape and weight can easily hole a hull given the opportunity. Below decks, batteries have to be tied down, locker doors strong and secure—no friction or magnetic catches—books fiddled or lashed in place, stove gimbals closed, etc. Even floor boards should be able to be fastened, perhaps with button catches. In a knockdown, you will have a mess below, but any heavy object or glass or sharp implement can cause major injuries or even death. Try to avoid the worst. At the beginning of the season, it's even a good idea to tighten the engine bed fastenings. There have been cases of engines tearing loose from their mountings and causing boats to founder. Be sure to secure all hatches, ventilators, hatchboards and seacocks.

Much of what has been said above applies to the crew. Safety harnesses are *de rigueur* at night and in anything over a Force 5. They ought to be to government standard and constructed with two lanyards with proofed hooks/snaps. The deck attachment points must be through-bolted. Lacking such, or in emergencies, crew can lash themselves to binnacle or tracks.

How you will actually handle the boat in heavy weather depends to a great extent on its size, the capacity of the crew and the size of the seas and the strength of the wind. Proximity to land plays a major role in deciding tactics. In a storm, with a lee shore in sight, the inability to beat to windward and inexperienced crew, anchoring—providing the

Sail reduction should be planned to keep the boat moving at optimum speed while retaining a balanced sail plan. Under power, throttle-back to keep green water off the decks as much as possible.

Lying ahull.

Heaving to.

proper ground tackle is aboard—may be the only alternative. But every situation demands informed judgment.

The key man as the weather deteriorates is the helmsman. He or she needs to be fresh, alert, sensitive. He must keep a watch to windward for approaching waves, and must be alert to the need for sudden maneuvers. Keep him as protected, warm and dry as possible. When changing the guard, allow the relief to acclimatize himself to the course, conditions and "feel" of the helm before switching. A less experienced hand may require that sail be reduced to giver greater control. This is a decision the skipper must make giving due regard to approaching fronts, need to reach port, etc.

Sailing to windward demands not only a good eye. The necessity of pacing the boat to the height of the waves is vital. The helmsman should luff slightly as the boat comes down the face of a wave, slowing the boat and allowing the bows to rise to the oncoming crest. Otherwise there is a good chance of burying the bows and causing loss and damage to the deck gear and crew. The boat should have minimum steerage when approaching the crest of the next wave, as the speed generated surfing down the back of the wave will usually be sufficient to ascend the next one. The maneuver is one of weaving, increasing and decreasing speed off-wind and upwind to keep the boat moving with a reasonable motion and as little threat to ship and crew as possible.

In really heavy weather, sailing in a beam sea can be courting disaster. Cresting waves can fill cockpits, cause knockdowns, or stove in a deckhouse. In less momentous seas, a tendency to broach or a difficulty in steering will probably be experienced. Either shorten sail or head off with the wind on the quarter.

Running can be an exhilarating experience. However, when the seas build to a point where steering becomes difficult, extreme care will be needed at the helm to avoid a broach. In gale or storm conditions, don't play racer and try to carry spinnakers. Rather, reduce sail to a point where the boat is moving at optimum speed, neither in danger of surfing so fast as to be falling off the wave tops nor so slow as to lose steerage way. In mid-ocean monster storms, the need will almost always be to slow the boat down.

To reduce speed in severe running conditions, several methods are available. With most modern sailing vessels, the sea anchor is to be avoided. The strain it puts on the ship are greater than the advantages, and there is usually not enough forefoot to the vessel for it to keep the bows to the wind. Trailing warps does work. However, they must be many and attached so as to distribute the strains around the ship. Occasionally, anchors can be trailed from warps or bundles of chain. However, be sure to rig tripping devices or you may never get the goods aboard again. Ideally, you will let them out as needed. This does assume, however, that several hundred meters of heavy line are aboard. Oil spread overboard either from the toilet or by means of a can or bag can be effective, but very few modern yachts ever have the capacity or availability of product effectively to deploy this method of calming the seas. Also, such tactics demand a very slow-moving or still vessel. It may be most effective when lying ahull or heaving to.

Lying ahull is when all sail is stowed, tiller is lashed, and the ship left to look after herself. This can be a perfectly sound tactic, providing the sea room exists for leeward drift and some forward motion due to the area presented by rigging, spars and hull and tophamper. Some experiences have suggested that a shallow-hulled craft will be safer at the maneuver than a deep-draft one, as the deep keel can cause a tripping effect in certain sized seas, possibly causing a knockdown or rollover. It is also a good tactic for the singlehander in a small boat.

Heaving to is perhaps the simplest method of slowing a boat down and giving the crew rest in heavy going. The only maneuver required is to tack, leaving the headsail as is. Ease the main and lash the tiller to leeward. Then, depending upon adjustments of mainsheet and tiller, the boat will forereach slowly–dependent to some degree upon tophamper, sail area, keel depth, etc. The headsail should be brought in tightly before heaving to, and in heavier conditions, the main might well be dropped and secured. Of course, leeway will be made, and heaving to should not be attempted on a lee shore unless for a short time and with little sail and a deep-draft hull. Even then, adjustments must be made to allow for as little leeway as possible, perhaps by trimming the main to allow stronger forereaching. Chafe is always a problem when hove to; the practice is better with a working jib or storm jib than with a genoa or lapper. In very heavy going, some chafe protection around the sheet–rags, tubing– where it crosses the shrouds will not be amiss.

In "survival conditions," Force 10 and upward, the only possible point of sail will be running. In fact, due to the strength of the wind and severity and height of the seas, you will run no matter what. In such circumstances, it is best to rid the decks of any and all impediments that may be carried away or hamper such working of the deck as is possible. As mentioned before, oil or trailing warps is probably the best tactic. The warps should be streamed one at a time until the speed of the ship is lowered to the point where control is possible and following seas present the least threat. Extraordinary concentration at the helm is necessary and watches may be only one hour. If the lines trailed are in a bight and long enough to coincide with the seas aft, the bight may well serve to inhibit crests and smooth the attacking demons. In any storm or "ultimate" seas, stay with the boat unless it is truly foundering. Life rafts, as shown by the Fastnet disaster in 1979, are too easily flipped, drift away or cannot be entered with any degree of safety. Even with improvements–ballast pockets, drogues, heavy tether lines–chances are that you will be safer in the mother ship so long as she remains tight. Whatever, be prepared!

HOLING

If you strike an object, immediately go below and check for damage. If a hole has been rent in the hull near the waterline, sail on the tack to keep the hole above water. More than likely, the hole will be hidden behind bunks or lockers or beneath immovable floorboards. There is only one solution: *Tear the furniture out!* It hurts, but failure to do so immediately will result in probable foundering. Using a pry bar or axe or large spanner, wrench the offending woodwork (or glasswork) away to clear a working opening.

Use either an umbrella patch or cushions stuffed into or against the hole to stop the major flow. Another interesting possibility is to use a plumber's helper over the hole, preferably from the outside. If the hole is well below the waterline, the inflow of water will be close to twice as fast as higher up, and may be much harder to reach. The storm jib, with lines at each corner, can be passed around the hull from outside to form a patch. Reduce the speed of the vessel to allow the sail to stay in position. Weight the corner with chain or odd fitments shackled together to allow it to sink below the water. No matter how hard and fast you work, a lot of water will enter the ship. The average bilge pump— 25 gallons per minute—will be next to useless when up against a flow of over 200 gallons per minute, which is what you can expect from a hole about 4 inches in diameter. Only a high-capacity engine-driven pump can handle a flow like that, and then only if the engine has not been flooded. A bucket brigade can be of help, but the key is speed in locating the hole and speed and efficiency in stemming the flow.

Once the flow is stopped, or slowed to a leak, more permanent repairs can be effected. Perhaps the best material, in anything but a wood boat, is underwater-hardening epoxy paste. Follow directions, but do try to apply it on the outside first with some sort of temporary board or backing held in place. Then apply to the interior. Remember to spread the paste well past the area of the hole to allow for good surface adhesion. In a wooden ship, boards and caulking can be used to first seal the opening from within, with further repairs made from the outside as conditions allow.

JURY RIGS: Masts

Depending upon the damage inflicted to the mast, a jury rig may be an addition to what remains standing, or it may be an entire make-do structure. If the mast has broken above the spreaders, the storm trysail may work as a mainsail with only a forestay and backstay pieced together from spare wire and wire rope clips. If only the mizzen remains, a forestay can be fashioned—albeit at a very low angle—and a jib can be modified to be set flying from said stay. As long as the remaining bit of mast has retained the lower shrouds, a low efficient sailing rig is not

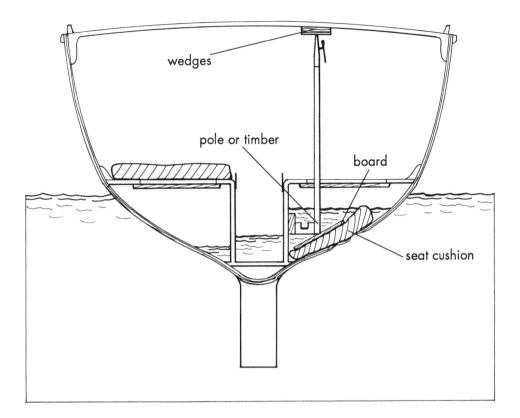

wedges

pole or timber

board

seat cushion

Any hole or breach in the hull's bottom is disastrous. Using a pad, bunk cushion of other comparatively dense and flexible material can be used to temporarily seal the opening.

only possible but relatively simple to fabricate.

If the mast breaks at or near deck level, a different set of criteria apply. First, see what is salvageable from the leavings of your once noble spar. It may be possible to save stays, hardware or a section of the spur itself. Before you decide what you will do, see what you have available to work with.

Having made an inventory of working materials—not forgetting oars, spinnaker and jockey poles, bunk fronts, etc.—sit below with a clean sheet of paper, some basic measurements (base of fore triangle, length of longest usable mast section, length of various salvaged wire, etc.) and a pencil and see what *might* be possible—what L. Francis Herreshoff called "thought experiments." It will be much easier than trying different combinations on deck in a seaway at night with the wind at Force 6. Perhaps the most important thing to remember is that the rig you design must be able to be created, hoisted and used by the available manpower and the available skills. If you are within sight of land, turn on the engine! However, if you are mid-ocean you will want to devise something that will take you where you want to go with the available rations and water aboard in whatever weather you may reasonably expect to have.

Having decided on the solution, gather the crew, explain the jury

Possible jury rigs when the mast breaks.

Jury rudders.

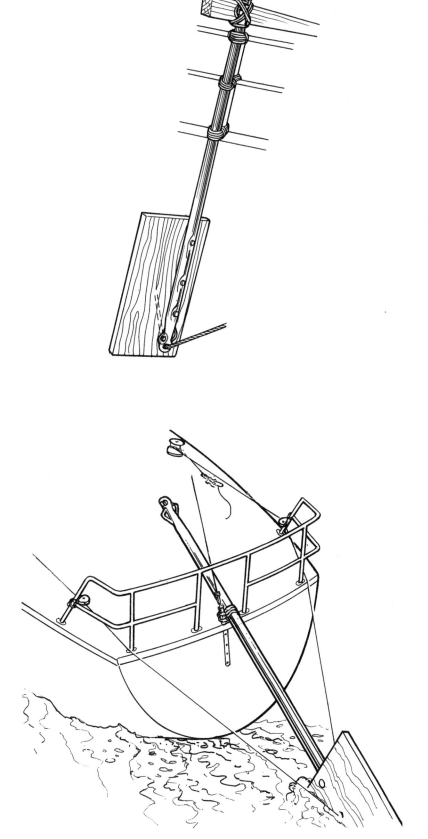

rig to them and delegate one crew member to each task needed to raise the rig. Collect and assemble all the necessary parts. Do as much as possible with the new rig *on deck*. The less you need to do aloft, the safer. Make sure, for example, that all the "masthead" fittings are secured, that the correct length wires and ropes are tied off. You don't want to have to lower the whole mess if you can avoid it.

Depending on size and weight, raising the rig can be a job for one with a winch and a tripod arrangement or it can take the muscles of ten strong men. You wish to get the thing up with minimal effort. The illustrations give some possible solutions.

Setting sail may mean adopting some odd and back-ended configurations. Jibs may be turned on end, or sewn together. Storm sails may be the best driving sails for a reduced rig, and setting them flying may be the best, and safest, means of propulsion. What is most important is to devise a sail combination that will get you where you wish to go. Quite often sprit sails, lateen rigs, makeshift schooners and squaresails will serve the purpose quite well if you know anything about them. Unfortunately, the modern sailor has little use for working sails of the past. The illustrations demonstrate their uses.

JURY RIGS: Rudders

If the rudder is inboard and the stock has been bent, ignore it. Instead, you will have to fashion a rudder of sweep to work off the transom. If the blade is damaged, it may still be possible to steer the boat, albeit with reduced sail. However, if the response is minimal and you are still some distance from port, some sort of jury-rigged rudder will have to be constructed.

Should the steering gear be damaged beyond repair, an emergency tiller should be aboard. Since many more yachts are wheel-steered now than even twenty years ago, essential spares should be carried— cable, clamps, sprocket wheels, gears, etc. Obviously, you will never be covered for all contingencies. And, sooner or later, you will have to rig that emergency tiller. Accidents do happen that will incapacitate both wheel and rudder.

The simplest repairs are to a transom-hung rudder, which can be shipped and patched, or even replaced from parts fashioned from floorboards, hatchboards, etc. If the pintles and gudgeons are not bent or broken, repairs should be fairly straightforward, and if the rudder is wood, can be accommodated with screws and bolts. If the rudder is fiberglass, the same methods can be used but reinforcement will be necessary in the form of load-spreading washers (of metal or wood) and lashings. However, if the major portion of the blade has been torn away, and the fastenings between rudder and hull are left without integrity, a new rudder assembly will have to be fashioned.

Inboard rudders pose a different set of problems. If the rudder bearing has been broken, and the rudder is slamming back and forth, potential exists for major hull damage or rupture, especially in a seaway. Some means of locking the rudder in position, or even of shipping the entire assembly, will have to be devised. One good precaution is to drill a small hole in the trailing edge of the blade, with the foreknowledge that this will be used, should an emergency occur, to lead lines outboard and to the cockpit for steering. If the blade can be set, a rudder aft will still have to be fashioned. Some self-steering wind vanes can be adapted to act as an auxiliary rudder. This potential might well be investigated when contemplating the purchase of a vane.

To actually construct a new rudder, first gather the necessary materials: a pole—boom, spinnaker pole, oar (if long enough); a blade substitute such as a hatchboard or section of floorboard; line, lashings, bolts, tools needed, etc. Fasten the pole to the blade with through bolts, U-bolts, or anything that will produce a rigid structure. Next, determine how to attach the assembly to the stern. As long as the blade will be deeply immersed, any method will do. However, stern shape will determine the most appropriate way of accomplishing this.

Perhaps the easiest stern to mount your new rudder will be virtually plumb, utilizing the pushpit horizontals as fastening points, with stout lashings to hold the two together. Reverse-counter transoms will demand a more deck-level approach with some fitting being used to hold the lashing. Traditional forward-sloping counters will best use the pushpit as above. Lacking guard rails aft, deck-level lashings will have to be used, remembering that with a single-point lashing some means will have to be devised to hold the blade in the water. Ballasting is one possibility. Another is to run lines from a hold in the *forward* edge of the blade near the bottom, outboard and forward to strong points on deck. The backstay can also be used as a second lashing point for the pole/stock, remembering that any lashing used here will put enormous strains on the entire rig and should be used advisedly in heavy weather.

To ease steering, lines can be led through snatch blocks attached to the pushpit at either outboard corner, or a spar can be slashed to the pushpit, or deck and blocks can be attached to either end, in either case with lines leading from the new rudder "stock" through the blocks and thence to winches or cleats in the cockpit.

Despite advice to the contrary, it is always better to attempt to fix the tiller at the centerline. Even without a pushpit, some makeshift arrangement can be worked out on the afterdeck, usually by lashing a spar to the mooring cleats at the quarters and affixing the rudder stock to the spar.

A drogue can be utilized for steering—tire, bucket or proper drogue—with steering lines attached to the drogue line with rolling hitches. To give the needed steering leverage, the ends of the steering lines should be led through blocks on either end of a fairly long spar lashed to the stern. Be sure to rig a tripping line for the drogue. You will find recov-

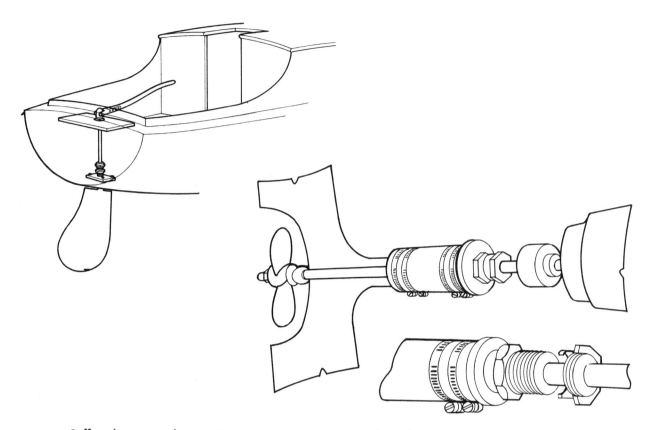

Suffing boxes, under constant moving pressures, need regular inspection and adjustment.

Every seacock, in fact every through-hull, should have a softwood plug attached to it by a lanyard, to be hammered home in the event of a fracture or inrush of water.

When anchored off a lee shore, always lay out a second anchor, carrying it out in the dinghy in the direction safest to allow making a safe departure.

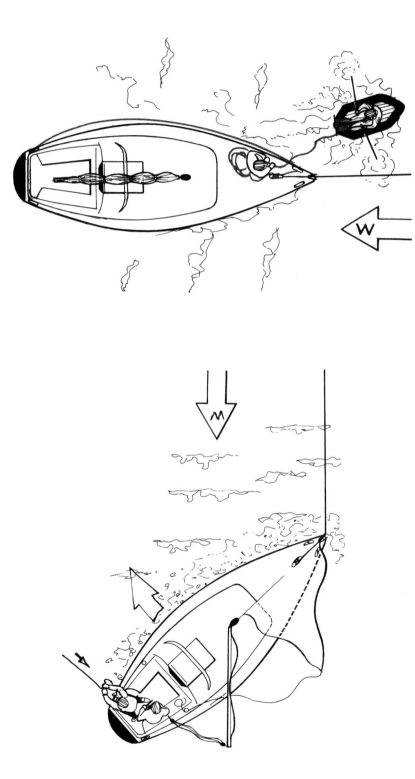

ery difficult otherwise. Also, this arrangement, although the easiest to rig, will not offer the control of a jury rudder.

LEAKS

Locating a leak may be much more difficult than you might imagine. Likely spots are seacocks, rudder gland, stuffing box, keelbolts, hull-to-deck join, deck fittings—in fact anywhere the hull or deck has been drilled, cut or opened to receive a fitting, including water, waste or fuel tanks. Too often, the leak is far from the spot at which water, etc., collects. You may have to trace the course.

A deck leak may be uncomfortable, but a hull leak, fitting or otherwise (skegs and keel sumps can crack from wracking strains in heavy seas), can be downright dangerous. Though the pumps may be able to cope, track it down. And don't forget the obvious: head intake hoses are usually not looped high enough. At rest this may be unnoticeable, but underway, especially when heeled, the head can overflow and cause a boat to founder. If the boat has sealed-off compartments, or if an area can be sealed off by makeshift means, do so until repairs can be safely effected.

Attempt to stop the leak with rags, caulking cotton, foam or neoprene or plugs. (Incidentally, all through hulls, even those with seacocks, should have a tapered softwood plug of appropriate size tied to the fitting with a lanyard.) Rubber and silicon caulking will *not* hold to wet surfaces. Underwater epoxy will, and should be kept aboard for such emergencies.

LEE SHORES

Under most conditions a lee shore should be avoided only because of the possibility of heavy weather. If no choice exists, try to anchor as far out as is possible with safety. If the engine is powerful, motoring or motor-sailing should be attempted before trying to leave under sail alone.

In truly horrendous conditions, boats have survived by sailing in a half-circle and dropping as many anchors as are on board. Under these conditions it will not be possible to set anything from the dinghy and no other choice will exist.

Careful planning and coordination from all the crew will be necessary for these maneuvers to work. It will be difficult to keep the headsail from flogging itself to death and the jib sheets from fouling. However, your safety depends on this, and a crew member should be stationed at what will be the leeward winch to haul in as soon as the anchor line has been released. Another must be stationed at the mainsheet, leaving the helmsman free to concentrate.

When alone or shorthanded, it may be an advantage to sail the yacht out under only one sail, whichever is most efficient, keeping the decks relatively clear. If you must lose an anchor, do so...it costs less than the ship.

LIFERAFTS

It should be obvious that a life raft must be kept on deck or in a special raft locker. Nevertheless, many yachtsmen place it in a cockpit or lazarette locker where accumulations of gear and debris block access to it. Under-the-sole lockers are not recommended; too many people will be in the cockpit to make for easy access. The best location is either lashed to the coachroof fore or aft or the mast, or on the afterdeck or beneath the helmsman seat. Some newer boats have special recesses within the transom; these are fine if, in practice, you can get to them without endangering the crew. Keep all safety gear inboard if possible.

Don't use lashings that end up like the Gordian knot. They must be slashable with one stroke of a knife, or with a single tug on a line—some variant of a slippery hitch, for example. The lashings are best done up on natural cordage, as synthetics will slip too much. Manila or hemp— if you can find them—are good. Patent hold-down systems can be acceptable, providing they are constantly checked for corrosion or chafe. Like anything mechanical they are liable to seizure and breakdown when most needed.

Servicing is vital to life raft performance. Kept on deck, the raft, even in a fiberglass cannister, is subject to moisture penetration, fabric deterioration and valve failure. Yearly servicing by an authorized service center is vital. Yes, it is expensive. Yes, you need to do it. While we are on the subject, do buy a cannister raft. Valises are too subject to kicks, seepage and puncture. They should be avoided at all costs, no matter how well-protected you believe the raft to be. Also, pay a few dollars or pounds more and get a raft that is up to SOLAS standards. The difference, especially offshore, is worth it both in terms of construction and materials specifications and in terms of equipment.

The crew, every member of it, must be given proper instruction in abandon-ship and life-raft drill. Don't wait until it is too late. This is not to suggest you should inflate the raft to practice, but do use the dinghy to get the crew used to boarding a raft in rough seas and in a state of mock panic, something best done at one's moorings. Show them how to undo lashings, how to toss the raft overboard and how to inflate it. Make sure, when underway, that each crew member is supplied with a sharp and properly protected knife.

Depending where the raft is located, the painter should be tied to a deck fitting which is *through-bolted*. The strains upon raft and painter in rough seas when thrown are great. Stanchion bases, mast step, coachroof rails, pushpit are all appropriate.

Never attempt to inflate the raft while it is on board! What with rigging, deck gear, trampling crew, wheel or tiller, etc., you will never be able to get into the water, and if you do, the chances are you will rip the fabric or tear off a fitting or two. Always throw it clear of the ship.

Liferafts should be thown clear of the ship, tethered securely. Never inflate until clear of the ship. Before entering the raft, make sure the canopy and floors are secure and safe.

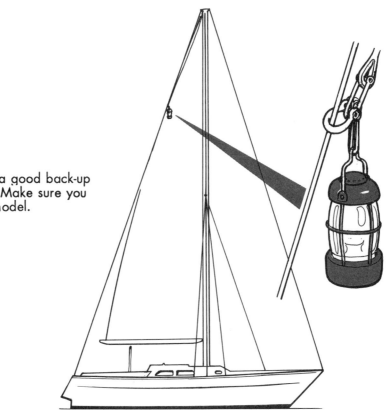

An oil lamp is always a good back-up for any electric fixture. Make sure you get a truly windproof model.

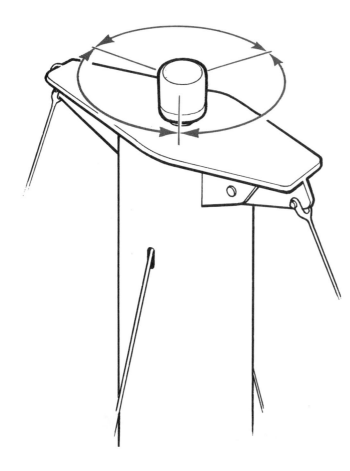

In heavy weather, a masthead light is probably the only light visible from another vessel.

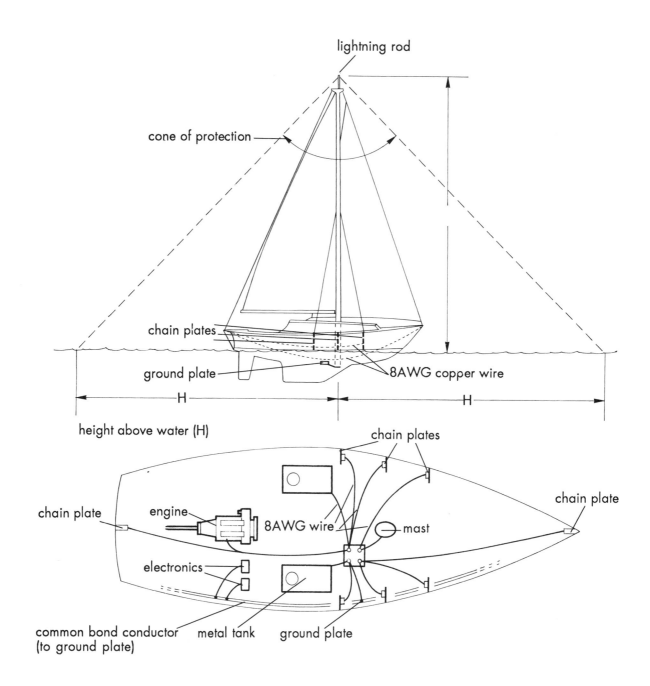

lightning rod

cone of protection

chain plates

ground plate

8AWG copper wire

H

H

height above water (H)

chain plates

chain plate

engine

8AWG wire

mast

electronics

chain plate

common bond conductor
(to ground plate)

metal tank

ground plate

A correctly designed and installed lightning protection system will assure crew safety. However, even with all in place, the chance of damage to the boat exists. In any lightning storm, stay away from any metal, stay below and be prepared for a possible fire or damage control action.

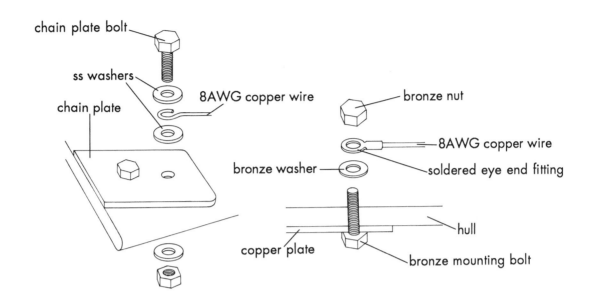

Connecting bonding wire to chain plate.

The painter can become tangled. First make sure it is clear, then tug firmly. The throw of the raft may start inflation, but it is always best to make sure by giving the painter the approved and appropriate pull. If the raft does not inflate, or only partially fills, get one person to attempt to start pumping.

Should abandonment of the mother vessel become imperative, make sure *all* members of the crew are aboard the raft before cutting the painter. Rafts drift—especially in the conditions likely at the time—at a remarkable rate. There is little or no chance that contact can be reestablished with the yacht. As tragic experience has unfortunately shown, all too often, in panic, some crew member cuts that figurative umbilical cord prematurely. Someone is sure to be the worse for it.

LIGHTNING

Lightning is always unpredictable. Though it will rarely strike a yacht enough cases exist, especially along the American eastern seaboard, to take all possible precautions. Since lightning will follow the most direct path to the water, it is up to you to provide such a path to help it on its way.

Though copper wire #8 is generally recommended for a lightning ground, much better is to use copper tubing, flattened at the ends connecting the lightning rod at the masthead with a keel bolt in a boat with an encapsulated keel, a grounding plate should be attached to the hull as far below the waterline as is feasible.

Because very few European boats are fitted with lightning protection, in a sudden storm a length of chain, shackled to the cap shroud and dangled overboard (make sure it is long enough to remain under water) will act as a satisfactory substitute. If time exists, tape the shackle end of the chain to the shroud to ensure positive contact. Obviously, the helmsman remains in greater danger than the rest of the crew, especially if steering with a wheel. If possible, anchor; when at sea, heave to and join the rest of the crew below.

LIGHTS

If the lights aboard go, hoist a lantern, preferably on the backstay. If hoisted to the spreaders, it will not be seen from leeward. Despite the International Rules, incorrect lights are often shown. Fishing boats are prime culprits, but yachts and merchant ships can also be offenders. Always attempt to discern exactly what lights are being shown where on an approaching vessel before taking evasive action. Likewise, even in approved anchorages, always hoist an anchor light. Strobe lights, *not* in accordance with the International Rules, should be used only for distress and then only when necessary, as they can confuse a watch officer on the bridge of a large ship.

MAN OVERBOARD

All boats should have a life ring with man-overboard pole, flag, whistle, light and possibly a sea anchor attached. A horseshoe buoy will be easier for the person in the water to slip into. For the pole to be sighted, it must be at least 8 feet (2.5m) long with a bright orange flag attached to the top. In heavy seas even this will be difficult to spot, and a longer pole is not a bad idea. Equally, the flag should be as large as is practical to aid in sighting. A whistle will help in locating the victim in any weather, while a light, preferably self-activating, will be a necessity in low-visibility conditions and at night. Sea anchors are often in bad repute, but a small cloth cone on a long bridle will certainly slow any drift and permit easier spotting and a more planned pick-up. No matter what the equipment, it should be mounted *outboard* of all rails, lifelines and deck encumbrances. Nothing can be worse than to attempt to release the gear and have it foul where it may be impossible to release it. Ideally, devices must be mounted on both sides of the cockpit at the stern within reach and ready-release by the helmsman. The pole can be fitted into a special release socket or very lightly lashed to the backstay. *Very lightly* is important: the lashings must break only through the initial pull of the life ring or horseshoe. Obviously, the idea is to have the entire kit in the water and as close to the man overboard as quickly as possible. Conditions exist where the shock of falling overboard will be enough to totally disorient and

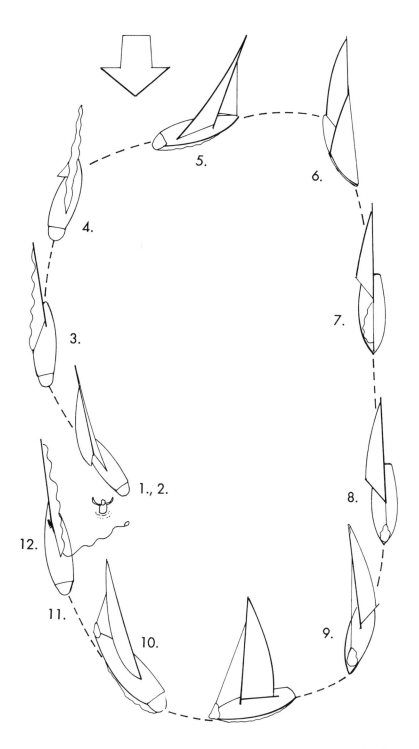

Man overboard recovery is dangerous, panic-making and difficult. It must be practiced in calm water again and again. Here's how to go about it.
1. Whoever see the incident shout shout "Man Overboard". A spotter must be assigned immediately. 2. Get a life ring or other floatation gear in the water as close to the victim as possible. 3. Bring the boat head to wind. 4. Back the sails to slow down or throw the transmission in neutral, then reverse very slowly to bring the boat to a complete stop. 5. Get the boat turned so the wind is slightly aft of amidships. 7. Douse headsail(s) and haul in the main. 8. Hold the downwind course until victim is beam on. 9. Jibe. 10. Approach from ca. 45° off the wind. 11. Use a heaving line to the victim. 12. Get the victim aboard from the windward side.

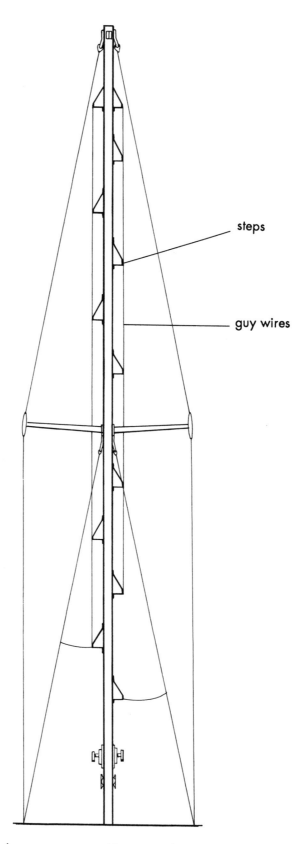

steps

guy wires

Getting aloft at sea is a dangerous game. However, there are times when it simply has to be done to retrieve a lost halyard, unstick a sheave or replace an antenna. One solution is to permanently install mast steps alternating up the mast. Note the guy wire to prevent sheets or sails from hanging-up on the steps.

196   *Emergencies*

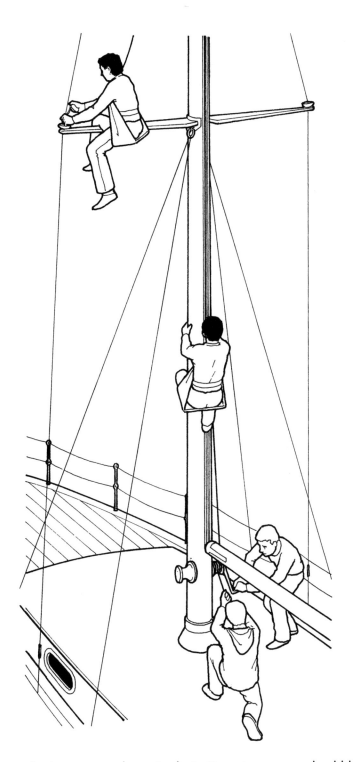

A more tradition method is to use a bosun's chair. Two strong crew should be positioned below, one to winch and one to tail. The person in the chair should have a loop of rope around the mast to keep him from swinging out and a guy to the deck to steady his rise, payed out by the tailer. A bosun's chair can be used solo with blocks and tackle and led to the bitter end of the halyard, but it is not recommended except at the dock in perfectly settled conditions.

Emergencies 197

weaken the victim. It becomes absolutely necessary to get the floatation device to him or her and as near as possible quickly. In addition, the victim may have been hurt or possibly incapacitated in the fall. Finally, in heavy going and cold, survival chances are greatly lessened, and the less activity required of the person in the water, the less the heat loss and the chance of hypothermia.

It is not easy to see someone in heavy seas. It is actually difficult to see a man overboard in almost any weather. The need for a crew member with good eyes and better powers of concentration is obvious. But for such a person to be truly effective, he must be left alone, not bothered, not expected to do anything but *keep an eye on the victim!* This cannot be too highly stressed. If the man in the water is lost sight of for even an instant, he may never again be spotted. Certainly, every sailor has practiced man overboard drills, but usually in gentle conditions and without panic or the sense of urgency required when a real living mass of flesh goes over the side. It's a lot different in reality.

Once the flotation materials are launched and a spotter is at work, then and only then should maneuvers to recover the person take place. Under sail, turn into the wind. This will allow the boat to keep way, yet slow her down by enough to prepare the crew for recovery measures. What you want to do is to get into a position to be able to pick up the man in the water from windward.

Under power, there is less to do on working the boat, but perhaps greater potential danger to the victim. Under "slow ahead" describe a circle in the water so that you approach the person in the water from behind and to windward. When you are in drifting reach or just alongside (the forward third of the hull), *stop the propellers from turning.* Obviously, you can throw the gears into neutral. In calm weather, shut off the engine if you are in clear water. The danger from the propellers is frightening, and cases are on record of persons being dismembered or killed by a fast-turning prop. On a powerboat, the freeboard, even aft (except on a fishing boat) will be appreciably higher than aboard a similar-length sailing vessel. If a stern door or swim platform is available, the person can best be hauled up from there. However, getting a soaked body up a meter or more of slick topsides is a maneuver that demands some forethought.

What you are doing in the above steps is *heaving to.* It allows the abandonment of actual sailing work, and the best apportionment of crew for retrieving the person in the water. Boat speed can be easily corrected by using the main or repositioning the rudder for angle or drift. Depending on what course you are at the time of the accident, different maneuvers are more or less appropriate for successful positioning of the boat. See the diagrams.

If you cannot see the person overboard and conditions are good, sail or motor a reciprocal course. If the weather is foul or shows signs of deteriorating, begin a search upwind of the approximate position you lost your crew. Keep records of time and distance sailed, and take into account current, tides and wind speed, all of which will affect the drift of the person in the water to a much greater degree than the ship. The search may be carried out to windward, on a reach or running. In each case you will have to tack back and forth, running parallel lines over the search area.

Once you have him spotted, and the boat is under control, you must be prepared to get him into the boat. An average man in foul weather gear and several layers of clothing will add as much as 50 pounds (23.5 kilos) to his dry weight with immersion. This is not inconsiderable, and must be taken into account in any maneuver to get him back on board. *The man in the water should practice a few precautionary measures to prolong his strength and chances of survival. He must keep his clothing on to preserve body heat. He must not scream or attempt to swim toward the boat. This will only confuse the crew and deplete his energies. He should utilize the gear thrown to him if possible and wait, activating any light and using the whistle only when the mother ship is in sight. Do not panic!*

To get the survivor on board, several methods are possible. If he is injured or exhausted, lower a sail with all corners secured by lines to the ship. If he can do some of the work himself, a bosun's chair or bight of rope can be lowered to swing around his arms, allowing him to sit in it and be winched aboard. If a platform or boarding ladder is permanently attached to the stern, have him grab a bight of rope and maneuver him to the stern with a crew member on each quarter to assist boarding. In boats with transom-mounted rudders, a set of steps can be installed on the rudder blade from below the water line to allow easier boarding. *Do not attempt to haul the victim aboard by his arms!*

Singlehanded sailors have the most to worry about in man-overboard situations. You must always trail a poly (floating) line with a buoy attached to the end of it. This should be about 25 meters long. If you are sailing under self-steering gear, some means of disengaging the gear is necessary. One possibility is suggested in the illustration. A permanently mounted ladder with a lanyard attached to release the lower half, or the transom steps mentioned above, should be included in fitting out the boat. In powerboats, the trailing line must be bridled to avoid fouling the propeller and might be rigged either to shift the gears into neutral or shut down the ignition when given a sharp jerk.

MAST CLIMBING

First ascertain if there is a way to free the line or ignore the damage without going up. If you are near port, you may be able to jury-rig an arrangement to get you in without trying to work in a seaway at the masthead. Remember, the pitching moment is much greater high up, especially if 75 kilos of mass is suddenly hanging on for dear life. Most

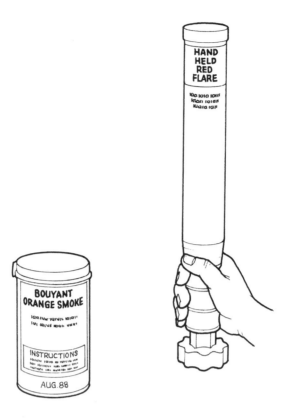

Day and night signals are a must aboard any boat venturing more than a few hundred yards away from the shore.

repair jobs at the top are two-handed affairs, and for effective work both body and legs must be secured and braced. If any possible way exists to carry on without clambering up, take it, *unless the crew or ship will be endangered through failure to take action.*

Tearing along at hull speed will in no way aid the crew who must be at the masthead, either once there or climbing. Lower the boat speed as much as possible while maintaining steering way. A reach will steady the boat and, depending upon the tack, can actually provide a more secure position at mast top. Sail may have to be reduced.

The traditional bosun's chair is both uncomfortable and potentially dangerous. The wood seat can slam into the mast, causing more damage. The newer, all-cloth models with restraining straps and tool pockets can be both safer and allow for more efficient and quicker work. The crew who has volunteered to go up must be *totally* secured before ascending. A downhaul must be rigged to the chair, and a line with snap hook or some other expedient means of wrapping around the mast to keep the occupant in position should be affixed, preferably around the person, not just to the seat. A safety harness can be employed, providing that the tether is not too long. All the tools that might be needed should be secured by lanyards if possible. In fact, it is a good idea to keep basic tools permanently ensconced with the bosun's chair: visegrips, screwdriver, marlinspike, adjustable wrench /spanner, etc. The assumption of rigging the chair on a spare halyard demands some forethought. Spinnaker halyards may be too light to be safe, the main halyard may be jammed, and the jib needed to maintain forward motion. In such a situation, it may be wise to use the spinnaker halyard as a messenger to carry a heavier line through its masthead sheave. In a fractionally rigged boat, a spare main halyard might well be permanently rigged.

Hauling a person aloft demands a strong wincher, enough turns (at least four) around the winch and a good braking turn around a cleat. The point is to get someone up safely, not fast. A second crew member on the deck should handle the downhaul, keeping it taut and making sure that swing is kept to a minimum. If the main is down, the safety line should be used by the man aloft, breaking it only at the spreaders.

Frankly, the precautions mentioned above should be adhered to in *all* weathers. At night, a flashlight/torch should be carried aloft, possibly taped to the upper arm with gaffer's tape. Gloves are another recommendation, but they must be full-fingered and leather. Anything else will either chafe or slip. Deck boots will protect the legs and a foam-filled life vest will help absorb bumps while not overly hindering the wearer's movements.

If for some reason the bosun's chair is not usable or one isn't on board, a substitute will have to be devised. Lots of possibilities exist, of course, but whatever is used must be of irreproachable integrity: a bowline on a bight or an emergency boarding ladder. Do *not* use a fender unless it is the type that allows the line to run through it; standard inflatable fenders are not reliable enough in their grommeting to hold a man's weight under stress conditions. And, should you use one of the other alternatives, remember to pad it well. Raw wood or rope can cause serious injury aloft in high winds and rolling conditions. The poor sucker at the masthead has enough to worry about!

There will be times when no halyard is available for hauling a bosun's chair. A rope or plastic ladder, or a wood and rope ladder, can be used but demands much vigilance and agility as well as a messenger line to haul it up: it's usually far too much bother and too time-consuming when you need it. The main can be slacked slightly (only in fairly large boats) and used as a ladder. However, the slides *must* be metal. Plastic slugs can fracture, causing a rapid descent of catastrophic speed and force. Follow safety precautions!

MEDICAL EMERGENCIES

Do you need to save a life?

Do you need to prevent the situation from getting worse?

Must you relieve pain and suffering?

Do you need outside assistance?

The above questions are not meant to solve any specific problem, but they must be asked in any situation concerning injury or sickness. Though most accidents aboard will be minor—cuts, seasickness, sunburn, colds and flu—many others will require more than two aspirin and a cup of tea. You must be prepared to cope with anything short of major surgery, especially if you intend a trans-oceanic passage of any length. To this degree, every yacht should be equipped with an up-to-date and constantly renewed first-aid kit, including appropriate medications for the areas to which you plan to voyage. Also aboard must be a modern first-aid manual *that has been read by at least two crew.* Any member of the crew who has a specific chronic ailment, drug allergy or medication requirement should inform the captain of such *before* setting sail. It is up to the captain to assess the situation and make the decision of the crew's suitability based on the remoteness of the landfall, the conditions likely to be encountered and the general physical condition of the crew member.

If the person has stopped breathing or has no discernable heartbeat you must act immediately to save that person's life. Bleeding will kill a person much less quickly, unless it is a major hemorrhage of an artery, than lack of oxygen or no heartbeat.

If the person is not subject to any immediate threat, you must decide if the condition might worsen. Many injuries and illnesses can get more serious, but the most common might include: burns, infections, exposure, poisoning, concussion, fractures, unconsciousness, open wounds and chest pain. If you decide that the person is in no immediate danger, continue to port. Otherwise, consult your medical guidebook or radio for further advice.

The greatest concurrent problem with any injury at sea may be fear. Not only take appropriate action, but reassure the injured person. Care, concern and will can play as important a part as anything to help alleviate distress and aid someone on the path to recovery.

Can you cope? Certain medical conditions will be beyond your ability to treat. If you are far from shore, you must use your judgment and common sense, and do everything in your power to aid the patient with what you have at hand. Certain infections can be held at bay with antibiotics. Certain fractures can be immobilized until a doctor is at hand. But other conditions may be impossible to do much about. Internal hemorrhaging, heart attack, certain types of poisoning, extreme hypothermia may be beyond you.

PROPELLER
Failure to shut down the engine could cause damage to the gearbox.

Since a crewmember will have to dive to clear the obstruction, follow the methods set out in the section on DIVING. Stopping the vessel will aid immeasurably. Try to anchor out of a tidal stream and be sure that anyone going overboard is tethered to ship.

It may help to raise the stern of the boat by concentrating weights forward. Also, a partially inflated dinghy can make a useful work area as well as cushioning the stern in any sort of swell. In heavy seas and well away from land, towing warps or a drogue may keep the boat at a reasonable speed and allow steerage. Do not attempt to go overboard in these conditions. Danger from the pitching, heaving hull is too great. It will probably be easier to saw rather than cut the rope turns on the prop. A hacksaw blade or keyhole saw will be most effective and can be lashed to a makeshift wood handle.

PUMPS: Bilge

Most modern bilge pumps are of the diaphragm type. These will function in situations where older pumps would have long since failed or clogged. However, even a pump that has a capacity of 30 gallons per minute (115 liters) will not be very effective with a major hull breach. In such a case, only an engine-driven pump will suffice. And if the engine ceases to function, a bucket brigade will do far more than either.

Always carry spares for all pumps. A new diaphragm can be installed in approximately five minutes, providing access is reasonable. The same is true of strainers; you must be able to reach them.

Installation is vital to proper pump efficiency and safety. Too often, bilge pumps are mounted so that a cockpit locker lid must be opened to operate them. Mount cockpit pump with a through-deck fitting, properly capped and watertight and accessible to the helmsman. Any offshore boat should have a second pump operable from below. Most stock boats are equipped with pumps of much too small capacity. Minimum should be 25 gallons per minute (95 liters).

Pump handles will break. Either keep a factory spare, make sure the interior and exterior pumps have identical handles or carry a hardwood dowel or length of pipe of correct dimensions. Also, it is a good idea to drill a hole through the handle and tie it with a light lanyard to a spot where it is always at hand, near the pump. A spring clip will also work well.

RIGGING

If any part of the standing rigging fails, immediately remove or decrease strain on that side of the rig. Depending on conditions, you can continue sailing. If calm when the forestay fails, it's best to let things alone, rather than risk the chance of the mast falling aft into the cockpit. When things get rough, this will not be possible and getting the sails down and the rigging break mended takes priority. If the backstay

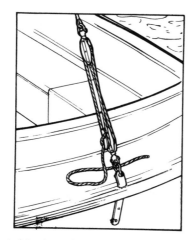

A block-and-tackle can be used to repair a broken stay.

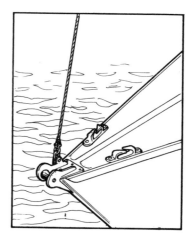

A spare halyard can double as a forestay.

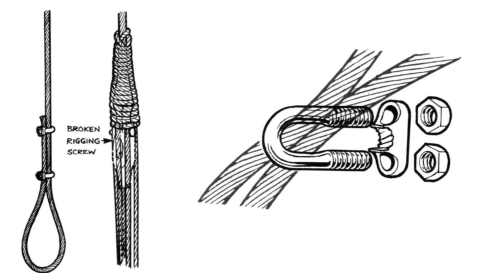

BROKEN RIGGING SCREW

Bulldog clips should always be carried aboard any boat, sail or power. They can be used to join wires or loop a broken wire. Vital for rigging, steering cable and engine control cable repairs.

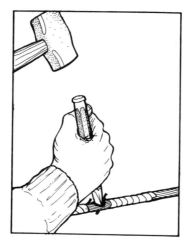

A cold chisel will cut away rigging if the cable cutters have gone west.

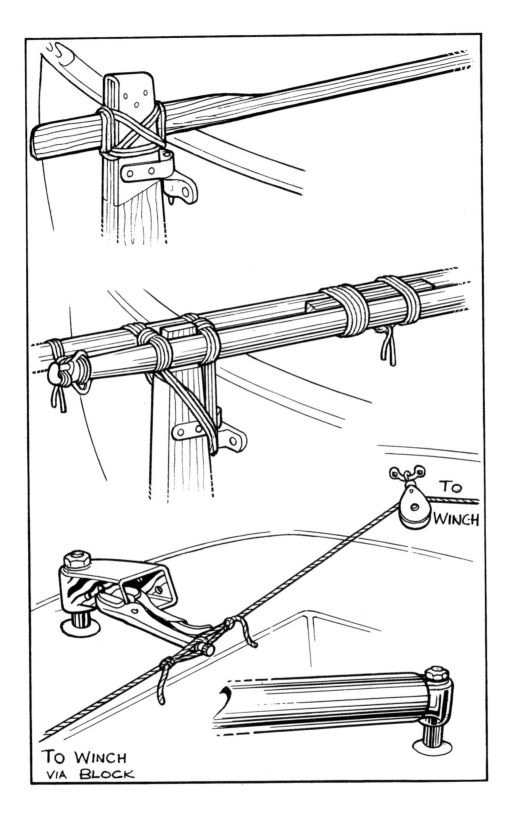

To WINCH

WINCH

TO WINCH
VIA BLOCK

Jury tillers.

parts, head upwind, lead a halyard aft and tension with a Spanish windlass or block and tackle. If the forestay ruptures, head downwind, and use a spare halyard shackled to the stem for support. If long enough, lead the halyard aft to a winch for greater tensioning.

Should a shroud go, immediately tack–jibing will place undue strain on the rig, and could carry it away–and head off so as to put the least strain on the failed part of the rig. Try to take sea state into account, as undue pitching and rolling can cause almost as much damage as the original fitting letting go.

Your most useful equipment for jury-rigging, besides a spare halyard, will be wire rope or bulldog clips. These should be galvanized, not stainless steel, which has a tendency to slip. If a stay has fractured at the turnbuckle fitting end, form a bight or loop with the wire and use at least two clips to form an eye, which may be lashed or shackled to the turnbuckle or attached directly to the chainplate with a block and tackle. If the stay has broken at the masthead, sooner or later someone will have to go aloft. If no spare length of wire is aboard, the eye should be made at the end of wire aloft (do this while still on deck), which can then be shackled to the masthead fitting or tang. The now shorter stay can be attached to the chainplate or turnbuckle with shackles and a length of chain. If the wire has broken midway, make two eyes and fasten them with shackles, lashings or chain.

Rarely does it occur, but when a turnbuckle fractures or lets go, the solution is actually much simpler than when the shroud or stay breaks. Either replace it with another turnbuckle, use a lanyard or lash the stay in place. Times come, though, when the turnbuckle is frozen tight. This is the result of lax maintenance, and you should curse yourself soundly. Since you are presumably sailing on a tack that takes the strain off the fitting, remove the offender by slipping a clevis, lash the stay temporarily, and use two mole wrenches to break the freeze. Replace the turnbuckle.

Should wire need to be cut, use either wire cutters or a cold chisel. However, whip or tape the wire to either side of the proposed cut first to prevent unlaid strands or eye-damaging bits of flying steel. Wire rope is prone to a life of its own, and another crew member should hold it fast. Lacking the personnel, lash the wire with light stuff to keep it in place.

SAIL REPAIR

Should the main rip along a seam, or should the stitching come undone, and the tear is below the reef points, reefing is the simplest immediate solution. If the tear is high up, lower the sail immediately, and continue to sail under foresail alone. Or hoist the storm trysail in its place until repairs can be effected. With roller reefing, there is greater latitude in just how large or small the reef can be, but after a certain point the main will lose any efficiency, driving power or ability to balance the foresail, and should be dropped and replaced.

Should the sailcloth, not a seam, tear, best patch it on *both* sides, either with rigging tape or even better, the special self-sticking sail-repair patches sold for the purpose. In calm conditions, patches of sailcloth and "instant" waterproof glue can effect a temporary repair. The best solution is to drop the sail, replace it with another and have the sail sent below for proper stitched repair. A stitched sail repair requires, in synthetic cloths, fine needles, not the canvas-piercing monsters of old, Terylene/Dacron thread, and a comfortable sewing palm. Beeswax is not really necessary with modern materials. Double the thread, knot the two loose ends, and close the tears with a series of herringbone stitches. With synthetic cloth, anything from six to ten stitches per inch, depending on the weight of cloth, thread, etc., should be adequate. If the tear is larger than your four fingers minus the thumb can enter, it should be patched. A patch can be done in several ways. Use approximately the same weight cloth as that of the sail. Use two layers—one on either side—of lighter cloth. Seal or fold under the edges. Tape the patch in place. Fasten using a seam stitch. *Note:* try to line up the weave of the sailcloth and the patch if possible. With very large rips this may not be achievable with the materials at hand. Any patch is better than none. Adhesive-backed sail-repair patches are sold for small jobs. These will usually work for a while, but are neither permanent nor particularly suited for heavy weather. They can be temporarily used until you or your sailmaker makes a permanent repair.

Lost slides are all too common, especially with plastic and nylon. A few spares ought be carried, and can easily be sewn on or, if the sail has been grommeted along its luff, can be lashed with light synthetic twine or tape.

Boltropes are easily repaired with a patch around the rope on either side, extending several inches outward from the rope. Sew through both sides, remembering to keep the patch around the rope as tight as possible, increasing the diameter as little as possible and avoiding jams in slots and in hoisting.

If the clew fitting goes by the board, a stout lashing will temporarily suffice. More permanently, sew in a new grommet, sew in a rope grommet, sew in a D-ring or O-ring replacement. In any case, make sure that the corner of the sail is heavily reinforced, and the stitching is doubled or quadrupled. All sewn repairs are similar: if overlap is possible, do it. If you can double-stitch, do it. If both sides can be patched, do it.

SALVAGE

A salvor must establish certain proofs to make a claim:

The vessel was in peril.

He made a voluntary decision to aid the distressed vessel.

He risked his life and vessel to save the distressed vessel.

He achieved his aim and succeeded in aiding.

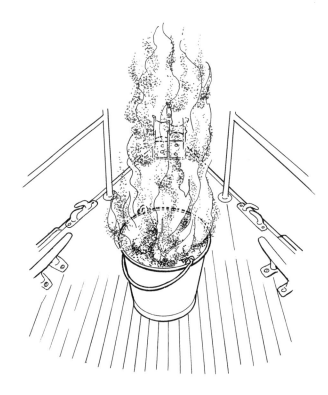

In emergencies, when the flares are exhausted, a steel bucket, filled with oil-soaked rags, set alight on the foredeck will make a very effective signal. Be careful. Have someone, armed with a fire extinguisher, stationed near the bucket. In any sort of heavy weather, don't even try it for fear of wind-spread fire or sliding bucket. In any case, chock the bucket to the deck.

If a contract is agreed upon *before* rescue efforts commence, no further claims can be made. A verbal agreement with witnesses present is adequate, legal and binding.

No matter what, few claims are settled without court or arbitrator attentions. Be prepared for a long and complicated procedure. Seek legal advice, specialized if necessary. The procedures are not related to land law and can easily overwhelm an amateur. Accepting tows or aid does *not* entitle the aiding party to claim salvage, nor claim ownership of property. Consult a qualified attorney or solicitor to determine the extent of claims or damages.

SIGNALS

Far too often distress signals are sent for inappropriate reasons or for no reason at all. If the engine has died and you are merely becalmed, *no* reason exists to send any signal. Patience is the solution.

Don't use flares in the daytime and smoke signals at night. Don't use an EPIRB when five miles from port. Don't attempt using VHF distress channel in mid-ocean. Common sense should dictate the signal most appropriate for any situation. Equally a question of propriety, don't waste signals, especially pyrotechnics. Unless you are near land, or sight another ship, chances are your visual signal will not be seen.

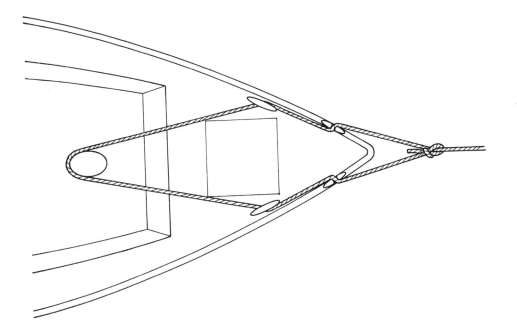

When being towed, make sure the load is spread as evenly as possible. A bridle arrangement, such as this, will allow strains to be evened out in bumpy seas and the chocks, cleats and mast will spread the load, with less chance of ripping anything out of the deck. Make sure everything is padded where the rope rounds it.

This is especially true of open water passages, a great many of which are away from shipping lanes.

Pyrotechnics, either hand-held or fired, must be used with caution. If any way exists to practice legally, avail yourself of it. When the time comes to use them, do so without panic. Potentially fatal accidents can and have occurred. The chance of starting a fire exists. Always set off flares away from tanks, gas bottles, engines, etc. In a pinch, a metal bucket of flaming rags, a fired gun or a signal mirror can work. Obviously, the burning materials must be used with extreme caution, and are not advised aboard GRP boats. A signal mirror, even if torn from the head's bulkhead, can, providing the weather cooperates, be extremely effective. It is seen from the bridge of a large ship with greater ease than dye markers or other daytime visual signals.

Important: all signals must be used cautiously, calmly and with a regard for the realities of the seas. If you can, whatever the manner, get safely to port, do so on your own. The cost to others should be considered before haphazardly requesting assistance.

STEERING

A wheel will lock if some obstruction or flotsam jams the rudder. Likewise, the same effect can occur if any of the linkages in the steer-

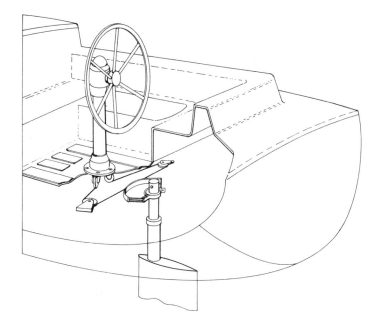

Quadrant/cable steering system. Loose cables will wear and break. Turnbuckles should be secured with locknuts.

Emergency tiller should be keyed to fit directly atop rudderpost.

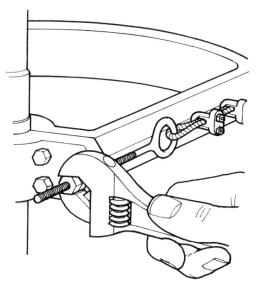

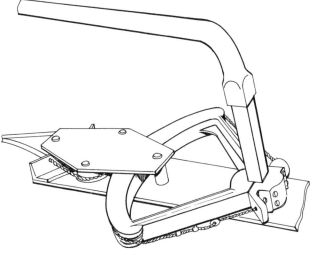

Rod steering. Keep linkages lubricated.

Rod steering. Keep linkages lubricated.

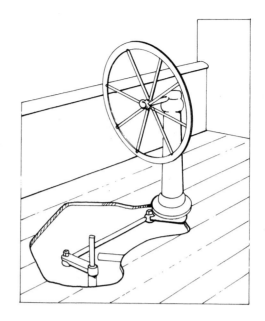

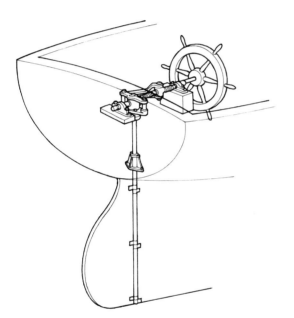

Rack-and-pinion steering. Make sure seats are secure and gears are lubricated.

Hydraulic steering. Check for leaks in hoses and tight connections. The resevoir should be checked periodically.

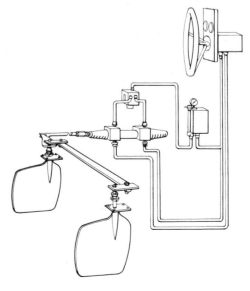

ing system become jammed—whether they are cables, rods or gears. Since the vessel will become all but uncontrollable should this occur, stop the vessel immediately. If inshore, anchor; if offshore, either set a drogue or allow the vessel to drift, providing the weather is settled. First check to see if any internal mechanical problems prevent the wheel from turning. If all checks out, someone will have to go over the side to make repairs.

If the wheel has no effect on the rudder, some mechanical link has gone by the boards. In cable and quadrant systems, this is usually caused by a broken cable. Wire-rope clips can be effective in making repairs, providing the cable thus reconnected does not have to pass through a sheave. In a rod system, the problem will most likely be a bent linkage clamp. This may be unrepairable at sea. In a hydraulic system, the lack of response will be due to a leaking hydraulic cylinder, lack of hydraulic fluid or a split hose. Repairs depend on your spares at hand.

Looseness is invariably due to slack cables or a loose crank arm (in a rod-controlled system). Taking up slack or making sure all connections are tight will usually solve the problem. Looseness in a hydraulic system will usually be caused by a loose hose connection or a leaking hose or fitting. The entire system may have to be bled after repair. Follow manufacturer's instructions.

All wheel-steering boats should have provision for access to the rudder head and an emergency tiller designed to be *easily* fitted so that the ship can be controlled and conned from a readily accessible position.

TILLER: Breakage

Cheeks at the rudder head may be damaged. Scrap plywood can be used as reinforcement on either side, lashed temporarily. Later, when time permits, drill three staggered holes through ply and rudder cheeks and throughbolt. Makeshift tiller can still be sashed between the new cheeks or else drilled and then throughbolted, making for a stronger, more responsive jury tiller.

If nothing else is at hand, use two long fiddles, such as are often found to keep settee cushions in place. These are usually fastened with self-tapping screws and can easily be refitted later; they make an elegant, either-side-of-the-rudder-head tiller.

Cheek fittings are usually bronze or stainless steel and the wood may have swelled between them, the tiller having broken slightly above the fitting. Knock out retaining bolt and swelled wood fragments. This will require a chisel and mallet. The same tools can be used to shape the wood replacement. Remember, any jury tiller will be weaker and offer a less than ideal position for maximum leverage.

TOWING

If you are the vessel to be towed:

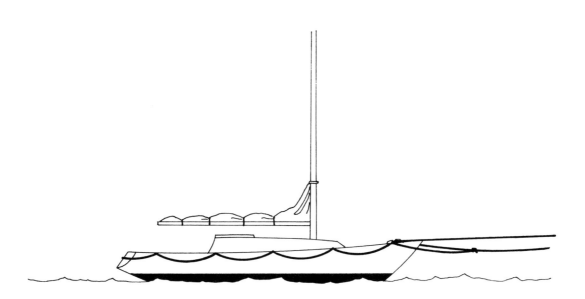

Another good idea is to carry a second line completely around the hull to act as a safety line, should the primary towing line break Depending on the seas running, and the size of your boat, you'll need at least 200-300 feet of 3/4-inch nylon.

1. Drop sails and secure.
2. Position one crew member at the helm.
3. Secure bitter end of hawser to strong point on deck (see below).
4. When towing boat approaches from leeward side. heave hawser to her waiting crew.
5. Instruct towing vessel as to your maximum speed and allow her to proceed, stationing a crew member forward to pass signals.

If you are towing a vessel:

1. Approach the vessel to be towed from her leeward side.
2. When crossing her bows, either pass or accept towing hawser.
3. Try to fasten the towline to strong points forward of the rudder-post to aid in maneuverability.
4. Proceed ahead slowly, handing out the towline until taut.
5. Position one crew member aft to see that line remains taut (to avoid fouling your prop) and to accept hand signals from the disabled boat.

Towing under sail:

1. Pass the disabled vessel's bows from leeward.
2. Heave towline as you pass her bows.
3. Head off on a reach or run.

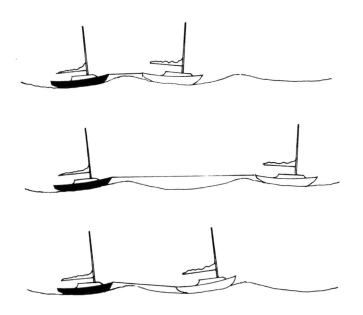

The towline must be watched and adjusted so the two boats are in sync with one another, depending on the length and height of the seas running at the time. In a steady breeze, boats can be towed under much-reduced sail.

Dropping sail is obviously not applicable in a powerboat. However, if there is a sea running, a very small steadying sail aft may make steering easier for the towed boat and maneuverability greater for the towboat. Crew should be positioned at the helm, forward and at standby. All must be ready for immediate action, especially as might concern recovery of the towline.

Many contemporary boats do not have adequate foredeck cleats. A towing hawser handed by a commercial vessel will be quite large, and even if the cleats were enormous, very likely they would only be through-bolted to a backing pad. Decks have been ripped up. The ideal foredeck attachment point will be a samson post properly locked into the keel or stem. Lacking this, it is perhaps best to secure the towline around the base of the mast, or, on a powerboat, around the entire house. Alternatively, the towline can be attached to a bridle led around either side of the house to the cockpit winches and then cleated. In any case, it is a good idea to bend a piece of (comparatively) light stuff to the hawser and tie its bitter end to a deck cleat; the bend to the hawser should be forward of the stemhead. In case the towline slips or chafes through at the stem, this "safety" line will make it that much easier to retrieve it.

Always approach from the leeward side of the disabled vessel. You

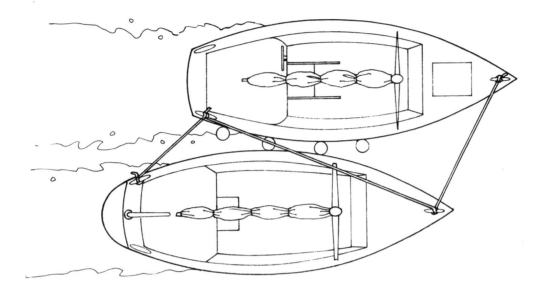

When shore is in sight, bring the disabled boat alongside, as shown. The tow boat should be slightly abaft to maintain control, more easily done pushing than pulling.

will then be able to avoid either drifting down on the vessel or over-shooting it. Whether you should accept a towline or pass over your own is not a clear point of maritime law.

All tows must be undertaken at slow rates of speed. Quite often, commercial ship operators do not fully understand the limits that can be imposed safely upon a yacht under tow. What happens is either the towrope snaps or your foredeck has a good chance of disintegrating. Hand signals are the only way to communicate properly during a tow. These must be arranged prior to the actual commencement of towing, and crew should be stationed on both vessels expressly for the purpose of signaling.

If you are the towing vessel, a bridle, carrying the towrope to either quarter or to the winches, will enable you to maintain a straighter tow and allow for more fluid handling, as well as keeping the rope clear of the propeller. It will prevent your vessel from skewing from side to side and will better distribute the towing strains.

Under sail, tows can be very efficient. They also allow for better communication between vessels, and more precise handling, believe it or not. Since the sails can be trimmed to help steer the boat, there will be less strain on the rudder assembly. Also, there will be little chance of dragging the disabled vessel at imprudent speeds.

Emergencies   **215**

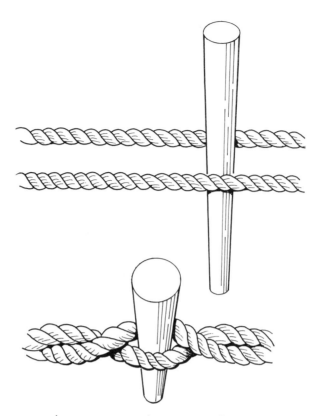

A Spanish windlass is used to tension two lines in parallel or a doubled length of rope. It is most useful for hauling together two parts of a broken fitting or in any other place where something must be temporarily joined.

WATER

Rainwater can be caught in awnings, buckets, from the mainsail, etc. Allow it to run for a few minutes to rinse off any salt adhering to the catchment. Distillation can be carried out using a large pot on the stove with a funnel-like cover secured over it. A tube should run up and over, then down to another container. Wrap the central portion of the tube with rags. As the water boils, pour cold seawater on the rags; this will condense the steam in the tube and leave the crystalized salt in the pot, producing reasonably salt-free water.

Household bleach can be used to purify and make palatable drinking water that may be tainted or old. Use 2 drops per quart or liter of clear water, double if the water is cloudy. Iodine (2%) can be used instead in the ration of 5 drops per quart or liter of clear water, double if the water is cloudy. Let stand for an hour before using and aerate by pouring back and forth between containers.

The Bosun's Locker

Everything for repairs, painting, spares and emergencies collectively can be called the bosun's locker. One should plan this equipment with reference to the size of the boat, stowage space aboard, type of voyaging expected and cost. Obviously, if you are planning a voyage to the South Seas of three years' duration, what you must plan for and carry with you is likely to be vastly more and different than if you take a two-week coastal cruise every summer. Unfortunately, many seamen stock up on everything—at great cost and with little forethought—without taking into account what it's all for!

The need for specific items depends on your boat's construction, size, engine, rig and type. A large powerboat will not need spare shrouds for a long passage, obviously, but it will pay to take a spare propeller and shaft, especially in out-of-the-way spots. Also, one would need tools or means to pull the prop with the boat careened or beached at low water. Likewise, 4 gallons of bottom paint make sense carried along on a year's cruise. There's no need for any paint aboard the weekend boat. Following are several lists of spares and tools to be kept aboard different-size yachts. None are to be taken as gospel, as each of us has different needs and aims.

FOR BOATS UNDER 30 FEET (9 METERS)

Tools
8" (20 cm) adjustable wrench
medium-size pliers
medium-blade screwdriver
10" (25 cm) vise grips
pocket rigging knife with spike
waterproof pouch to carry tools

Sail repair kit
scissors

sailmaker's wax
palm
seam ripper
hot knife
3 spools waxed polyester thread
assorted needles
1 roll ripstop tape
3'x3' (1x1 meter) piece of adhesive, sticky-backed
    Dacron/Terylene
light thread for spinnaker repair
telltale yarn
waterproof ditty bag

Spare parts
assorted stainless steel nuts, bolts, washers, sheet metal screws
bulbs for compass and running lights
winch pawls and springs
cam cleat springs
assorted cotter pins and split rings
clear, compartmented box to hold all

Miscellaneous
1 roll duct tape
tube of clear silicone seal
1 spray can penetrating oil
small can general-purpose lubricating oil
can of Teflon spray lubricant
indelible marking pen

FOR BOATS FROM 30-45 FEET (9-14 METERS)

Tools
Allen wrenches
chisels (1 cold chisel)
hand drill plus set of bits
files (8" or 20 cm mill bastard, 1 medium rattail, 1 triangular)
medium ballpeen hammer
50' (15 meters) measuring tape
nail set
oil stone
pliers (10" or 25 cm channel lock, needle nose, regular)
hacksaw with extra high-speed blades
6 assorted-size regular screwdrivers
2 Phillips screwdrivers
1 set jeweler's screwdrivers
vise grips (7" and 10" or 18 and 25 cm)

wire brush
wire cutters
work gloves
wrenches (8" and 10" or 20 and 25 cm adjustable, set of
  combination–open end and box)
toolbox

Electrical parts
spare bulbs for each light aboard
3 each spare fuses for each type aboard
assorted wire crimps
wire strippers/crimpers
flashlight (torch) batteries and bulbs
continuity tester
black electrician's tape

Engine and mechanical spares
3 cans oil for hydraulics
hydraulic hose and assorted end fittings
transmission fluid
set of engine filters
assorted grits wet/dry sandpaper
complete set of engine belts
one complete oil change
new voltage regulator for each alternator
6'x6' (2x2 meters) canvas drop cloth with grommets
length of 2x4 lumber
section of marine grade sheet plywood
assorted stainless steel hose clamps
drift punch
spare water pump impeller

Spares
assorted nuts, bolts and washers
assorted cotter pins
assorted clevis pins
assorted D-shackles
assorted snap shackles
1 spare turnbuckle with toggle
1 genoa car
winch pawls
winch pawl springs
winch roller bearings
spare winch handle

A buntline hitch will hold fittings more securely than a bowline, but must be snugged-up tightly. Use it when you want to encircle something tightly around.

Sail repair kit
scissors
sailmaker's wax
2 palms
2 seam rippers
hot knife
light thread for spinnaker repairs
6 spools waxed polyester thread
assorted needles
ripstop tape
3'x6' (1x2 meters) piece of sticky-backed Dacron/Terylene
yarn for telltales
25' (8 meters) stainless-steel or monel seizing wire
3 D-rings
sailmaker's pliers
ditty bag

Sealants and lubricants
2-part epoxy
2 tubes clear silicone sealant
2 cans spray penetrating oil
1 can general-purpose lubricating oil

1 can Teflon spray lubricant
2 rolls duct tape
silicone or lanolin grease
indelible ink markers
1 spray can seize preventative

FOR YACHTS 45 FEET (14 METERS) AND LARGER

Tools
Allen wrenches (long and short)
awls (small and large)
block plane
chisels (1 cold, 2 wood)
hand drill with set bits
variable-speed rechargeable electric drill with set bits
files (8", 10", 12" or 20, 25, 30 cm mill bastards, 3 wood files,
    2 rattails, 1 triangular)
hammers (16-oz. or 500-gram ballpeen, baby sledge, claw,
    rubber mallet)
measures (100' or 30 meters tape, fold-up rule, calipers)
mirror (1 retrieving)
nail sets (5 assorted)
oil stone
pipe cutter
pipe, 18" or 1/2 meter (as battering ram and as Spanish windlass)
pliers (2 channel lock, 2 needle nose, 4 regular in assorted sizes)
2 putty knives (1" or 2.5 cm)
saws (crosscut, hacksaw and 40 blades, jigsaw and 12 blades)
screwdrivers (17 assorted regular, 6 assorted Phillips, 2 offset,
    1 jeweler's set)
tap and die set (sized to your needs)
tin snips
propane torch with varying tips
vise
vise grips in assorted sizes
wire brushes (steel and brass)
wire cutters
work gloves (leather palms)
wrenches (6", 8", 10" or 15, 20, 25 cm adjustables, 14" or 36 cm pipe
    wrench, strap wrench, complete 3/8" or 1 cm drive socket wrench
    set, set combination wrenches, set open-ended wrenches)
X-Acto knife and 6 blades
tool box

Electrical parts
compass-light assembly

palm-and-needle whipping

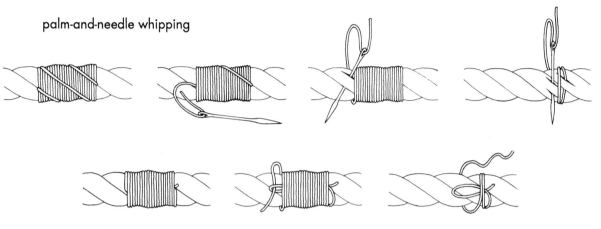

common whipping

All line ends should be tightly whipped to prevent unravelling.

running-light bulbs
spare bulbs for each lamp aboard
3 of each type of fuse aboard
assorted wire crimps
wire strippers-crimpers
flashlight (torch) batteries and bulbs
assorted lengths and gauges electrical wire
black electrician's tape
silicone grease
multimeter
solder
soldering gun or iron (12-volt or flame heating)
spare anemometer cups
spare wind vane
spare knotmeter transducer
storage box

Sealants and lubricants
2-part epoxy
2 tubes clear silicone sealant
2 cans spray penetrating oil

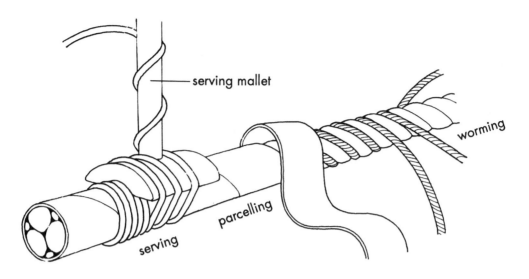

serving mallet

worming

parcelling

serving

For best chafe protection, especially in terminating rigging, worm and parcel with the lay of the line, then turn the line end-to-end and serve.

2 cans spray silicone lubricant
2 cans multipurpose lubricating oil
2 rolls duct tape
2 indelible ink markers
silicone or lanolin grease
2 cans antiseizing spray

Sail repair kit
scissors
sailmaker's wax
2 palms
2 seam rippers
hot knife with spare tip
light thread for spinnaker repairs
8 spools waxed polyester thread
assorted needles
2 rolls ripstop tape
2 pieces 3'x6' (1x2 meters) sticky-backed Dacron/Terylene
    yarn for telltales
2 weights seizing wire (25' or 8 meters each)
3 D-rings

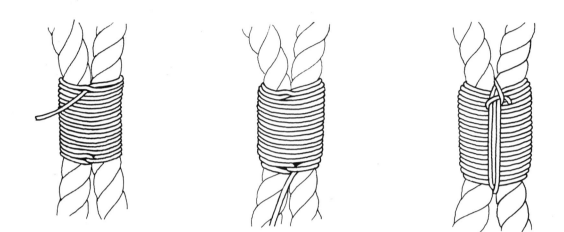

Round seizing is used to join to lines or make a bight in a line.

3 O-rings
50' (15 meters) tubular webbing
sailmaker's pliers
assorted weight sailcloth
roll 5 oz. Dacron tape, 6" (15 cm) wide
spool of light stuff for flag halyards, etc.
6 awls
grommet set (stainless steel or brass)
ditty bag

Rigging parts
Nicopress (Talurit) tool (sized to halyards and shrouds,
   2 preferably)
12 Nicopress (Talurit) sleeves for each size wire aboard
assorted stainless steel thimbles
assorted snap shackles
assorted D shackles
assorted stainless steel wire in 36" (1 meter) lengths
spare turnbuckles and toggles
assorted clevis pins
assorted track cars

link plate set
spare main halyard
spare jib halyard
one length stainless steel wire 2' longer than longest stay or
   shroud

Engine and mechanical spares
1 gallon (2.5 liters) oil for hydraulics
10' (3 meters) length hydraulic hose with fittings
2 cans transmission fluid
oil for engine oil change
set engine filters, gaskets
complete set engine belts
voltage regulator for each alternator
6'x6' (2x2 meters) canvas drop cloth with grommets
assorted stainless steel hose clamps
section of marine grade sheet plywood
2-3' (1 meter) lengths 2x4s
drift punch
set of injectors
grease gun with lithium grease
2 cans starting spray
keel-bolt wrench
rudder-packing wrench
spare impellers for engine pumps (4)
spare set steering cables
master links (12) for steering chain

Spares
assorted cotter pins
assorted nuts, bolts, washers
head repair kit: pump parts, diaphragms, etc.
hand pump for oil changes
high volume bilge pump mounted on board
electric drill pump with hoses
bronze wool
assorted wet/dry sandpaper
assorted crocus cloth and emery paper
spare packing for propeller and rudder glands
winch spares: pawls, pawl springs, assorted roller bearings, split rings,
   toothbrush, tweezers, dental pick, extra handles

Optional
banding tool, bands, clips
spare propeller and shaft
300' (100 meters) nylon line equal to heaviest line aboard

assorted softwood plugs sized to all through hulls

Needless to say, putting everything on a small boat would quickly lead to foundering. Nevertheless, you should have on board all the basics needed to make those repairs which are vital to the voyage you are undertaking.

OTHER BOSUNRY

In addition to the tools and spares above you should have other spare supplies on hand, logged in and replaced when necessary.

Paints

For the average yachtsman, this is a once-per-season job and paint need not be carried aboard. However, if you are planning any long voyage, the bare minimum would be enough bottom paint for a complete recoating. If you have a wood boat, paint for the hull and deck, along with sandpaper, brushes, solvents, scrapers, etc.

Adhesives

A tube of silicone sealant, a package of 2-part underwater epoxy, a small can of 2-part patching compound, a tube of all-purpose cement.

Rope

At least 100 feet (30 meters) of the heaviest line used aboard, spare halyard, extra dock lines, extra anchor rode (nylon), assorted small stuff for sail ties, lashings, etc.

Miscellaneous

Rigging knife, extra flashlights, spare batteries for every piece of equipment aboard, anchor light, stove fuel, spare engine oil, emergency flares, etc.

International Regulations for Preventing Collisions at Sea

No one expects you to memorize these rules, but for your own sake, liability and safety-in-general, you should be familiar with the basic premises stated herein. Since the entire point of them is to avoid collision at sea, any prudent yachtsman would be advised to read them with an eye for rights of way, lights and shapes and conduct in approach situations.

1972, WITH AMENDMENTS ADOPTED IN 1983

PART A. GENERAL

RULE 1

Application

(*a*) These Rules shall apply to all vessels upon the high seas and in all waters connected therewith navigable by seagoing vessels.

(*b*) Nothing in these Rules shall interfere with the operation of special rules made by an appropriate authority for roadsteads, harbours, rivers, lakes or inland waterways connected with the high seas and navigable by seagoing vessels. Such special rules shall conform as closely as possible to these Rules.

(*c*) Nothing in these Rules shall interfere with the operation of any special rules made by the Government of any State with respect to additional station or signal lights, shapes or whistle signals for ships of war and vessels proceeding under convoy, or with respect to additional station or signal lights or shapes for fishing vessels engaged in fishing as a fleet. These additional station or signal lights, shapes or whistle signals shall, so far as possible, be such that they cannot be mistaken for any light, shape or signal authorized elsewhere under these Rules.

(*d*) Traffic separation schemes may be adopted by the Organization for the purpose of these Rules.

(*e*) Whenever the Government concerned shall have determined that a vessel of special construction or purpose cannot comply fully with the provisions of any of these Rules with respect to the number, position, range or arc of visibility of lights or shapes, as well as to the disposition and characteristics of sound-signalling appliances, without interfering with the special function of the vessel, such vessel shall comply with such other provisions in regard to the number, position, range or arc of visibility of lights or shapes, as well as to the disposition and characteristics of sound-signalling appliances, as her Government shall have determined to be the closest possible compliance with these Rules in respect to that vessel.

RULE 2

Responsibility

(*a*) Nothing in these Rules shall exonerate any vessel, or the owner, master or crew thereof, from the consequences of any neglect to comply with these Rules or of the neglect of any precaution which may be required by the ordinary practice of seamen, or by the special circumstances of the case.

(*b*) In construing and complying with these Rules due regard shall be had to all dangers of navigation and collision and to any special circumstances, including the limitations of the vessels involved, which may make a departure from these Rules necessary to avoid immediate danger.

RULE 3

General definitions

For the purpose of these Rules, except where the context otherwise requires:

(*a*) The word "vessel" includes every description of water craft, including non-displacement craft and seaplanes, used or capable of being used as a means of transportation on water.

(*b*) The term "power-driven vessel" means any vessel propelled by machinery.

(c) The term "sailing vessel" means any vessel under sail provided that propelling machinery, if fitted, is not being used.

(d) The term "vessel engaged in fishing" means any vessel fishing with nets, lines, trawls or other fishing apparatus which restrict manoeuvrability, but does not include a vessel fishing with trolling lines or other fishing apparatus which do not restrict manoeuvrability.

(e) The word "seaplane" includes any aircraft designed to manoeuvre on the water.

(f) The term "vessel not under command" means a vessel which through some exceptional circumstance is unable to manoeuvre as required by these Rules and is therefore unable to keep out of the way of another vessel.

(g) The term "vessel restricted in her ability to manoeuvre" means a vessel which from the nature of her work is restricted in her ability to manoeuvre as required by these Rules and is therefore unable to keep out of the way of another vessel.

The term 'vessels restricted in their ability to manoeuvre' shall include but not be limited to:
(i) a vessel engaged in laying, servicing or picking up a navigation mark, submarine cable or pipeline;

(ii) a vessel engaged in dredging, surveying or underwater operations;

(iii) a vessel engaged in replenishment or transferring persons, provisions or cargo while underway;

(iv) a vessel engaged in the launching or recovery of aircraft;

(v) a vessel engaged in mine clearance operations;

(vi) a vessel engaged in a towing operation such as severely restricts the towing vessel and her tow in their ability to deviate from their course.

(h) The term "vessel constrained by her draught" means a power-driven vessel which because of her draught in relation to the available depth of water is severely restricted in her ability to deviate from the course she is following.

(i) The word "underway" means that a vessel is not at anchor, or made fast to the shore, or aground.

(*j*) The words "length" and "breadth" of a vessel mean her length overall and greatest breadth.

(*k*) Vessels shall be deemed to be in sight of one another when one can be observed visually from the other.

(*l*) The term "restricted visibility" means any condition in which visibility is restricted by fog, mist, falling snow, heavy rainstorms, sandstorms or any other similar causes.

PART B. STEERING AND SAILING RULES

Section I. Conduct of vessels in any condition of visibility

RULE 4

Application

Rules in this Section apply in any condition of visibility.

RULE 5

Look-out

Every vessel shall at all times maintain a proper look-out by sight and hearing as well as by all available means appropriate in the prevailing circumstances and conditions so as to make a full appraisal of the situation and of the risk of collision.

RULE 6

Safe speed

Every vessel shall at all times proceed at a safe speed so that she can take proper and effective action to avoid collision and be stopped within a distance appropriate to the prevailing circumstances and conditions.

In determining a safe speed the following factors shall be among those taken into account:

(*a*) By all vessels:

(i) the state of visibility;

(ii) the traffic density including concentrations of fishing vessels or any other vessels;

(iii) the manoeuvrability of the vessel with special reference to stopping distance and turning ability in the prevailing conditions;

(iv) at night the presence of background light such as from shore lights or from back scatter of her own lights;

(v) the state of wind, sea and current, and the proximity of navigational hazards;

(vi) the draught in relation to the available depth of water.

(b) Additionally, by vessels with operational radar:

(i) the characteristics, efficiency and limitations of the radar equipment;

(ii) any constraints imposed by the radar range scale in use;

(iii) the effect on radar detection of the sea state, weather and other sources of interference;

(iv) the possibility that small vessels, ice and other floating objects may not be detected by radar at an adequate range;

(v) the number, location and movement of vessels detected by radar;

(vi) the more exact assessment of the visibility that may be possible when radar is used to determine the range of vessels or other objects in the vicinity.

RULE 7

Risk of collision

(a) Every vessel shall use all available means appropriate to the prevailing circumstances and conditions to determine if risk or collision exists. If there is any doubt such risk shall be deemed to exist.

(b) Proper use shall be made of radar equipment if fitted and operational, including long-range scanning to obtain early warning of risk of collision and radar plotting or equivalent systematic observation of detected objects.

(*c*) Assumptions shall not be made on the basis of scanty information, especially scanty radar information.

(*d*) In determining if risk of collision exists the following considerations shall be among those taken into account:

(i) such risk shall be deemed to exist if the compass bearing of an approaching vessel does not appreciably change;

(ii) such risk may sometimes exist even when an appreciable bearing change is evident, particularly when approaching a very large vessel or a tow or when approaching a vessel at close range.

RULE 8

Action to avoid collision

(*a*) Any action taken to avoid collision shall, if the circumstances of the case admit, be positive, made in ample time and with due regard to the observance of good seamanship.

(*b*) Any alteration or course and/or speed to avoid collision shall, if the circumstances of the case admit, be large enough to be readily apparent to another vessel observing visually or by radar; a succession of small alterations of course and/or speed should be avoided.

(*c*) If there is sufficient sea room, alteration of course alone may be the most effective action to avoid a close-quarters situation provided that it is made in good time, is substantial and does not result in another close-quarters situation.

(*d*) Action taken to avoid collision with another vessel shall be such as to result in passing at a safe distance. The effectiveness of the action shall be carefully checked until the other vessel is finally past and clear.

(*e*) If necessary to avoid collision or allow more time to assess the situation, a vessel shall slacken her speed or take all way off by stopping or reversing her means of propulsion.

RULE 9

Narrow channels

(*a*) A vessel proceeding along the course of a narrow channel or fairway shall keep as near to the outer limit of the channel or fairway which lies on her starboard side as is safe and practicable.

(*b*) A vessel of less than 20 metres in length or a sailing vessel shall not impede the passage of a vessel which can safely navigate only within a narrow channel or fairway.

(*c*) A vessel engaged in fishing shall not impede the passage of any other vessel navigating within a narrow channel or fairway.

(*d*) A vessel shall not corss a narrow channel or fairway if such crossing impedes the passage of a vessel which can safely navigate only within such channel or fairway. The latter vessel may use the sound signal prescribed in Rule 34 (*d*) if in doubt as to the intention of the crossing vessel.

(*e*)
   (i) In a narrow channel or fairway when overtaking can take place only if the vessel to be overtaken has to take action to permit safe passing, the vessel intending to overtake shall indicate her intention by sounding the appropriate signal prescribed in Rule 34 (*c*) (i). The vessel to be overtaken shall, if in agreement, sound the appropriate signal prescribed in Rule 34 (*c*) (ii) and take steps to permit safe passing. If in doubt she may sound the signals prescribed in Rule 34 (*d*).
   (ii) This Rule does not relieve the overtaking vessel of her obligation under Rule 13.

(*f*) A vessel nearing a bend or an area of a narrow channel or fairway where other vessels may be obscured by an intervening obstruction shall navigate with particular alertness and caution and shall sound the appropriate signal prescribed in Rule 34 (*e*).
   (*g*) Any vessel shall, if the circumstances of the case admit, avoid anchoring in a narrow channel.

RULE 10

Traffic separation schemes

(*a*) This Rule applies to traffic separation schemes adopted by the Organization:

(*b*) A vessel using a traffic separation scheme shall:

   (i) proceed in the appropriate traffic lane in the general direction of traffic flow for that lane;

(ii) so far as practicable keep clear of a traffic separation line or separation zone;

(iii) normally join or leave a traffic lane at the termination of the lane, but when joining or leaving from either side shall do so at as small an angle to the general direction of traffic flow as practicable.

(*c*) A vessel shall so far as practicable avoid crossing traffic lanes, but if obliged to do so shall cross as nearly as practicable at right angles to the general direction of traffic flow.

(*d*) Inshore traffic zones shall not normally be used by through traffic which can safely use the appropriate traffic lane within the adjacent traffic separation scheme. However, vessels of less than 20 metres in length and sailing vessels may under all circumstances use inshore traffic zones.

(*e*) A vessel other than a crossing vessel or a vessel joining or leaving a lane shall not normally enter a separation zone or cross a separation line except:

(i) in cases of emergency to avoid immediate danger;

(ii) to engage in fishing within a separation zone;

(*f*) A vessel navigating in areas near the terminations of traffic separation schemes shall do so with particular caution.

(*g*) A vessel shall so far as practicable avoid anchoring in a traffic separation scheme or in areas near its terminations.

(*h*) A vessel not using a traffic separation scheme shall avoid it by as wide a margin as practicable.

(*i*) A vessel engaged in fishing shall not impede the passage of any vessel following a traffic lane.

(*j*) A vessel of less than 20 metres in length or a sailing vessel shall not impede the safe passage of a power-driven vessel following a traffic lane.

(*k*) A vessel restricted in her ability to manoeuvre when engaged in an operation for the maintenance of safety of navigation in a traffic separation scheme is exempted from complying with this Rule to the extent necessary to carry out the operation.

(*l*) A vessel restricted in her ability to manoeuvre when engaged in an operation for the laying, servicing or picking up of a submarine cable, within a traffic separation scheme, is exempted from complying with this Rule to the extent necessary to carry out the operation.

Section II. Conduct of vessels in sight of one another

RULE 11

Application

Rules in this Section apply to vessels in sight of one another.

RULE 12

Sailing vessels

(*a*) When two sailing vessels are approaching one another, so as to involve risk of collision, one of them shall keep out of the way of the other as follows:

(i) when each has the wind on a different side, the vessel which has the wind on the port side shall keep out of the way of the other;

(ii) when both have the wind on the same side, the vessel which is to windward shall keep out of the way of the vessel which is leeward;

(iii) if a vessel with the wind on the port side sees a vessel to windward and cannot determine with certainty whether the other vessel has the wind on the port or on the starboard side, she shall keep out of the way of the other.

(b) For the purposes of this Rule the windward side shall be deemed to be the side opposite to that on which the mainsail is carried or, in the case of a square-rigged vessel, the side opposite to that on which the largest fore-and-aft sail is carried.

RULE 13

Overtaking

(*a*) Notwithstanding anything contained in the Rules of Part B, Sections I and II any vessel overtaking any other shall keep out of the way of the vessel being overtaken.

International Regulations for Preventing Collisions at Sea   235 (*b*) A vessel shall be deemed to be overtaking when coming up with another vessel from a direction more than 22.5 degrees abaft her beam, that is, in such a position with reference to the vessel she is overtaking, that at night she would be able to see only the sternlight of that vessel but neither of her sidelights.

(*c*) When a vessel is in any doubt as to whether she is overtaking another, she shall assume that this is the case and act accordingly.

(*d*) Any subsequent alteration of the bearing between the two vessels shall not make the overtaking vessel a crossing vessel within the meaning of these Rules or relieve her of the duty of keeping clear of the overtaken vessel until she is finally past and clear.

RULE 14

Head-on situation

(*a*) When two power-driven vessels are meeting on reciprocal or nearly reciprocal courses so as to involve risk of collisions each shall alter her course to starboard so that each shall pass on the port side of the other.

(*b*) Such a situation shall be deemed to exist when a vessel sees the other ahead or nearly ahead and by night she could see the masthead lights of the other in a line or nearly in a line and/or both sidelights and by day she observes the corresponding aspect of the other vessel.

(*c*) When a vessel is in any doubt as to whether such a situation exists she shall assume that it does exist and act accordingly.

RULE 15

Crossing situation

When two power-driven vessels are crossing so as to involve risk of collision, the vessel which has the other on her own starboard side shall keep out of the way and shall, if the circumstances of the case admit, avoid crossing ahead of the other vessel.

RULE 16

Action by give-way vessel

Every vessel which is directed to keep out of the way of another vessel shall, so far as possible, take early and substantial action to keep well clear.

RULE 17

Action by stand-on vessel

(*a*)

(i) Where one of two vessels is to keep out of the way the other shall keep her course and speed.

(ii) The latter vessel may however take action to avoid collision by her manoeuvre alone, as soon as it becomes apparent to her that the vessel required to keep out of the way is not taking appropriate action in compliance with these Rules.

(*b*) When, from any cause, the vessel required to keep her course and speed finds herself so close that collision cannot be avoided by the action of the give-way vessel alone, she shall take such action as will best aid to avoid collision.

(*c*) A power-driven vessel which takes action in a crossing situation in accordance with sub-paragraph (*a*) (ii) of this Rule to avoid collision with another power-driven vessel shall, if the circumstances of the case admit, not alter course to port for a vessel on her own port side.

(*d*) This Rule does not relieve the give-way vessel of her obligation to keep out of the way.

RULE 18

Responsibilities between vessels

Except where Rules 9, 10 and 13 otherwise require:

(*a*) A power-driven vessel underway shall keep out of the way of:

(i) a vessel not under command;

(ii) a vessel restricted in her ability to manoeuvre;

(iii) a vessel engaged in fishing;

(iv) a sailing vessel.

(*b*) A sailing vessel underway shall keep out of the way of:

(i) a vessel not under command;

(ii) a vessel restricted in her ability to manoeuvre;

(iii) a vessel engaged in fishing.

(*c*) A vessel engaged in fishing when underway shall, so far as possible, keep out of the way of:

(i) a vessel not under command;

(ii) a vessel restricted in her ability to manoeuvre;

(*d*)
(i) Any vessel other than a vessel not under command or a vessel restricted in her ability to manoeuvre shall, if the circumstances of the case admit, avoid impeding the safe passage of a vessel constrained by her draught, exhibiting the signals in Rule 28.

(ii) A vessel constrained by her draught shall navigate with particular caution having full regard to her special condition.

(*e*) A seaplane on the water shall, in general, keep well clear of all vessels and avoid impeding their navigation. In circumstances, however, where risk of collision exists, she shall comply with the Rules of this Part.

Section III. Conduct of vessels in restricted visibility

RULE 19

Conduct of vessels in restricted visibility

(*a*) This Rule applies to vessels not in sight of one another when navigating in or near an area of restricted visibility.

(*b*) Every vessel shall proceed at a safe speed adapted to the prevailing circumstances and conditions of restricted visibility. A power-driven vessel shall have her engines ready for immediate manoeuvre.

(*c*) Every vessel shall have due regard to the prevailing circumstances and conditions of restricted visibility when complying with the Rules of Section I of this Part.

(*d*) A vessel which detects by radar alone the presence of another vessel shall determine if a close-quarters situation is developing and/or risk of collision exists. If so, she shall take avoiding action in ample time, provided that when such action consists of an alteration of course, so far as possible the following shall be avoided:

(i) an alteration of course to port for a vessel forward of the beam, other than for a vessel being overtaken;

(ii) an alteration of course towards a vessel abeam or abaft the beam.

(e) Except where it has been determined that a risk of collision does not exist, every vessel which hears apparently forward of her beam the fog signal of another vessel, or which cannot avoid a close-quarters situation with another vessel forward of her beam, shall reduce her speed to the minimum at which she can be kept on her course. She shall if necessary take all her way off and in any event navigate with extreme caution until danger of collision is over.

PART C. LIGHTS AND SHAPES

RULE 20

Application

(a) Rules in this Part shall be complied with in all weathers.

(b) The Rules concerning lights shall be complied with from sunset to sunrise, and during such times no other lights shall be exhibited, except such lights as cannot be mistaken for lights specified in these Rules or do not impair their visibility or distinctive character, or interfere with the keeping of a proper look-out.

(c) The lights prescribed by these Rules shall, if carried, also be exhibited from sunrise to sunset in restricted visibility and may be exhibited in all other circumstances when it is deemed necessary.

(d) The Rules concerning shapes shall be complied with by day.

(e) The lights and shapes specified in these Rules shall comply with the provisions of Annex I to these Regulations.

RULE 21

Definitions

(a) "Masthead light" means a white light placed over the fore and aft centreline of the vessel showing an unbroken light over an arc of the horizon of 225 degrees and so fixed as to show the light from right ahead to 22.5 degrees abaft the beam on either side of the vessel.

(b) "Sidelights" means a green light on the starboard side and a red light on the port side each showing an unbroken light over an arc of the horizon of 112.5 degrees and so fixed as to show the light from right ahead to 22.5 degrees abaft the beam on its respective side. In a vessel of less than 20 metres in length the sidelights may be combined in one lantern carried on the fore and aft centreline of the vessel.

(c) "Sternlight" means a white light places as nearly as practicable at the stern showing an unbroken light over an arc of the horizon of 135 degrees and so fixed as to show the light 67.5 degrees from right aft on each side of the vessel.

(d) "Towing light" means a yellow light having the same characteristics as the "sternlight" defined in paragraph (c) of this Rule.

(e) "All round light" means a light showing an unbroken light over an arc of the horizon of 360 degrees.

(f) "Flashing light" means a light flashing at regular intervals at a frequence of 120 flashes or more per minute.

RULE 22

Visibility of lights

The lights prescribed in these Rules shall have an intensity as specified in Section 8 of Annex I to these Regulations so as to be visible at the following minimum ranges:

(a) In vessels of 50 metres or more in length:

—a masthead light, 6 miles;

—a sidelight, 3 miles;

—a sternlight, 3 miles;

—a towing light, 3 miles;

—a white, red, green or yellow all-round light, 3 miles.

(b) In vessels of 12 metres or more in length but less than 50 metres in length:

-a masthead light, 5 miles; except that where the length of the vessel is less than 20 metres, 3 miles;

-a sidelight, 2 miles;

-a sternlight, 2 miles;

-a towing light, 2 miles;

-a white, red, green or yellow all-round light, 2 miles.

(c) In vessels of less than 12 metres in length:

-a masthead light, 2 miles;

-a sidelight, 1 mile;

-a sternlight, 2 miles;

-a towing light, 2 miles;

-a white, red, green or yellow all-round light, 2 miles.

(d) In inconspicuous, partly submerged vessel or objects being towed:

-a white all-round light, 3 miles.

RULE 23

Power-driven vessels underway

(a) A power-driven vessel underway shall exhibit:

(i) a masthead light forward;

(ii) a second masthead light abaft of and higher than the forward one; except that a vessel of less than 50 metres in length shall not be obliged to exhibit such light but may do so;

(iii) sidelights;

(iv) a sternlight.

(b) An air-cushion vessel when operating in the non-displacement mode shall, in addition to the lights prescribed in paragraph (a) of this Rule, exhibit an all-round flashing yellow light.

(c)

(i) A power-driven vessel of less than 12 metres in length may in lieu of the lights prescribed in paragraph (a) of this Rule exhibit an all-round white light and sidelights;

(ii) a power-driven vessel of less than 7 metres in length whose maximum speed does not exceed 7 knots may in lieu of the lights prescribed in paragraph (a) of this Rule exhibit an all-round white light and shall, if practicable, also exhibit sidelights;

(iii) the masthead light or all-round white light on a power-driven vessel of less than 12 metres in length may be displaced from the fore and aft centreline of the vessel if centreline fitting is not practicable, provided that the sidelights are combined in one lantern which shall be carried on the fore and aft centreline of the vessel or located as nearly as practicable in the same fore and aft line as the masthead light or the all-round white light.

RULE 24

Towing and pushing

(a) A power-driven vessel when towing shall exhibit:

(i) instead of the light prescribed in Rule 23 (a) (i) or (a)

(ii), two masthead lights in a vertical line. When the length of the tow, measuring from the stern of the towing vessel to the after end of the tow exceeds 200 metres, three such lights in a vertical line;

(ii) sidelights;

(iii) a sternlight;

(iv) a towing light in a vertical line above the sternlight;

(v) when the length of the tow exceeds 200 metres, a diamond shape where it can best be seen.

(b) When a pushing vessel and a vessel being pushed ahead are rigidly connected in a composite unit they shall be regarded as a power-driven vessel and exhibit the lights prescribed in Rule 23.

(*c*) A power-driven vessel when pushing ahead or towing alongside, except in the case of a composite unit shall exhibit:

    (i) instead of the light prescribed in Rule 23 (*a*) (i) or (*a*) (ii), two masthead lights in a vertical line;

    (ii) sidelights;

    (iii) a sternlight.

(*d*) A power-driven vessel to which paragraphs (*a*) or (*c*) of this Rule apply shall also comply with Rule 23 (*a*) (ii).

(*e*) A vessel or object being towed, other than those mentioned in paragraph (*g*) of this Rule, shall exhibit:

    (i) sidelights,

    (ii) a sternlight;

    (iii) when the length of the tow exceeds 200 metres, a diamond shape where it can best be seen.

(*f*) Provided that any number of vessels being towed alongside or pushed in a group shall be lighted as one vessel,

    (i) a vessel being pushed ahead, not being part of a composite unit, shall exhibit at the forward end, sidelights;

    (ii) a vessel being towed alongside shall exhibit a sternlight and at the forward end, sidelights.

(*g*) An inconspicuous, partly submerged vessel or object, or combination of such vessels or objects being towed, shall exhibit:

    (i) if it less than 25 metres in breadth, one all-round white light at or near the forward end and one at or near the after end except that dracones need not exhibit a light at or near the forward end.

    (ii) if it is 25 metres or more in breadth, two additional all-round white lights at or near the extremities of its breadth;

    (iii) if it exceeds 100 metres in length, additional all-round white lights between the lights prescribed in sub-paragraphs (i) and (ii) so that the distance between the lights shall not exceed 100 metres;

(iv) a diamond shape at or near the aftermost extremity of the last vessel or object being towed and if the length of the tow exceeds 200 metres as additional diamond shape where it can best be seen and located as far forward as is practicable.

(*h*) Where from any sufficient cause it is impracticable for a vessel or object being towed to exhibit the lights of shapes prescribed in paragraph (*e*) or (*g*) of this Rule, all possible measures shall be taken to light the vessel or object towed or at least to indicate the presence of such vessel or object.

(*i*) Where from any sufficient cause it is impracticable for a vessel not normally engaged in towing operations to display the lights prescribed in paragraph (*a*) or (*c*) of this Rule, such vessel shall not be required to exhibit those lights when engaged in towing another vessel in distress or otherwise in need of assistance. All possible measures shall be taken to indicate the nature of the relationship between the towing vessel and the vessel being towed as authorized by Rule 36, in particular by illuminating the towline.

RULE 25

Sailing vessels underway and vessels under oars

(*a*) A sailing vessel under shall exhibit:

(i) sidelights;

(ii) a sternlight.

(*b*) In a sailing vessel of less than 20 metres in length the lights prescribed in paragraph (*a*) of this Rule may be combined in one lantern carried at or near the top of the mast where it can best be seen.

(*c*) A sailing vessel underway may, in addition to the lights prescribed in paragraph (*a*) of this Rule, exhibit at or near the top of the mast, where they can best be seen, two all-round lights in a vertical line, the upper being red and the lower green, but these lights shall not be exhibited in conjunction with the combined lantern permitted by paragraph (*b*) of this Rule.

(*d*)
(i) A sailing vessel of less than 7 metres in length shall, if practicable, exhibit the lights prescribed in paragraph (*a*) or (*b*) of this Rule, but if she does not, she shall have ready at hand an electric torch or lighted lantern showing a white light which shall be ex-

hibited in sufficient time to prevent collision.

(ii) A vessel under oars may exhibit the lights prescribed in this Rule for sailing vessels, but if she does not, she shall have ready at hand an electric torch or lighted lantern showing a white light which shall be exhibited in sufficient time to prevent collision.

(e) A vessel proceeding under sail when also being propelled by machinery shall exhibit forward where it can best be seen a conical shape, apex downwards.

RULE 26

Fishing Vessels

(a) A vessel engaged in fishing, whether underway or at anchor, shall exhibit only the lights and shapes prescribed in this Rule.

(b) A vessel when engaged in trawling, by which is meant the dragging through the water of a dredge net or other apparatus used as a fishing appliance, shall exhibit:

(i) two all-round lights in a vertical line, the upper being green and the lower white, or a shape consisting of two cones with their apexes together in a vertical line one above the other; a vessel of less than 20 metres in length may instead of this shape exhibit a basket;

(ii) a masthead light abaft of and higher than the all-round green light; a vessel of less than 50 metres in length shall not be obliged to exhibit such a light but may do so;

(iii) when making way through the water, in addition to the lights prescribed in this paragraph, sidelights and a sternlight.

(c) A vessel engaged in fishing, other than trawling, shall exhibit:

(i) two all-round lights in a vertical line, the upper being red and the lower white, or a shape consisting of two cones with apexes together in a vertical line one above the other; a vessel of less than 20 metres in length may instead of this shape exhibit a basket;

(ii) when there is outlying gear extending more than 150 metres horizontally from the vessel, an all-round white light or a cone apex upwards in the direction of the gear;

(iii) when making way through the water, in addition to the lights prescribed in this paragraph, sidelights and a sternlight.

(*d*) A vessel engaged in fishing in close proximity to other vessels engaged in fishing may exhibit the additional signals described in Annex II to these Regulations.

(*e*) A vessel when not engaged in fishing shall not exhibit the lights or shapes prescribed in this Rule, but only those prescribed for a vessel of her length.

RULE 27

Vessels not under command or restricted in their ability to manoeuvre

(*a*) A vessel not under command shall exhibit:

(i) two all-round red lights in a vertical line where they can best be seen;

(ii) two balls or similar shapes in a vertical line where they can best be seen;

(iii) when making way through the water, in addition to the lights prescribed in this paragraph, sidelights and a sternlight.

(*b*) A vessel restricted in her ability to manoeuvre, except a vessel engaged in mine clearance operations, shall exhibit:

(i) three all-round lights in a vertical line where they can best be seen. The highest and lowest of these lights shall be red and the middle light shall be white;

(ii) three shapes in a vertical line where they can best be seen. The highest and lowest of these shapes shall be balls and the middle one a diamond.

(iii) when making way through the water, a masthead light or lights, sidelights and a sternlight, in addition to the lights prescribed in sub-paragraph (i);

(iv) when at anchor, in addition to the lights or shapes prescribed in sub-paragraphs (i) and (ii), the light, lights or shape prescribed in Rule 30.

(*c*) A power-driven vessel engaged in a towing operation such as severely restricts the towing vessel and her tow in their ability to deviate from their course shall, in addition to the lights or shapes prescribed in Rule 24 (*a*), exhibit the lights or shapes prescribed in sub-paragraphs (*b*) (i) and (ii) of this Rule.

(*d*) A vessel engaged in dredging or underwater operations, when restricted in her ability to manoeuvre, shall exhibit the lights and shapes prescribed in sub-paragraph (*b*) (i), (ii) and (iii) of this Rule and shall in addition when an obstruction exists, exhibit:

(i) two all-round red lights or two balls in a vertical line to indicate the side on which the obstruction exists;

(ii) two all-round green lights or two diamonds in a vertical line to indicate the side on which another vessel may pass;

(iii) when at anchor the lights or shapes prescribed in this paragraph instead of the lights or shape prescribed in Rule 30.

(*e*) Whenever the size of a vessel engaged in diving operations makes it impracticable to exhibit all lights and shapes prescribed in paragraph (*d*) of this Rule, the following shall be exhibited:

(i) three all-round lights in a vertical line where they can best be seen. The highest and lowest of these lights shall be red and the middle light shall be white;

(ii) a rigid replica of the International Code Flag "A" not less than 1 metre in height. Measures shall be taken to ensure its all-round visibility.

(*f*) A vessel engaged in mine clearance operations shall in addition to the lights prescribed for a power-driven vessel in Rule 23 or to the lights or shape prescribed for a vessel at anchor in Rule 30 as appropriate, exhibit three all-round green lights or three balls. One of these lights or shapes shall be exhibited near the foremast head and one at each end of the fore yard. These lights or shapes indicate that it is dangerous for another vessel to approach with 1000 metres of the mine clearance vessel.

(*g*) Vessels of less than 12 metres in length, except those engaged in diving operations shall not be required to exhibit the lights and shapes prescribed in this Rule.

(*h*) The signals prescribed in this Rule are not signals of vessels in distress and requiring assistance. Such signals are contained in Annex IV to these Regulations.

RULE 28

Vessels constrained by their draught

A vessel constrained by her draught may, in addition to the lights prescribed for power-driven vessels in Rule 23, exhibit where they can best be seen three all-round red lights in a vertical line, or a cylinder.

RULE 29

Pilot vessels

(a) A vessel engaged on pilotage duty shall exhibit:

(i) at or near the masthead, two all-round lights in a vertical line, the upper being white and the lower red;

(ii) when underway, in addition, sidelights and a sternlight;

(iii) when at anchor, in addition to the lights prescribed in sub-paragraph (i), the light, lights or shape prescribed in Rule 30 for vessels at anchor.

(b) A pilot vessel when not engaged on pilotage duty shall exhibit the lights or shapes prescribed for a similar vessel of her length.

RULE 30

Anchored vessels and vessels aground

(a) A vessel at anchor shall exhibit where it can best be seen:

(i) in the fore part, an all-round white light or one ball;

(ii) at or near the stern and at a lower level than the light prescribed in sub-paragraph (i), an all-round white light.

(b) A vessel of less than 50 metres in length may exhibit an all-round white light were it can best be seen instead of the lights prescribed in paragraph (a) of this Rule.

(c) A vessel at anchor may, and a vessel of 100 metres and more in length shall, also use the available working or equivalent lights to illuminate her decks.

(*d*) A vessel aground shall exhibit the lights prescribed in paragraph (*a*) or (*b*) of this Rule and in addition, where they can best be seen:

(i) two all-round red lights in a vertical line;

(ii) three balls in a vertical line.

(*e*) A vessel of less than 7 metres in length, when at anchor, not in or near a narrow channel, fairway or anchorage, or where other vessels normally navigate, shall not be required to exhibit the lights or shape prescribed in paragraphs (*a*) and (*b*) of this Rule.

(*f*) A vessel of less than 12 metres in length, when aground, shall not be required to exhibit the lights or shapes prescribed in sub-paragraphs (*d*) (i) and (ii) of this Rule.

RULE 31

Seaplanes

Where it is impracticable for a seaplane to exhibit lights and shapes of the characteristics or in the positions prescribed in the Rules of this Part she shall exhibit lights and shapes as closely similar in characteristics and position as is possible.

PART D. SOUND AND LIGHT SIGNALS

RULE 32

Definitions

(*a*) The word "whistle" means any sound signalling appliance capable of producing the prescribed blasts and which complies with the specifications in Annex III to these Regulations.

(*b*) The term "short blast" means a blast of about one second's duration.

(*c*) The term "prolonged blast" means a blast of from four to six seconds' duration.

RULE 33

Equipment for sound signals

(*a*) A vessel of 12 metres or more in length shall be provided with a whistle and a bell and a vessel of 100 metres or more in length shall, in addition , be provided with a gong, the tone and sound of which cannot be confused with that of the bell. The whistle, bell and gong shall comply with the specifications in Annex III to these Regulations. The bell or gong or both may be replaced by other equipment having the same respective sound characteristics, provided that manual sounding of the prescribed signals shall always be possible.

(*b*) A vessel of less than 12 metres in length shall not be obliged to carry the sound signalling appliances prescribed in paragraph (*a*) of this Rule but if she does not, she shall be provided with some other means of making an efficient sound signal.

RULE 34

Manoeuvring and warning signals

(*a*) When vessels are in sight of one another, a power-driven vessel underway, when manoeuvring as authorized or required by these Rules, shall indicate that manoeuvre by the following signals on her whistle:

—one short blast to mean "I am altering my course to starboard";

—two short blasts to mean "I am altering my course to port";

—three short blasts to mean "I am operating astern propulsion".

(*b*) Any vessel may supplement the whistle signals prescribed in paragraph (*a*) of this Rule by light signals, repeated as appropriate, whilst the manoeuvre is being carried out:

(i) these lights signals shall have the following significance:

—one flash to mean "I am altering my course to starboard";

—two flashes to mean "I am altering my course to port";

—three flashes to mean "I am operating astern propulsion".

(ii) the duration of each flash shall be about one second, the interval between flashes shall be about one second, and the interval between successive signals shall not be less than ten seconds;

(iii) the light used for this signal shall, if fitted, be an all-round white light, visible at a minimum range of 5 miles, and shall comply with the provisions of Annex I to these Regulations.

(c) When in sight of one another in a narrow channel or fairway:

(i) a vessel intending to overtake another shall in compliance with Rule 9(e) (i) indicate her intention by the following signals on her whistle:

–two prolonged blasts followed by one short blast to mean "I intend to overtake you on your starboard side";

–two prolonged blasts followed by two short blasts to mean "I intend to overtake you on your port side".

(ii) the vessel about to be overtaken when acting in accordance with Rule 9 (e) (i) shall indicate her agreement by the following signal on her whistle:

–one prolonged, one short, one prolonged and one short blast, in that order.

(d) When vessels in sight of one another are approaching each other and from any cause either vessel fails to understand the intentions or actions of the other, or is in doubt whether sufficient action is being taken by the other to avoid collision, the vessel in doubt shall immediately indicate such doubt by giving at least five short and rapid blasts on the whistle. Such signal may be supplemented by a light signal of at least five short and rapid flashes.

(e) A vessel nearing a bend or an area of a channel or fairway where other vessels may be obscured by an intervening obstruction shall sound one prolonged blast. Such signal shall be answered with a prolonged blast by any approaching vessel that may be within hearing around the bend or behind the intervening obstruction.

(f) If whistles are fitted on a vessel at a distance apart of more than 100 metres, one whistle only shall be used for giving manoeuvring and warning signals.

RULE 35

Sound signals in restricted visibility

In or near an area of restricted visibility, whether by day or night, the signals prescribed in this Rule shall be used as follows:

(*a*) A power-driven vessel making way through the water shall sound at intervals of not more than 2 minutes one prolonged blast.

(*b*) A power-driven vessel underway but stopped and making no way through the water shall sound at intervals of not more than 2 minutes two prolonged blasts in succession with an interval of about 2 seconds between them.

(*c*) A vessel not under command, a vessel restricted in her ability to manoeuvre, a vessel constrained by her draught, a sailing vessel, a vessel engaged in fishing and a vessel engaged in towing or pushing another vessel shall, instead of the signals prescribed in paragraphs (*a*) or (*b*) of this Rule, sound at intervals of not more than 2 minutes three blasts in succession, namely one prolonged followed by two short blasts.

(*d*) A vessel engaged in fishing, when at anchor, and a vessel restricted in her ability to manoeuvre when carrying out her work at anchor, shall instead of the signals prescribed in paragraph (*g*) of this Rule sound the signal prescribed in paragraph (*c*) of this Rule.

(*e*) A vessel towed or if more than one vessel is towed the last vessel of the tow, if manned, shall at intervals of not more than 2 minutes sound four blasts in succession, namely one prolonged followed by three short blasts. When practicable, this signal shall be made immediately after the signal made by the towing vessel.

(*f*) When a pushing vessel and a vessel being pushed ahead are rigidly connected in a composite unit they shall be regarded as a power-driven vessel and shall give the signals prescribed in paragraph (*a*) or (*b*) of this Rule.

(*g*) A vessel at anchor shall at intervals of not more than one minute ring the bell rapidly for about 5 seconds. In a vessel of 100 metres or more in length the bell shall be sounded in the forepart of the vessel and immediately after the ringing of the bell the gong shall be sounded rapidly for about 5 seconds in the after part of the vessel. A vessel at anchor may in addition sound three blasts in succession, namely one short, one prolonged and one short blast, to give warning of her position and of the possibility of collision to an approaching vessel.

(*h*) A vessel aground shall give the bell signal and if required the gong signal prescribed in paragraph (*f*) of this Rule and shall, in addition, give three separate and distinct strokes on the bell immediately before and after the rapid ringing of the bell. A vessel aground may in addition sound an appropriate whistle signal.

(*i*) A vessel of less than 12 metres, in length shall not be obliged to give the above-mentioned signals but, if she does not, shall make some other efficient sound signal at intervals of not more than 2 minutes.

(*j*) A pilot vessel when engaged on pilotage duty may in addition to the signals prescribed in paragraphs (*a*), (*b*) or (*f*) of this Rule sound an identity signal consisting of four short blasts.

RULE 36

Signals to attract attention

In necessary to attract attention of another vessel any vessel may make light or sound signals that cannot be mistaken for any signal authorized elsewhere in these Rules, or may direct the beam of her searchlight in the direction of danger, in such a way as not to embarrass any vessel. Any light to attract the attention of another vessel shall be such that it cannot be mistaken for any aid to navigation. For the purpose of this Rule the use of high intensity intermittent or revolving lights, such as strobe lights, shall be avoided.

RULE 37

Distress signals

When a vessel is in distress and requires assistance she shall use or exhibit the signals described in Annex IV to these Regulations.

PART E. EXEMPTIONS

RULE 38

Exemptions

Any vessel (or class of vessels) provided that she complies with the requirements of the International Regulations for Preventing Collisions at Sea, 1960, the keel of which is laid or which is at a corresponding state of construction before the entry into force of these Regulations may be exempted from compliance therewith as follows:

(*a*) The installation of lights with ranges prescribed in Rule 22, until four years after the date of entry into force of these Regulations.

International Regulations for Preventing Collisions at Sea   253

(b) The installation of lights with colour specifications as prescribed in Section 7 of Annex I to these Regulations, until four years after the date of entry into force of these Regulations.

(c) The repositioning of lights as a result of conversion from Imperial to metric units and rounding off measurement figures, permanent exemption.

(d)

(i) The repositioning of masthead lights on vessels of less than 150 metres in length, resulting from the prescriptions of Section 3 (a) of Annex I to these Regulations, permanent exemption.

(ii) The repositioning of masthead lights on vessels of 150 metres or more in length, resulting from the prescriptions of Section 3 (a) of Annex I to these Regulations, until nine years after the date of entry into force of these Regulations.

(e) The repositioning of masthead lights resulting from the prescriptions of Section 2 (b) of Annex I to these Regulations until nine years after the date of entry into force of these Regulations.

(f) The repositioning of sidelights resulting from the prescriptions of Sections 2 (g) and 3 (b) of Annex I to these Regulations until nine years after the date of entry into force of these Regulations.

(g) The requirements for sound signal appliances prescribed in Annex III to these Regulations until nine years after the date of entry into force of these Regulations.

(h) The repositioning of all-round lights resulting from the prescription of Section 9 (b) of Annex I to these Regulations, permanent exemption.

ANNEX I

Positioning and technical details of lights and shapes

1. *Definition*

The term "height above the hull" means height above the uppermost continuous deck. This height shall be measured from the position vertically beneath the location of the light.

2. *Vertical positioning and spacing of lights*

(a) On a power-driven vessel of 20 metres of more in length the masthead lights shall be placed as follows:

(i) the forward masthead light, or if only one masthead light is carried, then that light, at a height above the hull of not less than 6 metres, and, if the breadth of the vessel exceeds 6 metres, then at a height above the hull not less than such breadth, so however that the light need not be placed at a greater height above the hull than 12 metres;

(ii) when two masthead lights are carried the after one shall be at least 4.5 metres vertically higher than the forward one.

(b) The vertical separation of masthead lights of power-driven vessels shall be such that in all normal conditions of trim the after light will be seen over and separate from the forward light at a distance of 1,000 metres from the stem when viewed from sea level.

(c) The masthead light of a power-driven vessel of 12 metres but less than 20 metres in length shall be placed at a height above the gunwale of not less than 2.5 metres.

(d) A power-driven vessel of less than 12 metres in length may carry the uppermost light at a height of less than 2.5 metres above the gunwale. When however a masthead light is carried in addition to sidelights and a sternlight, then such masthead light shall be carried at least 1 metre higher than the sidelights.

(e) One of the two or three masthead lights prescribed for a power-driven vessel when engaged in towing or pushing another vessel shall be placed in the same position as either the forward masthead light or the after masthead light; provided that, if carried on the aftermast, the lowest after masthead light shall be at least 4.5 metres vertically higher than the forward masthead light.

(f)
(i) The masthead light or lights prescribed in Rule 23(a) shall be so placed as to be above and clear of all other lights and obstructions except as described in sub-paragraph (ii).

(ii) When it is impracticable to carry the all-round lights prescribed by Rule 27 (b) (i) or Rule 28 below the masthead lights, they may be carried above the after masthead light(s) or vertically in between the forward masthead light(s) and after masthead light(s), provided that in the latter case the requirement of Section 3 (c) of this Annex shall be complied with.

(g) The sidelights of a power-driven vessel shall be placed at a height above the hull not greater than three-quarters of that of the forward masthead light. They shall not be so low as to be interfered with by deck lights.

(h) The sidelights, if in a combined lantern and carried on a power-driven vessel of less than 20 metres in length, shall be placed not less than 1 metre below the masthead light.

(i) When the Rules prescribe two or three lights to be carried in a vertical line, they shall be spaced as follows:

(i) on a vessel of 20 metres in length or more such lights shall be spaced not less than 2 metres apart, and the lowest of these lights shall, except where a towing light is required, be placed at a height of not less than 4 metres above the hull;

(ii) on a vessel of less than 20 metres in length such lights shall be spaced not less than 1 metre apart and the lowest of these lights shall, except where a towing light is required, be placed at a height of not less than 2 metres above the hull;

(iii) when three lights are carried they shall be equally spaced.

(j) The lower of the two all-round lights prescribed for a vessel when engaged in fishing shall be at a height above the sidelights not less than twice the distance between the two vertical lights.

(k) The forward anchor light prescribed in Rule 30 (a) (i), when two are carried, shall not be less than 4.5 metres above the after one. On a vessel of 50 metres or more in length this forward anchor light shall be placed at a height of not less than 6 metres above the hull.

3. *Horizontal positioning and spacing of lights*

(a) When two masthead lights are prescribed for a power-driven vessel, the horizontal distance between them shall not be less than one-half of the length of the vessel but need not be more than 100 metres. The forward light shall be placed not more than one-quarter of the length of the vessel from the stem.

(b) On a power-driven vessel of 20 metres or more in length the sidelights shall not be placed in front of the forward masthead lights. They shall be placed at or near the side of the vessel.

(c) When the lights prescribed in Rule 27 (b) (i) or Rule 28 are placed vertically between the forward masthead light(s) and the after masthead light(s) these all-round lights shall be placed at a horizontal distance of not less than 2 metres from the fore and aft centreline of the vessel in the athwartship direction.

4. *Details of location of direction-indicating lights for fishing vessels, dredgers and vessels engaged in underwater operations*

(*a*) The light indicating the direction of the outlying gear from a vessel engaged in fishing as prescribed in Rule 26 (*c*) (ii) shall be placed at a horizontal distance of not less than 2 metres and not more than 6 metres away from the two all-round red and white lights. This light shall be placed not higher than the all-round white light prescribed in Rule 26 (*c*) (i) and not lower than the sidelights.

(*b*) The lights and shapes on a vessel engaged in dredging or underwater operations to indicate the obstructed side and/or the side on which it is safe to pass, as prescribed in Rule 27 (*d*) (i) and (ii), shall be placed at the maximum practical horizontal distance, but in no case less than 2 metres, from the lights of shapes prescribed in Rule 27 (*b*) (i) and (ii). In no case shall the upper of these lights or shapes be at a greater height than the lower of the three lights or shapes prescribed in Rule 27 (*b*) (i) and (ii).

5. *Screens for sidelights*

The sidelights of vessels of 20 metres or more in length shall be fitted with inboard screens painted matt black, and meeting the requirements of Section 9 of this Annex. On vessels of less than 20 metres in length the sidelights, if necessary to meet the requirements of Section 9 of this Annex, shall be fitted with inboard matt black screens. With a combined lantern, using a single vertical filament and a very narrow division between the green and red sections, external screens need not be fitted.

6. *Shapes*

(*a*) Shapes shall be black and of the following sizes:

(i) a ball shall have a diameter of not less than 0.6 metre;

(ii) a cone shall have a base diameter of not less than 0.6 metre and a height equal to its diameter;

(iii) a cylinder shall have a diameter of at least 0.6 metre and height of twice its diameter;

(iv) a diamond shall consist of two cones as defined in (ii) above having a common base.

(*b*) The vertical distance between shapes shall be at least 1.5 metre.

(*c*) In a vessel of less than 20 metres in length shapes of lesser dimensions but commensurate with the size of the vessel may be used and the distance apart may be correspondingly reduced.

7. *Colour specification of lights*

The chromaticity of all navigation lights shall conform to the following standards, which lie within the boundaries of the area of the diagram specified for each colour by the International Commission on Illumination (CIE).

The boundaries of the area for each colour are given by indicating the corner co-ordinates, which are as follows:

(i) *White*

x 0.525 0.525 0.452 0.310 0.310 0.443

y 0.382 0.440 0.440 0.348 0.283 0.382

(ii) *Green*

x 0.028 0.009 0.300 0.203

y 0.385 0.723 0.511 0.356

(iii) *Red*

x 0.680 0.660 0.735 0.721

y 0.320 0.320 0.265 0.259

(iv) *Yellow*

x 0.612 0.618 0.575 0.575

y 0.382 0.382 0.425 0.406

8. *Intensity of lights*

(a) The minimum luminous intensity of lights shall be calculated by using the formula:

$$I = 3.43 \times 106 \times T \times D2 \times K\text{-}D$$

where I is luminous intensity in candelas under service conditions,

T is threshold factor 2 x 10-7 lux.

D is range of visibility (luminous range) of the light in nautical miles,

K is atmospheric transmissivity.

For prescribed lights the value of K shall be 0.8, corresponding to a meteorological visibility of approximately 13 nautical miles.

(b) A selection of figures derived from the formula is given in the following table:

Range of visibility (luminous range) of light in nautical miles D

1
2
3
4
5
6

Luminous intensity of light in candelas for K= 0.8 I

0.9
4.3
12
27
52
94

Note: The maximum luminous intensity of navigation of lights should be limited to avoid undue glare. This shall not be achieved by a variable control of the luminous density.

9. Horizontal sectors

(a)

(i) In the forward direction, sidelights as fitted on the vessel shall show the minimum required intensities. The intensities shall decrease to reach practical cut-off between 1 degree and 3 degrees outside the prescribed sectors.

(ii) For sternlights and masthead lights and at 22.5 degrees abaft the beam for sidelights, the minimum required intensities shall be maintained over the arc of the horizon up to 5 degrees within the limits of the sectors prescribed in Rule 21. From 5 degrees within the prescribed sectors the intensity may decrease by 50 per cent up to the prescribed limits; it shall decrease steadily to reach practical cut-off at not more than 5 degrees outside the prescribed sectors.

(b) All-round lights shall be so located as not to be obscured by masts, top-masts or structures within angular sectors of more than 6 degrees, except anchor light prescribed in Rule 30 which need not be placed at an impracticable height above the hull.

10. *Vertical sectors*

(a) The vertical sectors of electric lights, as fitted, with the exception of lights on sailing vessels shall ensure that:

(i) at least the required minimum intensity is maintained at all angles from 5 degrees above to 5 degrees below the horizontal;

(ii) at least 60 per cent of the required minimum intensity is maintained from 7.5 degrees above to 7.5 degrees below the horizontal.

(b) In the case of sailing vessels the vertical sectors of electric lights as fitted shall ensure that:

(i) at least the required minimum intensity is maintained at all angles from 5 degrees above to 5 degrees below the horizontal;

(ii) at least 50 per cent of the required minimum intensity is maintained from 25 degrees above to 25 degrees below the horizontal.

(c) In the case of lights other than electric these specifications shall be met as closely as possible.

11. *Intensity of non-electric lights*

Non-electric lights shall so far as practicable comply with the minimum intensities, as specified in the Table given in Section 8 of this

Annex.

12. *Manoeuvring light*

Notwithstanding the provisions of paragraph 2 (*f*) of this Annex the manoeuvring light described in Rule 34 (b) shall be placed in the same fore and aft vertical plane as the masthead light or lights and, where practicable, at a minimum height of 2 metres vertically above the forward masthead light, provided that it shall be carried not less than 2 metres vertically above or below the after masthead light. On a vessel where only one masthead light is carried the manoeuvring light, if fitted, shall be carried where it can best be seen, not less than 2 metres vertically apart from the masthead light.

13. *Approval*

The construction of lights and shapes and the installation of lights on board the vessel shall be to the satisfaction of the appropriate authority of the State whose flag the vessel is entitled to fly.

ANNEX II

Additional signals for fishing vessels fishing in close proximity

1. *General*

The lights mentioned herein shall, if exhibited in pursuance of Rule 26 (*d*), be placed where they can best be seen. They shall be at least 0.9 metre apart but at a lower level than lights prescribed in Rule 26 (*b*) (i) and (*c*) (i). The lights shall be visible all round the horizon at a distance of at least 1 mile but at a lesser distance than the lights prescribed by these Rules for fishing vessels.

2. *Signals for trawlers*

(*a*) Vessels when engaged in trawling, whether using demersal or pelagic gear, may exhibit:

(i) when shooting their nets: two white lights in a vertical line;

(ii) when hauling their nets: one white light over one red light in a vertical line;

(iii) when the net has come fast upon an obstruction: two red lights in a vertical line.

(*b*) Each vessel engaged in pair trawling may exhibit:

(i) by night, a searchlight directed forward and in the direction of the other vessel of the pair;

(ii) when shooting or hauling their nets or when their nets have come fast upon an obstruction, the lights prescribed in 2 (*a*) above.

3. *Signals for purse seiners*

Vessels engaged in fishing with purse seine gear may exhibit two yellow lights in a vertical line. These lights shall flash alternately every second and with equal light and occultation duration. These lights may be exhibited only when the vessel is hampered by its fishing gear.

ANNEX III

Technical details of sound signal appliances

1. *Whistles*

(a) *Frequencies and range of audibility*

The fundamental frequency of the signal shall lie within the range 70-700Hz.

The range of audibility of the signal from a whistle shall be determined by those frequencies, which may include the fundamental and/or one or more higher frequencies, which lie within the range 180-700 Hz ($\pm$ 1 per cent) and which provide the sound pressure levels specified in paragraph 1 (*c*) below.

(b) *Limits of fundamental frequencies*

To ensure a wide variety of whistle characteristics, the fundamental frequency of a whistle shall be between the following limits:

(i) 70-200 Hz, for a vessel 200 metres or more in length;

(ii) 130-350 Hz, for a vessel 75 metres but less than 200 metres in length;

(iii) 250-700 Hz, for a vessel less than 75 metres in length.

(c) Sound signal intensity and range of audibility

A whistle fitted in a vessel shall provide, in the direction of maximum intensity of the whistle and at a distance of 1 metre from it, a sound pressure level in at least one 1/3rd-octave band within the range of frequencies 180-700 Hz (± 1 per cent) of not less than the appropriate figure given in the table below.

Length of vessel in metres
200 or more
75 but less than 200
20 but less than 75
Less than 20

1/3rd-octave band level at 1 metre in dB referred to
2 x 10-5 N/m2
143
138
130
120

Audibility range in nautical miles
2
1.5
1
0.5

The range of audibility in the table above is for information and in approximately the range at which a whistle may be heard on its forward axis with 90 per cent probability in conditions of still air on board a vessel having average background noise level at the listening posts (taken to be 68 dB in the octave band centred on 250 Hz and 63 dB in the octave band centred on 500 Hz).

In practice the range at which a whistle may be heard is extremely variable and depends critically on weather conditions; the values given can be regarded as typical but under conditions of strong wind or high ambient noise level at the listening post the range may be much reduced.

(d) Directional properties

The sound pressure level of a directional whistle shall be not more than 4dB below the prescribed sound pressure level on the axis at any direction in the horizontal plane with ± 45 degrees of the axis. The sound pressure level at any other direction in the horizontal plane shall be not more than 10 dB below the prescribed wound pressure level on the axis, so that the range in any direction will be at least half the range on the forward axis. The sound pressure level shall be measured in that 1/3rd-octave band which determines the audibility range.

(e) Positioning of whistles

When a directional whistle is to be used as the only whistle on a vessel, it shall be installed with its maximum intensity directed straight ahead.

A whistle shall be placed as high as practicable on a vessel, in order to reduce interception of the emitted sound by obstructions and also to minimize hearing damage risk to personnel. The sound pressure level of the vessel's own signal at listening posts shall not exceed 11o dB (A) and so far as practicable should not exceed 100 dB (A).

(f) Fitting of more than one whistle
If whistles are fitted at a distance apart of more than 100 metres, it shall be so arranged that they are not sounded simultaneously.

(g) Combined whistle systems
If due to the presence of obstructions the sound field of a single whistle or of one of the whistles referred to in paragraph 1 (f) above is likely to have a zone of greatly reduced signal level, it is recommended that a combined whistle system be fitted so as to overcome this reduction. For the purposes of the Rules a combined whistle system is to be regarded as a single whistle. The whistles of a combined system shall be located at a distance apart of not more than 100 metres and arranged to be sounded simultaneously. The frequency of any one whistle shall differ from those of the others by at least 10 Hz.

2. Bell or gong
(a) Intensity of signal
A bell or gong, or other device having similar sound characteristics shall produce a sound pressure level of not less than 110 dB at a distance of 1 metre from it.

(b) Construction

Bells and gongs shall be made of corrosion-resistant material and designed to give a clear tone. The diameter of the mouth of the bell shall be not less than 300 mm. for vessels of 20 metres or more in length, and shall be not less than 200 mm. for vessels of 12 metres or more but of less than 20 metres in length. Where practicable, a power-driven bell striker is recommended to ensure constant force but manual operation shall be possible. The mass of the striker shall be not less than 3 per cent of the mass of the bell.

3. *Approval*
The construction of sound signal appliances, their performance and their installation on board the vessel shall be to the satisfaction of the appropriate authority of the State whose flag the vessel is entitled to fly.

ANNEX IV

Distress signals

1. The following signals, used or exhibited either together or separately, indicate distress and need of assistance:

(a) a gun or other explosive signal fired at intervals of about a minute;

(b) a continuous sounding with any fog-signalling apparatus:

(c) rockets or shells, throwing red stars fired one at a time at short intervals;

(d) a signal made by radiotelegraphy or by any other signalling method consisting of the group ...---... (SOS) in the Morse Code;

(e) A signal sent by radiotelephony consisting of the spoken word "Mayday";

(f) the International Code Signal of distress indicated by N.C.;

(g) a signal consisting of a square flag having above or below it a ball or anything resembling a ball;

(h) flames on the vessel (as from a burning tar barrel, oil barrel, etc.);

(i) a rocket parachute flare or hand flare showing a red light;

(j) a smoke signal giving off orange-coloured smoke;

(k) slowly and repeatedly raising and lowering arms outstretched to each side;

(l) the radiotelegraph alarm signal

(*m*) the radiotelephone alarm signal;

(*n*) signals transmitted by emergency position-indicating radio beacons.

2. The use or exhibition of any of the foregoing signals except for the purpose of indicating distress and need of assistance and the use of other signals which may be confused with any of the above signals is prohibited.

3. Attention is drawn to the relevant sections of the International Code of Signals, the Merchant Ship Search and Rescue Manual and the following signals:
   (*a*) a piece of orange-coloured canvas with either a black square and circle or other appropriate symbol (for identification from the air);

   (*b*) a dye marker.

Index

Page numbers in italics indicate illustrations.